TABLE OF CONTENTS

CHRIS SCHWARZ, THE JOURNAL

Jeff Halper, left, is a Jewish professor at Ben Gurion University in Jerusalem and Salim Hassan Shawamreh is a Palestinian engineer. They are on a cross-Canada and U.S. tour promoting peace in the Middle East .

Jews and Palestinians rebuild homes

Destruction of houses brings two sides together

SUSAN HAGAN
Journal Staff Writer
EDMONTON

Salim Hassan Shawamreh's house on the outskirts of Jerusalem has been demolished twice.

The last time, his wife and six children had 15 minutes to gather their belongings while Israeli soldiers beat him. All the while, a bulldozer waited to tear through their home.

It is part of living in Israel as a Palestinian minority, Shawamreh said.

"My wife didn't speak for two months because she was so traumatized," said Shawamreh, a Palestinian engineer. "My kids were very good in school before

the demolition. Now, they are doing very poorly. The smallest two kids are scared to go to the bathroom at night. ... My daughter doesn't believe I can protect her."

Stories like these prompted Jeff Halper, a lifelong peace advocate and professor at Israel's Ben Gurion University, to launch a group called the Israeli Committee Against Housing Demolitions.

For the last five years, Palestinians and Jews have worked side by side to help Palestinians rebuild their lives after military action has torn away homes or destroyed crops.

Halper described the organization on Wednesday at a University of Alberta speaking engagement as a non-violent, direct-action, political group established to resist Israel's demolition of Palestinian houses on the West Bank and East Jerusalem.

The group has since expanded to help replant olive trees and ravaged orchards.

"I am not anti-Israel," Halper said. "You do have to look at both sides. I am not saying that Arabs don't have a responsibility, but Israel is a state against a non-state. ... Only if we find a win-win situation are both sides going to survive."

He has brought his message on tour to the U.S. and Canada to garner support. Since 1967, more than 7,000 Palestinian houses have been destroyed at random because the owners don't have legal permits to build, he said. He added that most Palestinians aren't granted permits even after they pay thousands of dollars just to apply.

Halper has dubbed the Israeli powers a "matrix of control" over occupied territories that excludes Palestinians from economic opportunities and restricts freedom.

"The Israeli people live in a bubble — we don't even know Palestinians," he said.

Halper said demolitions could

become even more common under prime minister-elect Ariel Sharon, who has said security comes first, peace second.

"The peace process is over," Halper said. "Sharon has never recognized Palestinians as anything but a nuisance."

Halper's group will passively, but illegally recruit hundreds of people to help Palestinian families rebuild.

Shawamreh is rebuilding, even though he may lose his home again. He wants to get his family out of a cramped, expensive apartment and back onto the land he invested his savings in, he said.

"I told the soldiers once I will not leave this land because I have nowhere else to go," he said. "I have to resist."

**MORE WORLD NEWS
A9, A11, A16**

Colombian leaders meet / A9

THE ISRAELI COMMITTEE AGAINST HOUSE DEMOLITIONS
(ICAHD)

The Israeli Committee Against House Demolitions (ICAHD) is a non-violent Israeli direct-action organization established to resist Israel's demolition of Palestinian houses in the Occupied Territories - over 12,000 homes destroyed since 1967 – and, ultimately, to end the Occupation. The motivation for demolishing these homes is purely political: to confine the three and a half million residents of the West Bank, East Jerusalem and Gaza to small, crowded, impoverished and disconnected enclaves, thus effectively foreclosing any viable Palestinian entity and ensuring Israeli control. Ninety-five percent of the homes demolished have nothing to do with security: their inhabitants did not commit any acts of terrorism and, indeed, were never charged with any crime. Israel's policy of house demolitions violates human rights and international law, and is a major obstacle to achieving peace and reconciliation between the two peoples.

Over the years ICAHD's resistance "on the ground" has extended to other manifestations of the Occupation as well: land expropriation, settlement expansion, the construction of "Israeli-only" highways that incorporate the West Bank into Israel proper, the closure, the building of the Separation Barrier/Wall, and the wholesale uprooting of fruit and olive trees. The fierce repression of Palestinian efforts to "shake off" the Occupation following the latest Intifada has only added urgency to our efforts.

ICAHD members represent many Israeli peace and human rights organizations, and it cooperates closely with Palestinian organizations seeking peace and co-existence.

ICAHD's activities include:

- *Resisting the demolition of Palestinian homes.* ICAHD members physically block bulldozers sent to demolish homes. ICAHD also mobilizes Israelis and Palestinians to rebuild them as acts of resistance. House has proven an effective vehicle of grassroots peace-making as well as a means of raising awareness of the Occupation.

- *Disseminating information and mobilizing public opinion.* ICAHD's familiarity with realities "on the ground" gives it a special authority and insight into the sources of the conflict. Our views are frequently sought by diplomats, journalists, fact-finding missions and the public, for whom we offer critical briefings and tours. ICAHD also sends speakers on informational tours abroad, initiates campaigns to secure of just peace for our region and participates in international conferences.

- *Providing strategic practical support to Palestinian families and communities.* ICAHD aids Palestinians seeking to protect their homes from demolition by arranging and subsidizing legal assistance, as well as offering them support and solidarity as they cope with the traumas and tribulations of life under Occupation. ICAHD also cooperates with other human rights organizations to present legal challenges to Israeli actions and policies in the Occupied Territories.

- *Community and Family Matching.* ICAHD links communities and families in Israel and abroad with Palestinians whose homes are threatened with demolition so as to introduce an element of people-to-people involvement. This brings hope and succor to families under Occupation, while empowering people abroad to do something constructive for the sake of reconciliation and a just peace.

For more information about our activities or to join us in our efforts, please contact us at the address above. Within the constraints of local laws, ICAHD's efforts are also supported by the following ICAHD chapters:

ICAHD-USA: Office phone: +1-919-933-3319; Fax: +1-919-967-6685; E-mail: <usa@icahd.org>
ICAHD-UK: Office phone: +44-20-7424 5400; Fax: +44-20-7837 7731
Website: www.icahduk.org

ICAHD's work is supported solely by donations, and we appreciate financial support. Checks may be sent to:

The Israeli Committee Against House Demolitions
PO Box 2030
Jerusalem 91020
Israel

For a tax-deductible donation in the US, Make checks payable to AJPME, with ICAHD-USA in the memo, and send to:
ICAHD-USA
PO Box 1354
Carrboro, NC 27510

Donations from the UK may be sent to:
ICAHD UK
33a Islington Park Street
London N1 1QB

United Kingdom

DESCRIPTIONS OF MAPS

Map 1: 1947 UN Partition of Palestine

The UN Partition Plan tried to divide the country according to demographic concentrations, but the Palestinian and Jewish populations were so intertwined that that became impossible. Although the Jews comprised only a third of the country's population (548,000 out of 1,750,000) and owned only 6% of the land, they received 55% of the country (including both Tel Aviv/Jaffa and Haifa port cities, the Sea of Galilee and the resource-rich Negev). In the area allocated to the Jewish state, only about 57% of the population was actually Jewish (538,000 Jews, 397,000 Arabs). The Jewish community accepted the Partition Plan; the Palestinians (except those in the Communist Party) and the Arab countries rejected it.

Map 2: Israel and the Occupied Palestinian Territories

By the end of the 1948 war – called the War of Independence by Israel and the *Naqba* ("Disaster") by the Palestinians – Israel controlled 78% of the country, including half the territory that had been allocated by the UN to the Palestinians. Some 750,000 Palestinians living in what became Israel were made refugees or "internally displaced" people; only 100,000 remained in their homes. More than 418 villages, two-thirds of the villages of Palestine, were systematically destroyed by Israel after their residents had left or been driven out. Of the Arab areas, now reduced to 22% of the country, the West Bank was taken by Jordan and Gaza by Egypt. The 1949 Armistice Line, today known as the "Green Line," *de facto* demarcates the State of Israel until today. Since 1988, when the Palestinians recognized Israel within that boundary, it has constituted the basis of the two-state option, with the Palestinians claiming a state on all the lands conquered by Israel in 1967: the West Bank, East Jerusalem and Gaza.

Maps 3-7: Five Elements Defining the Palestinian Bantusan

Israel defines its policy of ensuring permanent control over the Occupied Territories as "creating facts on the ground." In this conception, Israeli control must be made immune from any external or internal pressures to remove Israel from the Occupied Territories (which Israel vehemently denies is an occupation at all), as well as to foreclose forever the possibility of *a viable and truly sovereign* Palestinian state. Nevertheless, even Sharon recognizes that Israel needs a Palestinian state, since it can neither extend citizenship to the Territories' three and a half million Palestinians nor deny it to them. It also needs a Palestinian state to relieve itself of the necessity of accepting the refugees. A Bantustan, a cantonized Palestinian mini-state controlled by Israel yet possessing a limited independence, thus solves Israel's fundamental dilemma of how to keep control over the entire country yet "get rid of" its Palestinian population (short of actual "transfer"). The contours of that Bantustan are defined by five elements comprising Israel's Matrix of Control as illustrated in the following maps: (1) Areas A and B;

(2) the closure; (3) the settlement blocs; (4) the infrastructure; and (5) the Separation Barrier/Wall. A full (if complex) picture of the Matrix of Control is depicted in Map 10, and the truncated Palestinian mini-state Israel is creating in Map 11.

Map 3: Defining the Palestinian Bantustan. Element #1: West Bank Areas A, B and C

In the Oslo II agreement of 1995, the West Bank was divided into three Areas: A, under full Palestinian Authority control; B, under Palestinian civil control but joint Israeli-Palestinian security; and C, under full Israeli control. Although Area A was intended to expand until it included all of the West Bank except Israel's settlements, its military facilities and East Jerusalem – whose status would then be negotiated – in fact the division became a permanent feature. Area A comprises 18% of the West Bank, B another 22%, leaving a full 60%, Area C, including most of Palestinian farmland and water, under exclusive Israeli control. These areas, comprising 64 islands, shape the contours of the "cantons" Sharon has proposed as the basis of the future Palestinian state. Taken together with Gaza, which Israel will relinquish, the emerging Bantustan will consist of five truncated cantons – a northern one around Nablus and Jenin; a central one around Ramallah; a southern one around Bethlehem and Hebron; enclaves in East Jerusalem; and Gaza. In this scheme Israel will expand from its present 78% to 85-90%, with the Palestinian state confined to just 10-15% of the country.

Map 4: Defining the Palestinian Bantustan. Element #2: The Closure and House Demolitions

At the very beginning of the Oslo peace process Israel established an ever-constrictive system of permanent "closure" over the Occupied Territories, a regime both arbitrary and counter-productive. Arbitrary because there was no particular rise in terrorism or security threats during this time; the security situation was certainly better than it was during the first Intifada, when there was no closure whatsoever. And counter-productive because, rather than benefiting the Palestinians, it meant that the "peace process" had actually impoverished and imprisoned them, destroying their commerce and industry and de-developing their emerging country. The permanent checkpoints depicted on the map, together with hundreds of other "flying" checkpoints erected spontaneously throughout the Territories and earthen barriers to the entrances to virtually all the Palestinian cities, towns and villages, present some 750 obstacles to Palestinian movement on any given day. They serve to accustom the Palestinians to living in a collective space defined by Areas A and B. When these cantons finally become a truncated Palestinian state, the Palestinians will already be adapted to its narrow confines. So minimal will be the Palestinians' expectations that the addition of corridors linking the cantons will given them the feeling of "freedom," thus leading them to acquiesce to the Bantustan. Israel's policy of house demolitions, by which some 12,000 Palestinian homes have been demolished since 1967, is designed to confine the Palestinian population to the islands of A and B as well as small enclaves in East Jerusalem. (It is also a policy that impacts seriously on the Arab population within Israel).

Map 5: Defining the Palestinian Bantustan. Element #3: Israel's Settlement Blocs

When Ehud Barak proposed to "jump" to final status negotiations in 1999, he consolidated the settlements Israel sought to retain into "blocs," leaving the more isolated and less strategic ones vulnerable to dismantling. Thus, instead of dealing with 200 settlements, Barak had only to negotiate the annexation of seven settlement blocs: (1) the Jordan Valley Bloc; (2) the Ariel Bloc that divides the West Bank east and west and preserves Israeli control over the Territories largest water aquifer; (3) the Modi'in Bloc, connecting the Ariel settlements to Jerusalem; a "Greater Jerusalem" consisting of (4) the Givat Ze'ev Bloc to the northwest of the city, (5) the expansive Ma'aleh Adumim bloc extending to the northeast and east of Jerusalem and (6) the Etzion Bloc to the southwest; and (7) a corridor rising from the settlements in the south to incorporate the Jewish community of Hebron. While the extent of these settlements blocs is to some extent subject to negotiations, their function, however, is to further define and divide the Palestinian cantons. Representing some 25% of the West Bank, their annexation to Israel has been approved by the US in the bi-lateral Bush-Sharon Exchange of Letters in April 2004. (Within the settlement blocs are depicted both the settlements themselves and the master plans that surround and extend them.)

Map 6: Defining the Palestinian Bantustan. Element #4: The Infrastructure of Control

In order to incorporate the West Bank and East Jerusalem permanently into Israel proper, a $3 billion system of highways and "by-pass roads" has been constructed that integrates the settlement blocs into the metropolitan areas of Tel Aviv, Modi'in and Jerusalem, while creating additional barriers to Palestinian movement. This ambitious project articulates with the Trans-Israeli Highway, now being built along the entire length of the country, hugging the West Bank in its central portion. Shifting Israel's population center eastward from the coast to the corridor separating Israel's major cities from the settlement blocs it seeks to incorporate, the Trans-Israel Highway will become the new spine of the country, upon which the by-pass road network can be hung. The result is the reconfiguration of the country from two parallel north-south units – Israel and the West Bank, the basis of the two state idea – into one country integrated east-west. Besides ensuring Israeli control, the reorientation of traffic, residential and commercial patterns further weakens a truncated Palestinian mini-state; each Palestinian canton is integrated separately into Israel, with only tenuous connections one to the other.

Map 7: Defining the Palestinian Bantustan. Element #5: The Separation Barrier/Wall

The final defining element of the bantustan is the Separation Barrier, known by its opponents as the Apartheid Wall both because it serves to make permanent an apartheid situation between Israelis and Palestinians, and because it rises to a massive concrete wall of eight meters (26 feet) when reaching Palestinian population centers – replete with prison-like watch towers, gates, security roads, electronic fences and deadly armaments. While sold to the public as an innocent security device, the Barrier in fact defines the border between Israel (including the areas of the West Bank and East Jerusalem Israel seeks to annex) and the Palestinian mini-state. It follows not the Green Line but establishes a new demographic line that extends Israel eastward into the West Bank. Although the Barrier's overall route has been moved closer to the Green Line in light of the International Court of Justice's ruling, the addition of "supplementary security zones" and "special security zones" to the Barrier's complex still retains the convoluted route around the settlement blocs in order to ensure they are on the "right" side of the Barrier. When completed the Separation Barrier will be five times longer than the Berlin Wall (some 700 kms versus 155), in places twice as high and will unilaterally annex East Jerusalem and some 8% of the West Bank. As an installation costing $2 billion, it is not designed to be dismantled.

Map 8: The Palestinian Bantustan in the Gaza Strip

The Gaza Strip is a tiny area of land 45 km (30 miles) long and 5-12 km (3-9 miles) in length, surrounded by Israeli settlements and electronic fences and gates. As of this writing – two months before Sharon's plan of "disengagement" is scheduled to be completed – its 1.3 million Palestinian inhabitants live on 60% of the land, while 7000 Israeli settlers and the Israeli army control the other 40%, including much of the coastline. Gazans, once farmers, are today impoverished, their lands cleared of fruit and olive trees and other crops as "security measures." Some 75% of Gazans live on less than $2 a day, 80% are refugees living mainly in squalid camps. Gaza has the densest population concentration in the world – 9000 persons per square mile, almost four times the density of Bangladesh. Malnutrition among children is rampant; most of its water is taken by the settlers or is highly polluted; and more than 1200 homes have been demolished and thousands of more damaged in the course of the second Intifada. Gaza is divided into white, yellow, blue and green areas that divide Israelis and Palestinians. Gaza has also been carved into three separate cantons between which Palestinians cannot move. Israelis travel freely on special Israeli-only highways. Even if disengagement takes place, Gazans will still live in a cage, blockaded by sea, fenced in by land, unable to travel by air, prevented from seeking employment in Israel.

Map 9: The Matrix of Control

When all the elements are put together, the full extent and complexity Israel's Matrix of Control becomes evident. This raises the major question before us: Is the Occupation reversible? If it is not, if the Occupation can never be dismantled to the extent that a *viable* Palestine emerges, then should we continue supporting a "two-state solution"? To do so places us in a position of advocating for a Bantustan. If the Occupation is reversible, then we must ensure that the minimal conditions for a *viable* Palestinian state are achieved. In either case Israel's "facts on the ground," its Matrix of Control, are essential parts of the political equation.

Map 10: The Emerging Palestinian Bantustan in the West Bank

When the elements of the Matrix of Control are combined with American agreement for Israel's annexing its major settlement blocs, the outlines of a Palestinian Bantustan clearly emerge. It is a mini-state of four islands occupying 10-15% of the country with no international borders, no territorial contiguity, no freedom of movement internally or externally, little economic viability, limited access to Jerusalem, no control of its water or other major resources, no control of its airspace or even its communications sphere, a demilitarized entity lacking even the authority to enter into foreign alliances without Israeli approval. If Israel has succeeded in rendering the Occupation permanent, it is not because of the logistical difficulties in removing the settlements. A Peace Now poll found that fully 90% of the settlers (most of whom live in the Territories for economic and "quality of life" reasons) would leave if they were offered comparable housing inside Israel. It is only the will if the international community to force the Israel government to abandon its settlement enterprise that is lacking. If that is the case, the international community is confronted with two stark choices: either to accept and condone a new apartheid situation, or to work towards another just and sustainable solution – a single democratic state in the entire country, a regional confederation or some other option. It is to be hoped that apartheid, the only "solution" Israel is offering by rendering its Occupation irreversible, will not be acceptable.

Map 11: Three Alternative Bantustans

The problem is not obtaining a Palestinian state. Israel itself desperately needs a Palestinian state, since it can neither bestow citizenship on the Palestinians nor deny it to them permanently. In order to retain its Jewish character yet control the entire country, Israel must somehow "relieve itself" of the Palestinian population. The only way out (except for transfer, which is impossible in the present circumstances) is to establish a Bantustan. Sharon has suggested a Bantustan (he calls it a plan of "cantonization") on 40% of the West Bank, but has indicated that he is willing to unilaterally "give" the Palestinians 60%, perhaps even a bit more. Labor, wishing to make a Bantustan cosmetically acceptable, would offer up to 85% of the Occupied Territories, knowing that Israel needs just a strategic 15% to retain control.

Map 12: Moveable Borders: 1947, 1949, 1967 and On

These maps illustrate the changing borders at the expense of the Palestinians over the years. The picture that emerges is one of displacement, whether actually driving the Palestinians out of the country or confining them to a sort of reservation.

Map 13: Municipal Jerusalem, with the Separation Barrier

In 1967 Israel annexed an area of 70 sq. kms., which it called "East" Jerusalem, to the 38 sq. kms. that had comprised Israeli "West" Jerusalem since 1948, even though the Palestinian side of the city under Jordan was just 6 sq. kms. It gerrymandered the municipal border according to two principles: incorporating as much unbuilt-upon Palestinian land as possible for future Israeli settlements (the "inner ring" of settlements depicted in blue), while excluding as much of the Palestinian population as possible so as to maintain a 72% Jewish majority in the city. As the concentrations of Palestinian population show (in brown), the municipal border cut in half a living urban fabric of communities, families, businesses, schools, housing and roads. Its placement of settlements prevents the urban development of Palestinian Jerusalem – the economic and cultural as well as religious center of Palestinian life – transforming its residential and commercial areas into disconnected enclaves. There are today more Israelis living in "East" Jerusalem (more than 200,000) than Palestinians. Since Palestinians cannot live in "West" Jerusalem, Israeli restrictions on building (combined with an aggressive campaign of house demolitions) have confined that population to a mere 6% of the urban land – although they are a third of the Jerusalem population. Discriminatory administrative and housing measures have led to the "Quiet Transfer" of thousands of Palestinian families out of the city, and to the loss of their Jerusalem residency.

Map 14: The Three Jerusalems: Municipal, Greater and Metropolitan

The "inner ring" of settlements that defines municipal Jerusalem is today being linked with an "outer ring" of settlements to transform Jerusalem from a city into a region that controls the entire central portion of the West Bank. "Greater Jerusalem," the master plan of which was formalized already in 1995, extends the city far into the West Bank. Yet an even more extensive "Jerusalem" exists: Metropolitan Jerusalem. Though not intended for annexation, it forms a planning unit designed to ensure that Ramallah and Bethlehem remain undeveloped satellite cities dependent upon Israeli Jerusalem even if they eventually fall across a political border separating Israel from Palestine. Indeed, by creating extensive buffer zones between the city of Jerusalem and the surrounding West Bank, Israel is eliminating the economic heart of any Palestinian state. In this way Israel keeps all the developmental potential of the city - and the country as a whole – firmly in its hands, rendering the Palestinian state a non-viable entity existing on a Third World subsistence level.

The map also shows the "E-1" area, 4000 acres annexed to Ma'aleh Adumim in a combined move by the Netanyahu and Barak governments. With the addition of E-1, Ma'aleh Adumim's master plan extends entirely across the West Bank from Jerusalem to Jericho, effectively severing the northern West Bank from the south. Palestinian traffic will likely be diverted into Israeli territory (along the "Eastern Ring Road" now being constructed in East Jerusalem), allowing Israel to control Palestinian movement even in the event that a Palestinian state emerges. E-1 reveals the subtle, sophisticated and effective use of planning for control employed by Israel.

Maps

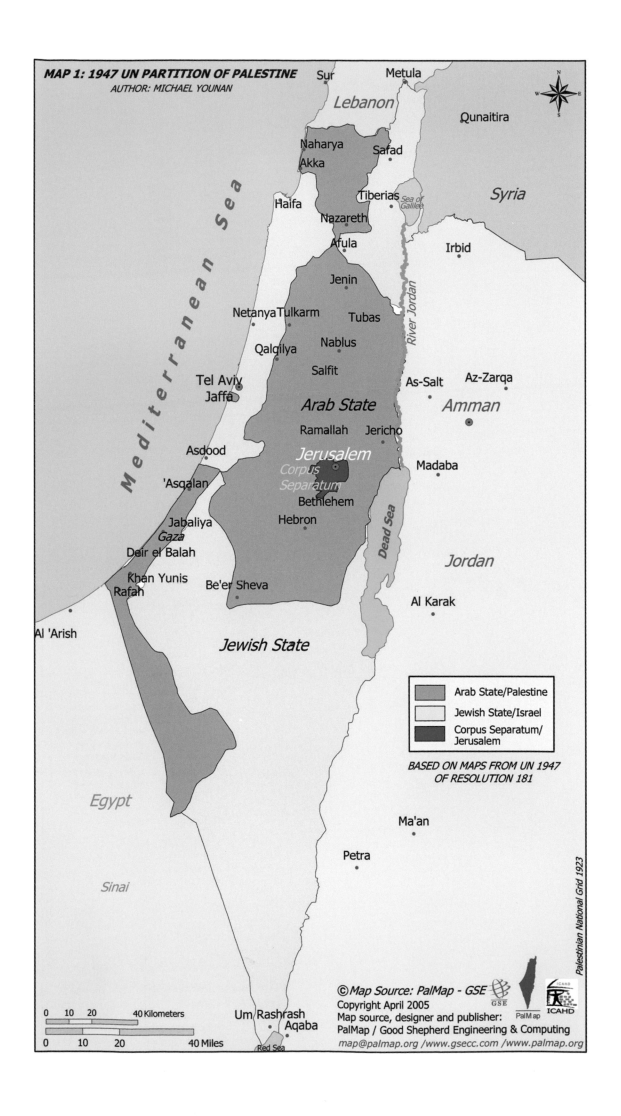

MAP 1: 1947 UN PARTITION OF PALESTINE
AUTHOR: MICHAEL YOUNAN

Lebanon

Syria

Sur
Metula
Qunaitira

Naharya
Akka
Safad

Haifa
Tiberias *Sea of Galilee*

Nazareth

Mediterranean Sea

Afula

Irbid

Jenin

Netanya Tulkarm
Tubas

Qalqilya
Nablus

River Jordan

Salfit

As-Salt
Az-Zarqa

Tel Aviv
Arab State
Amman

Jaffa

Ramallah
Jericho

Asdood
Jerusalem

Corpus Separatum
Madaba

'Asqalan

Bethlehem

Jabaliya
Gaza
Hebron

Deir el Balah
Dead Sea

Khan Yunis
Jordan

Rafah

Be'er Sheva
Al Karak

Al 'Arish

Jewish State

	Arab State/Palestine
	Jewish State/Israel
	Corpus Separatum/ Jerusalem

BASED ON MAPS FROM UN 1947 OF RESOLUTION 181

Egypt

Ma'an

Petra

Sinai

Palestinian National Grid 1923

0 10 20   40 Kilometers

0   10   20   40 Miles

Um Rashrash
Aqaba
Red Sea

GSE

ICAHD
PalMap

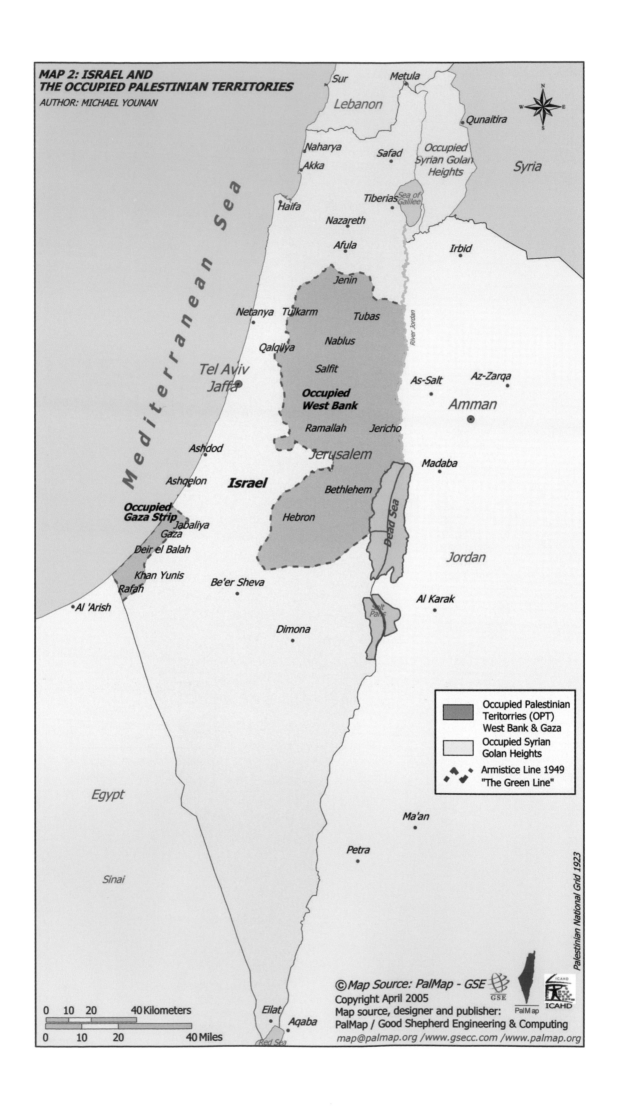

MAP 2: ISRAEL AND
THE OCCUPIED PALESTINIAN TERRITORIES
AUTHOR: MICHAEL YOUNAN

Sur
Metula
Lebanon
Qunaitira

Naharya
Safad
Occupied
Syrian Golan
Heights
Syria

Akka

Haifa
Tiberias   Sea of Galilee

Nazareth

Afula
Irbid

Jenin

Netanya   Tulkarm
Tubas

Qalqilya
Nablus

Salfit

Tel Aviv
Jaffa
Occupied
West Bank

As-Salt   Az-Zarqa

Amman

Ramallah   Jericho

Ashdod
Jerusalem

Madaba

Ashqelon   Israel

Bethlehem

Occupied
Gaza Strip
Dead Sea

Jabaliya
Hebron

Gaza

Deir el Balah

Khan Yunis
Jordan

Rafah
Be'er Sheva

Al 'Arish
Salt Pans

Al Karak

Dimona

Mediterranean Sea

Egypt

Ma'an

Petra

Sinai

	Occupied Palestinian Teritorries (OPT) West Bank & Gaza
	Occupied Syrian Golan Heights
◆◆◆	Armistice Line 1949 "The Green Line"

0 10 20   40 Kilometers

0   10   20   40 Miles

Eilat
Aqaba
Red Sea

© Map Source: PalMap - GSE
Copyright April 2005
Map source, designer and publisher:
PalMap / Good Shepherd Engineering & Computing
map@palmap.org /www.gsecc.com /www.palmap.org

GSE

PalMap

ICAHD

Palestinian National Grid 1923

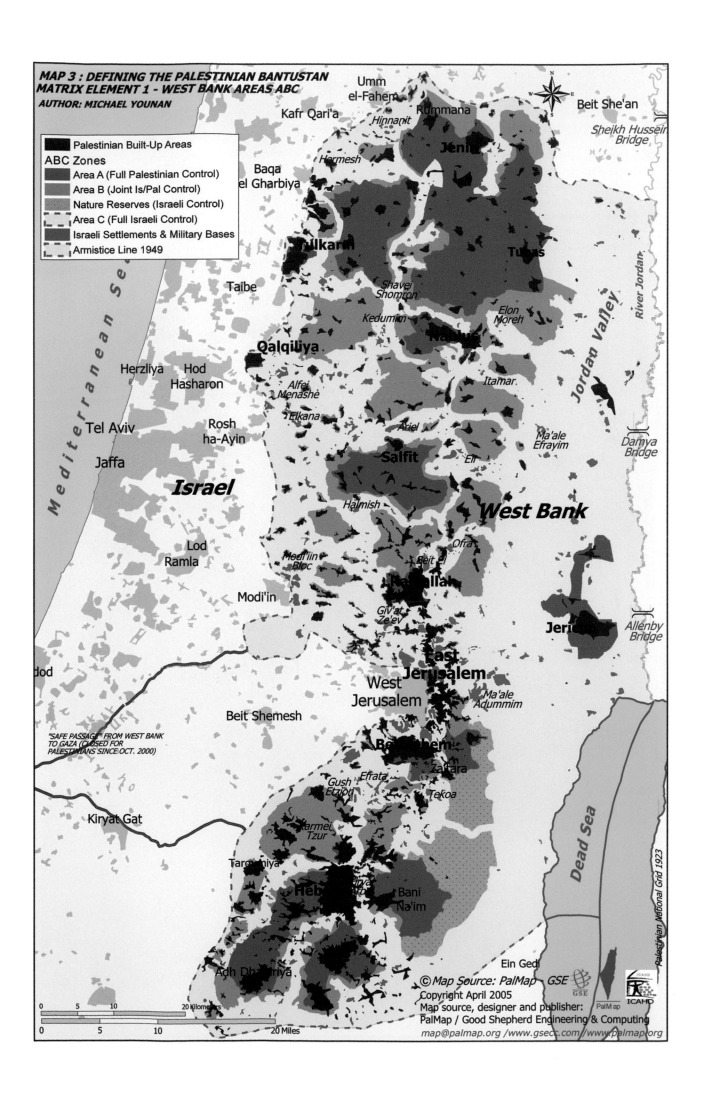

MAP 3 : DEFINING THE PALESTINIAN BANTUSTAN
MATRIX ELEMENT 1 - WEST BANK AREAS ABC
AUTHOR: MICHAEL YOUNAN

Legend:
- Palestinian Built-Up Areas
- **ABC Zones**
  - Area A (Full Palestinian Control)
  - Area B (Joint Is/Pal Control)
  - Nature Reserves (Israeli Control)
  - Area C (Full Israeli Control)
  - Israeli Settlements & Military Bases
  - Armistice Line 1949

Umm el-Fahem
Kafr Qari'a
Hinnanit
Rummana
Beit She'an
Sheikh Hussein Bridge
Jenin
Baqa el Gharbiya
Hermesh
Tulkarm
Tubas
Shavei Shomron
Elon Moreh
Taibe
Kedumim
Nablus
Qalqiliya
Herzliya
Hod Hasharon
Alfei Menashe
Itamar
Elkana
Ariel
Ma'ale Efrayim
Damya Bridge
Tel Aviv
Rosh ha-Ayin
Eli
Salfit
Jaffa
Israel
Halmish
West Bank
Lod
Ramla
Modi'in Bloc
Ofra
Beit El
Modi'in
Ramallah
Giv'at Ze'ev
Jericho
Allenby Bridge
East Jerusalem
West Jerusalem
Ma'ale Adummim
Beit Shemesh
"SAFE PASSAGE" FROM WEST BANK TO GAZA (CLOSED FOR PALESTINIANS SINCE OCT. 2000)
Bethlehem
Zaatara
Efrata
Gush Etzion
Tekoa
Kiryat Gat
Karmel Tzur
Bani Na'im
Taroumiya
Hebron
Kiryat Arba
Dead Sea
Adh Dhahriya
Ein Gedi

Mediterranean Sea
Jordan Valley
River Jordan

0 5 10 20 Kilometers
0 5 10 20 Miles

Palestinian National Grid 1923

© Map Source: PalMap — GSE
Copyright April 2005
Map source, designer and publisher:
PalMap / Good Shepherd Engineering & Computing
map@palmap.org / www.gsecc.com / www.palmap.org

ICAHD
GSE
PalMap

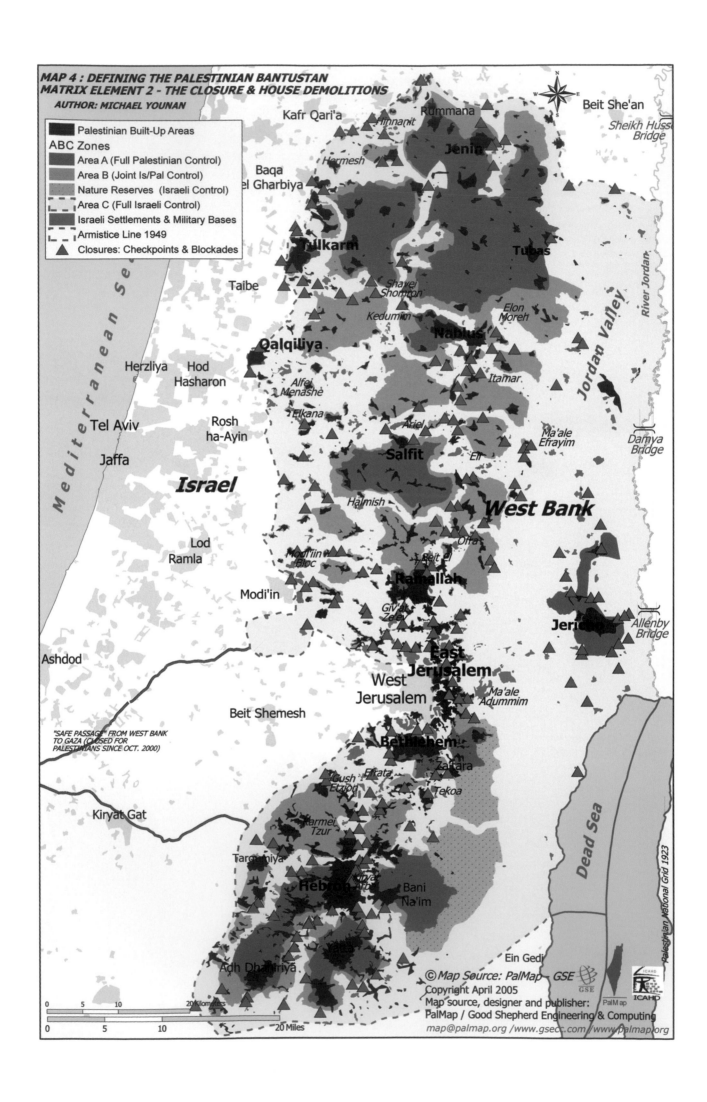

MAP 4 : DEFINING THE PALESTINIAN BANTUSTAN
MATRIX ELEMENT 2 - THE CLOSURE & HOUSE DEMOLITIONS
AUTHOR: MICHAEL YOUNAN

Palestinian Built-Up Areas
ABC Zones
Area A (Full Palestinian Control)
Area B (Joint Is/Pal Control)
Nature Reserves (Israeli Control)
Area C (Full Israeli Control)
Israeli Settlements & Military Bases
Armistice Line 1949
▲ Closures: Checkpoints & Blockades

Beit She'an
Sheikh Huss
Bridge
Kafr Qari'a
Rummana
Hinnapit
Jenin
Harmesh
Baqa
el Gharbiya
Tulkarm
Tubas
Taibe
Shavei
Shomron
Elon
Moreh
Kedumim
Qalqiliya
Nablus
Herzliya
Hod
Hasharon
Itamar
Alfei
Menashe
Rosh
ha-Ayin
Elkana
Tel Aviv
Ariel
Ma'ale
Efrayim
Jaffa
Salfit
Eli
Israel
Damya
Bridge
Halmish
West Bank
Lod
Ramla
Offra
Modi'in
Bloc
Beit El
Modi'in
Ramallah
Giv'at
Ze'ev
Jericho
Allenby
Bridge
Ashdod
East
Jerusalem
West
Jerusalem
Ma'ale
Adummim
Beit Shemesh
"SAFE PASSAGE" FROM WEST BANK
TO GAZA (CLOSED FOR
PALESTINIANS SINCE OCT. 2000)
Bethlehem
Zaftara
Efrata
Gush
Etzion
Tekoa
Kiryat Gat
Carmel
Tzur
Dead Sea
Targumiya
Bani
Na'im
Hebron
Kiryat
Arba
Yatta
Ein Gedi
Adh Dhahiriya

Mediterranean Sea

Jordan Valley

River Jordan

Palestinian National Grid 1923

0 5 10 20 Kilometers
0 5 10 20 Miles

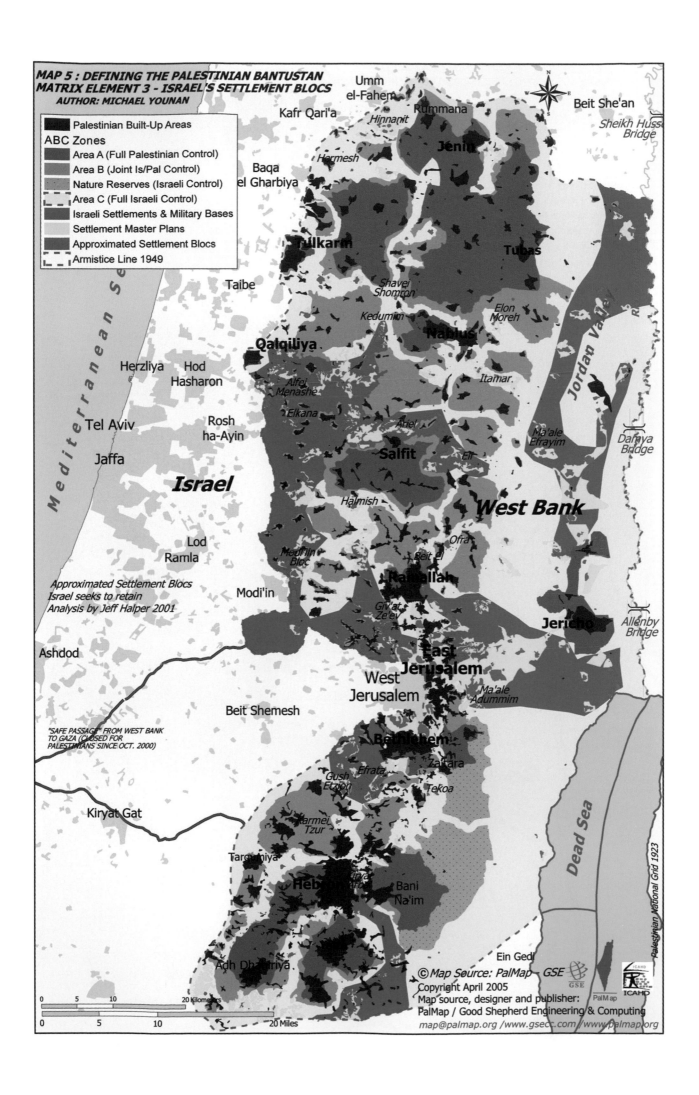

MAP 5 : DEFINING THE PALESTINIAN BANTUSTAN
MATRIX ELEMENT 3 - ISRAEL'S SETTLEMENT BLOCS
AUTHOR: MICHAEL YOUNAN

Legend:
- Palestinian Built-Up Areas
- ABC Zones
- Area A (Full Palestinian Control)
- Area B (Joint Is/Pal Control)
- Nature Reserves (Israeli Control)
- Area C (Full Israeli Control)
- Israeli Settlements & Military Bases
- Settlement Master Plans
- Approximated Settlement Blocs
- Armistice Line 1949

Approximated Settlement Blocs
Israel seeks to retain
Analysis by Jeff Halper 2001

"SAFE PASSAGE" FROM WEST BANK
TO GAZA (CLOSED FOR
PALESTINIANS SINCE OCT. 2000)

Mediterranean Sea

Umm el-Fahem
Kafr Qari'a
Rummana
Beit She'an
Sheikh Huss... Bridge
Hinnanit
Jenin
Harmesh
Baqa el Gharbiya
Tulkarm
Tubas
Shavei Shomron
Elon Moreh
Kedumim
Taibe
Qalqiliya
Nablus
Herzliya
Hod Hasharon
Itamar
Alfei Menashe
Elkana
Ariel
Tel Aviv
Rosh ha-Ayin
Eli
Jaffa
Salfit
Ma'ale Efrayim
Damiya Bridge
Israel
Halmish
West Bank
Jordan Valley
Lod
Ramla
Ofra
Beit El
Medi'in Bloc
Modi'in
Ramallah
Givat Ze'ev
Jericho
Allenby Bridge
Ashdod
East Jerusalem
West Jerusalem
Ma'ale Adummim
Beit Shemesh
Bethlehem
Zatara
Efrata
Tekoa
Kiryat Gat
Gush Etzion
Dead Sea
Karmei Tzur
Targumiya
Bani Na'im
Hebron
Adh Dhahiriya
Ein Gedi

0 5 10 20 Kilometers
0 5 10 20 Miles

Palestinian National Grid 1923

© Map Source: PalMap - GSE
Copyright April 2005
Map source, designer and publisher:
PalMap / Good Shepherd Engineering & Computing
map@palmap.org /www.gsecc.com /www.palmap.org

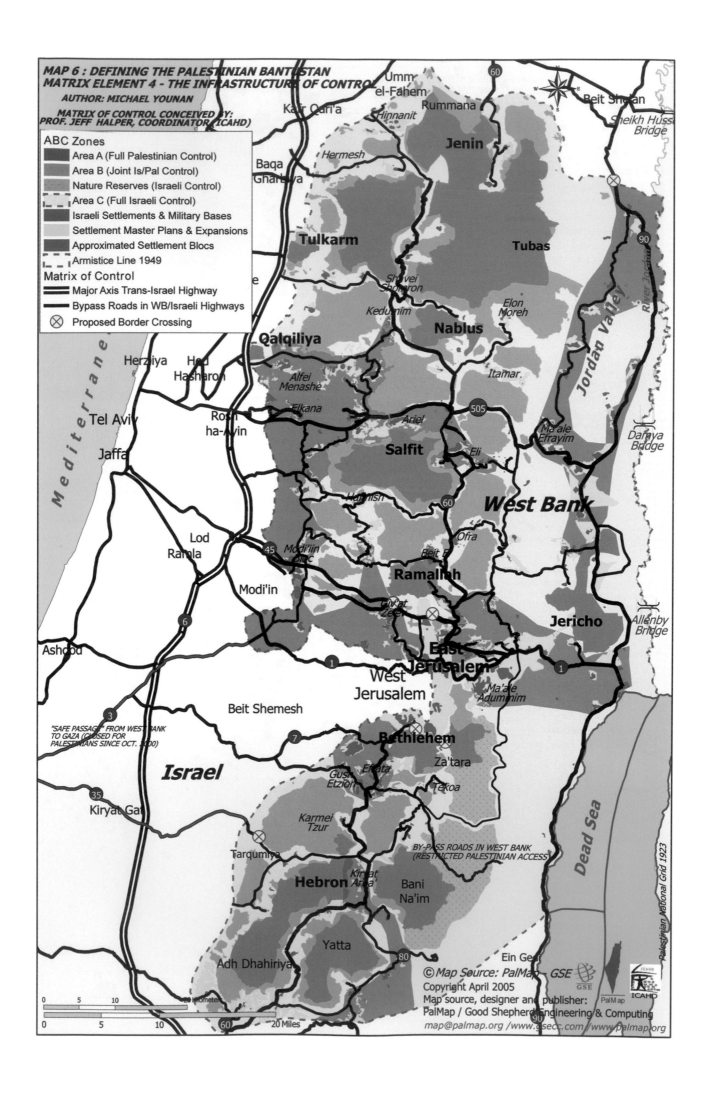

MAP 6 : DEFINING THE PALESTINIAN BANTUSTAN
MATRIX ELEMENT 4 - THE INFRASTRUCTURE OF CONTROL
AUTHOR: MICHAEL YOUNAN
MATRIX OF CONTROL CONCEIVED BY:
PROF. JEFF HALPER, COORDINATOR (ICAHD)

ABC Zones
Area A (Full Palestinian Control)
Area B (Joint Is/Pal Control)
Nature Reserves (Israeli Control)
Area C (Full Israeli Control)
Israeli Settlements & Military Bases
Settlement Master Plans & Expansions
Approximated Settlement Blocs
Armistice Line 1949

Matrix of Control
Major Axis Trans-Israel Highway
Bypass Roads in WB/Israeli Highways
Proposed Border Crossing

© Map Source: PalMap – GSE
Copyright April 2005
Map source, designer and publisher:
PalMap / Good Shepherd Engineering & Computing
map@palmap.org /www.gsecc.com /www.palmap.org

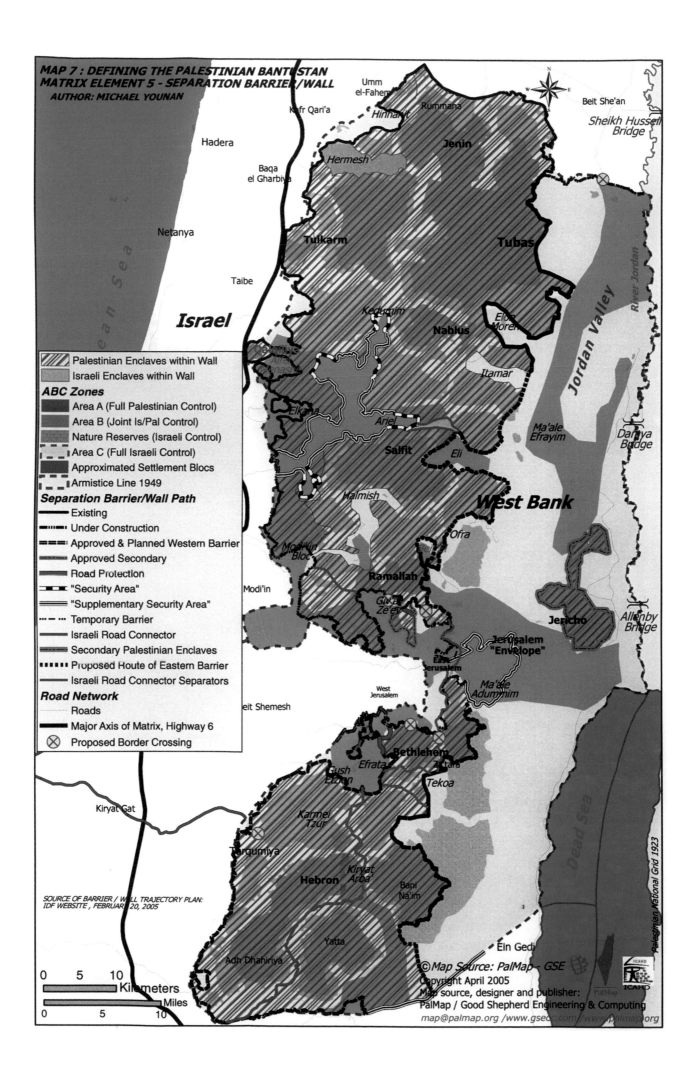

MAP 7 : DEFINING THE PALESTINIAN BANTUSTAN
MATRIX ELEMENT 5 - SEPARATION BARRIER/WALL
AUTHOR: MICHAEL YOUNAN

Hadera

Kafr Qari'a

Umm
el-Fahem

Rummana

Hinnanit

Jenin

Beit She'an

Sheikh Hussein
Bridge

Hermesh

Baqa
el Gharbiya

Netanya

Tulkarm

Tubas

Taibe

Israel

Kedumim

Elon
Moreh

Nablus

Jordan Valley

River Jordan

Itamar

Elkana

Ariel

Ma'ale
Efrayim

Daraya
Bridge

Salfit

Eli

Halmish

West Bank

Modi'in
Bloc

Ofra

Modi'in

Ramallah

Giv'at
Ze'ev

Jericho

Allenby
Bridge

Jerusalem
"Envelope"

East
Jerusalem

West
Jerusalem

Ma'ale
Adummim

eit Shemesh

Bethlehem

Gush
Etzion

Efrata

Tekoa

Kiryat Gat

Karmei
Tzur

Tarqumiya

Kiryat
Arba'

Hebron

Bani
Na'im

Dead Sea

Yatta

Ein Gedi

Adh Dhahiriya

©Map Source: PalMap - GSE
Copyright April 2005
Map source, designer and publisher:
PalMap / Good Shepherd Engineering & Computing
map@palmap.org /www.gseoc.com / www.palmap.org

Legend

| | Palestinian Enclaves within Wall |
| | Israeli Enclaves within Wall |

ABC Zones
Area A (Full Palestinian Control)
Area B (Joint Is/Pal Control)
Nature Reserves (Israeli Control)
Area C (Full Israeli Control)
Approximated Settlement Blocs
Armistice Line 1949

Separation Barrier/Wall Path
Existing
Under Construction
Approved & Planned Western Barrier
Approved Secondary
Road Protection
"Security Area"
"Supplementary Security Area"
Temporary Barrier
Israeli Road Connector
Secondary Palestinian Enclaves
Proposed Route of Eastern Barrier
Israeli Road Connector Separators

Road Network
Roads
Major Axis of Matrix, Highway 6
Proposed Border Crossing

SOURCE OF BARRIER / WALL TRAJECTORY PLAN:
IDF WEBSITE , FEBRUARY 20, 2005

0   5   10
Kilometers
Miles
0   5   10

Palestinian National Grid 1923

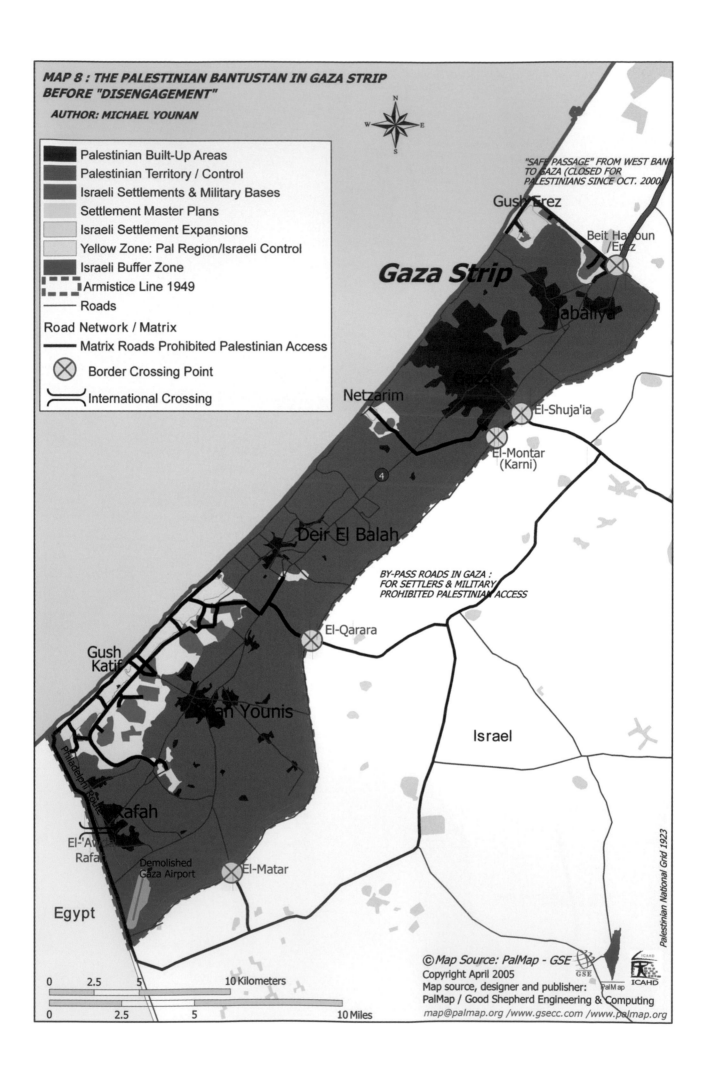

MAP 8 : THE PALESTINIAN BANTUSTAN IN GAZA STRIP BEFORE "DISENGAGEMENT"

AUTHOR: MICHAEL YOUNAN

Legend:
- Palestinian Built-Up Areas
- Palestinian Territory / Control
- Israeli Settlements & Military Bases
- Settlement Master Plans
- Israeli Settlement Expansions
- Yellow Zone: Pal Region/Israeli Control
- Israeli Buffer Zone
- Armistice Line 1949
- Roads

Road Network / Matrix
- Matrix Roads Prohibited Palestinian Access
- Border Crossing Point
- International Crossing

Gaza Strip

Gush Erez

"SAFE PASSAGE" FROM WEST BANK TO GAZA (CLOSED FOR PALESTINIANS SINCE OCT. 2000)

Beit Hanoun /Erez

Jabaliya

Gaza

Netzarim

El-Shuja'ia

El-Montar (Karni)

4

Deir El Balah

BY-PASS ROADS IN GAZA : FOR SETTLERS & MILITARY PROHIBITED PALESTINIAN ACCESS

El-Qarara

Gush Katif

Khan Younis

Israel

Philadelphi Route

Rafah

El-'Awda Rafah

Demolished Gaza Airport

El-Matar

Egypt

Palestinian National Grid 1923

0   2.5   5   10 Kilometers

0   2.5   5   10 Miles

©Map Source: PalMap - GSE
Copyright April 2005
Map source, designer and publisher:
PalMap / Good Shepherd Engineering & Computing
map@palmap.org /www.gsecc.com /www.palmap.org

GSE
ICAHD
PalMap

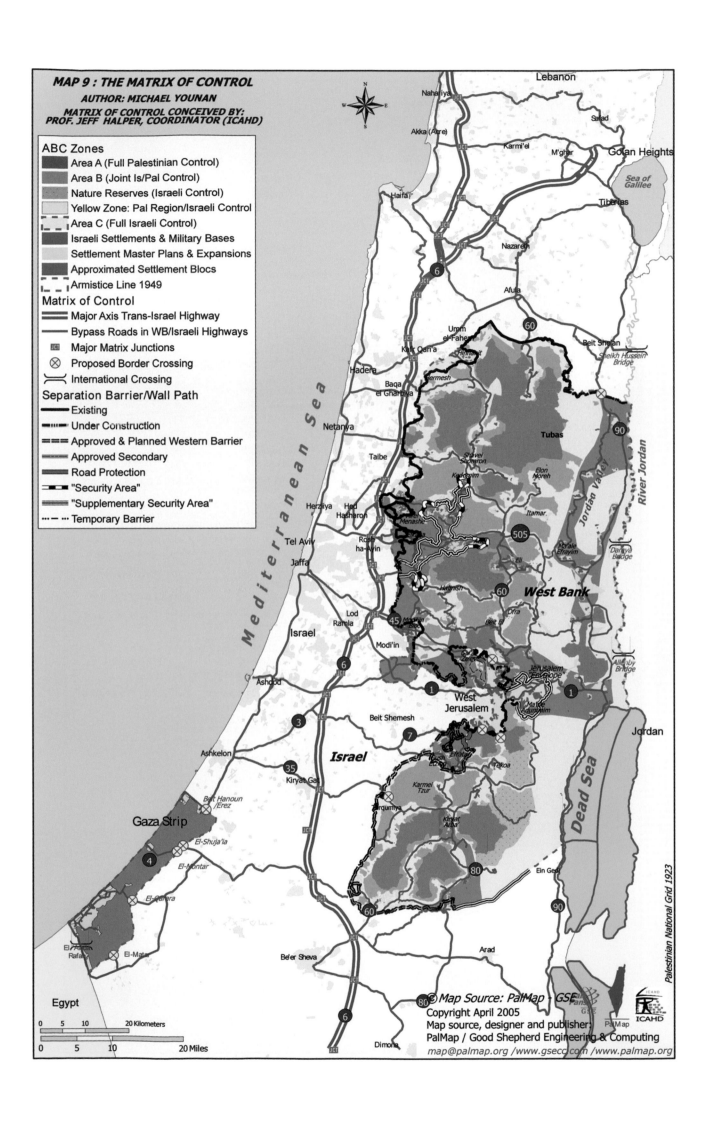

MAP 9 : THE MATRIX OF CONTROL
AUTHOR: MICHAEL YOUNAN
MATRIX OF CONTROL CONCEIVED BY:
PROF. JEFF HALPER, COORDINATOR (ICAHD)

ABC Zones
- Area A (Full Palestinian Control)
- Area B (Joint Is/Pal Control)
- Nature Reserves (Israeli Control)
- Yellow Zone: Pal Region/Israeli Control
- Area C (Full Israeli Control)
- Israeli Settlements & Military Bases
- Settlement Master Plans & Expansions
- Approximated Settlement Blocs
- Armistice Line 1949

Matrix of Control
- Major Axis Trans-Israel Highway
- Bypass Roads in WB/Israeli Highways
- Major Matrix Junctions
- Proposed Border Crossing
- International Crossing

Separation Barrier/Wall Path
- Existing
- Under Construction
- Approved & Planned Western Barrier
- Approved Secondary
- Road Protection
- "Security Area"
- "Supplementary Security Area"
- Temporary Barrier

Palestinian National Grid 1923

© Map Source: PalMap - GSE
Copyright April 2005
Map source, designer and publisher:
PalMap / Good Shepherd Engineering & Computing
map@palmap.org /www.gseco.com /www.palmap.org

0 5 10 20 Kilometers
0 5 10 20 Miles

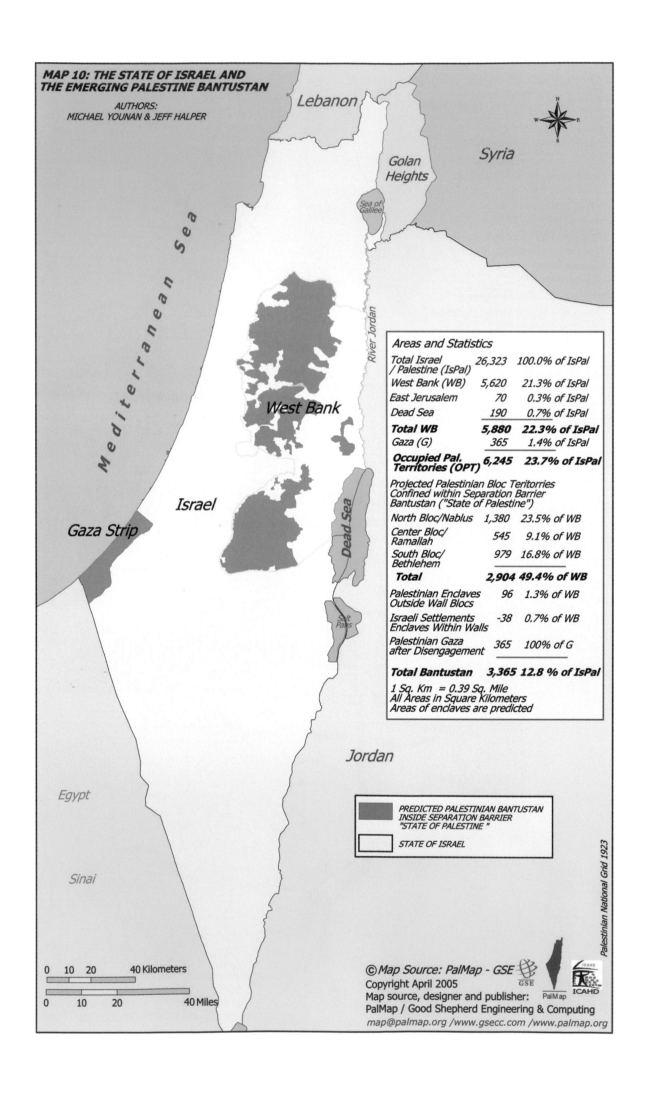

MAP 10: THE STATE OF ISRAEL AND THE EMERGING PALESTINE BANTUSTAN

AUTHORS:
MICHAEL YOUNAN & JEFF HALPER

Lebanon

Syria

Golan
Heights

Sea of
Galilee

Mediterranean Sea

River Jordan

West Bank

Israel

Dead Sea

Gaza Strip

Salt
Pans

Jordan

Egypt

Sinai

Areas and Statistics

Total Israel / Palestine (IsPal)	26,323	100.0% of IsPal
West Bank (WB)	5,620	21.3% of IsPal
East Jerusalem	70	0.3% of IsPal
Dead Sea	190	0.7% of IsPal
Total WB	**5,880**	**22.3% of IsPal**
Gaza (G)	365	1.4% of IsPal
Occupied Pal. Territories (OPT)	**6,245**	**23.7% of IsPal**

Projected Palestinian Bloc Teritorries
Confined within Separation Barrier
Bantustan ("State of Palestine")

North Bloc/Nablus	1,380	23.5% of WB
Center Bloc/ Ramallah	545	9.1% of WB
South Bloc/ Bethlehem	979	16.8% of WB
Total	**2,904**	**49.4% of WB**
Palestinian Enclaves Outside Wall Blocs	96	1.3% of WB
Israeli Settlements Enclaves Within Walls	-38	0.7% of WB
Palestinian Gaza after Disengagement	365	100% of G
Total Bantustan	**3,365**	**12.8 % of IsPal**

1 Sq. Km = 0.39 Sq. Mile
All Areas in Square Kilometers
Areas of enclaves are predicted

PREDICTED PALESTINIAN BANTUSTAN
INSIDE SEPARATION BARRIER
"STATE OF PALESTINE"

STATE OF ISRAEL

0 10 20 40 Kilometers

0 10 20 40 Miles

Palestinian National Grid 1923

© Map Source: PalMap - GSE
Copyright April 2005
Map source, designer and publisher:
PalMap / Good Shepherd Engineering & Computing
map@palmap.org /www.gsecc.com /www.palmap.org

GSE

PalMap

ICAHD

MAP 11: THREE ALTERNATIVES OF THE PALESTINE BANTUSTAN

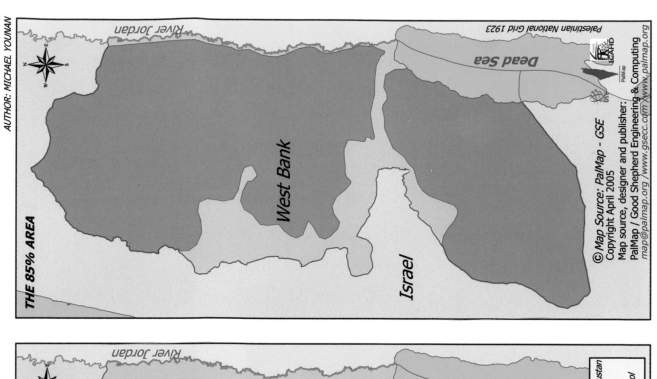

THE 85% AREA

West Bank

Israel

River Jordan

Dead Sea

Palestinian National Grid 1923

© Map Source: PalMap - GSE
Copyright April 2005
Map source, designer and publisher:
PalMap / Good Shepherd Engineering & Computing
map@palmap.org / www.palmap.org

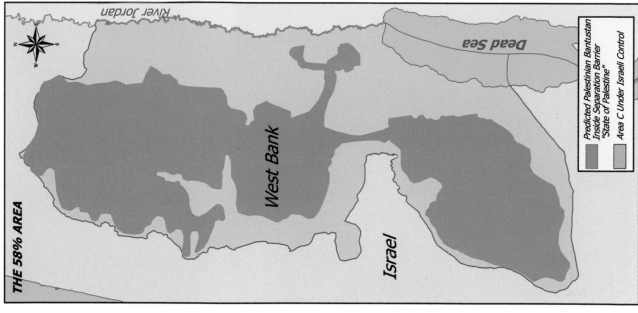

THE 58% AREA

West Bank

Israel

River Jordan

Dead Sea

Predicted Palestinian Bantustan
Inside Separation Barrier
"State of Palestine"

Area C Under Israeli Control

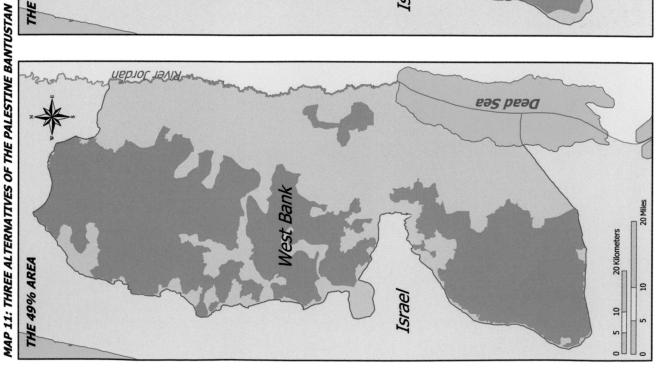

THE 49% AREA

West Bank

Israel

River Jordan

Dead Sea

0   5   10   20 Kilometers

0   5   10   20 Miles

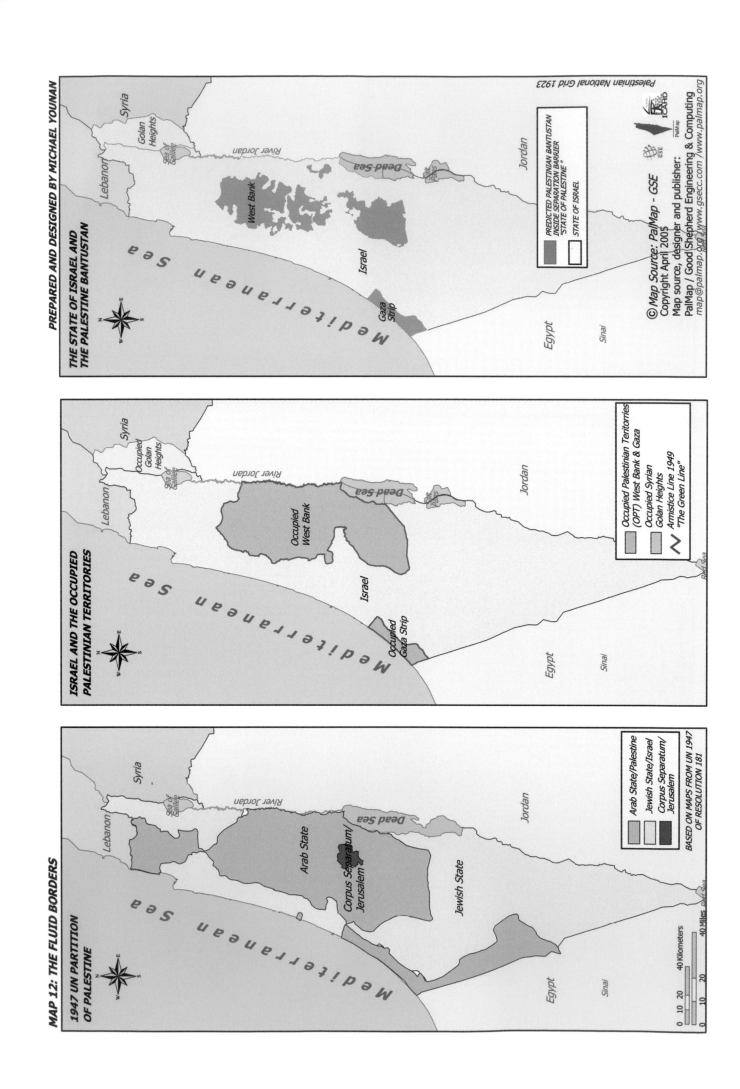

PREPARED AND DESIGNED BY MICHAEL YOUNAN

**THE STATE OF ISRAEL AND
THE PALESTINE BANTUSTAN**

Palestinian National Grid 1923

PREDICTED PALESTINIAN BANTUSTAN
INSIDE SEPARATION BARRIER
"STATE OF PALESTINE"

"STATE OF ISRAEL"

© Map Source: PalMap - GSE
Copyright April 2005
Map source, designer and publisher:
PalMap / Good\Shepherd Engineering & Computing
map@palmap.org / www.gsecc.com / www.palmap.org

West Bank

Israel

Gaza
Strip

Golan
Heights

Syria

Lebanon

Sea of
Galilee

River Jordan

Dead Sea

Salt
Pans

Jordan

Egypt

Sinai

Mediterranean Sea

**ISRAEL AND THE OCCUPIED
PALESTINIAN TERRITORIES**

Occupied Palestinian Territories
(OPT) West Bank & Gaza

Occupied Syrian
Golan Heights

Armistice Line 1949
"The Green Line"

Occupied
West Bank

Israel

Occupied
Gaza Strip

Occupied Golan
Heights

Syria

Lebanon

Sea of
Galilee

River Jordan

Dead Sea

Salt
Pans

Jordan

Egypt

Sinai

Red Sea

Mediterranean Sea

MAP 12: THE FLUID BORDERS

**1947 UN PARTITION
OF PALESTINE**

Arab State/Palestine

Jewish State/Israel

Corpus Separatum/
Jerusalem

BASED ON MAPS FROM UN 1947
OF RESOLUTION 181

Arab State

Corpus Separatum/
Jerusalem

Jewish State

Syria

Lebanon

Sea of
Galilee

River Jordan

Dead Sea

Jordan

Egypt

Sinai

Mediterranean Sea

0 10   20   40 Kilometers
0   10   20   40 Miles
Red Sea

MAP 13: MUNICIPAL JERUSALEM WITH SEPARATION BARRIER

AUTHOR: MICHAEL YOUNAN

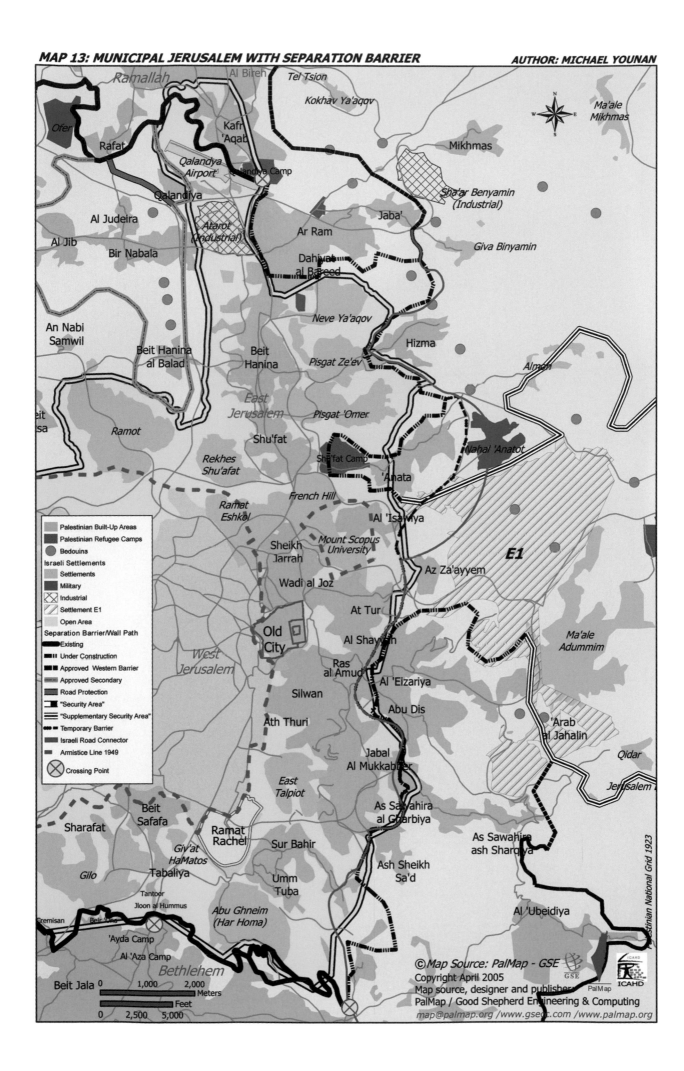

Legend:

- Palestinian Built-Up Areas
- Palestinian Refugee Camps
- Bedouins

Israeli Settlements
- Settlements
- Military
- Industrial
- Settlement E1
- Open Area

Separation Barrier/Wall Path
- Existing
- Under Construction
- Approved Western Barrier
- Approved Secondary
- Road Protection
- "Security Area"
- "Supplementary Security Area"
- Temporary Barrier
- Israeli Road Connector
- Armistice Line 1949
- Crossing Point

Place names:
Ramallah, Al Bireh, Tel Tsion, Kokhav Ya'aqov, Ma'ale Mikhmas, Ofer, Rafat, Kafr 'Aqab, Qalandya Airport, Qalandya Camp, Mikhmas, Qalandya, Al Judeira, Atarot (Industrial), Jaba', Sha'ar Benyamin (Industrial), Al Jib, Bir Nabala, Ar Ram, Dahiyat al Bareed, Giva Binyamin, An Nabi Samwil, Beit Hanina al Balad, Beit Hanina, Neve Ya'aqov, Pisgat Ze'ev, Hizma, Almon, Ramot, Pisgat 'Omer, Shu'fat, Rekhes Shu'afat, Shu'fat Camp, 'Anata, Nahal 'Anatot, French Hill, Ramat Eshkol, Al 'Isawiya, E1, Sheikh Jarrah, Mount Scopus University, Wadi al Joz, Az Za'ayyem, At Tur, Old City, Al Shayah, Ma'ale Adummim, West Jerusalem, Ras al Amud, Silwan, Al 'Eizariya, Abu Dis, Ath Thuri, Jabal Al Mukkabber, 'Arab al Jahalin, Qidar, Jerusalem, East Talpiot, As Sawahira al Gharbiya, Beit Safafa, Sharafat, Ramat Rachel, Sur Bahir, As Sawahira ash Sharqiya, Giv'at HaMatos, Tabaliya, Umm Tuba, Ash Sheikh Sa'd, Gilo, Tantoor, Jloon al Hummus, Abu Ghneim (Har Homa), Al 'Ubeidiya, Cremisan, Beir Yona, 'Ayda Camp, Al 'Aza Camp, Bethlehem, Beit Jala

Scale:
0 1,000 2,000 Meters
0 2,500 5,000 Feet

Palestinian National Grid 1923

©Map Source: PalMap - GSE
Copyright April 2005
Map source, designer and publisher:
PalMap / Good Shepherd Engineering & Computing
map@palmap.org /www.gsecc.com /www.palmap.org

ICAHD

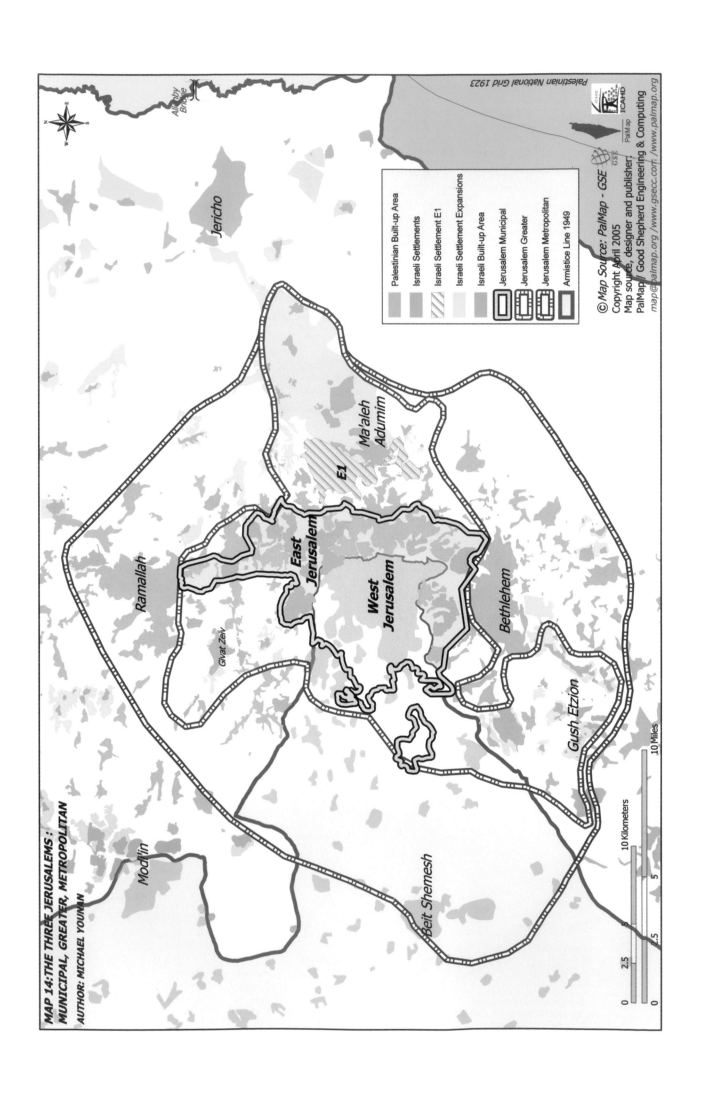

MAP 14: THE THREE JERUSALEMS :
MUNICIPAL, GREATER, METROPOLITAN

AUTHOR: MICHAEL YOUNAN

Allenby Bridge

Jericho

Ramallah

Giv'at Ze'ev

Modi'in

East Jerusalem

West Jerusalem

E1

Ma'aleh Adumim

Bethlehem

Gush Etzion

Beit Shemesh

Palestinian National Grid 1923

Palestinian Built-up Area
Israeli Settlements
Israeli Settlement E1
Israeli Settlement Expansions
Israeli Built-up Area
Jerusalem Municipal
Jerusalem Greater
Jerusalem Metropolitan
Armistice Line 1949

© Map Source: PalMap - GSE
Copyright April 2005
Map source, designer and publisher:
PalMap / Good Shepherd Engineering & Computing
map@palmap.org / www.gsecc.com / www.palmap.org

ICAHD

GSE PalMap

2.5   5   10 Kilometers
0   5   10 Miles
0

RE-FRAMING THE CONFLICT

"I must be frank, the demographic picture is very stark. Within the next decade or two, Jews will be a minority in the areas of Israel, the West Bank and the Gaza Strip. As Israeli settlements expand, and the population increases, it becomes ever more difficult to see how two peoples can be separated into two states….The fact is the settlements continue to grow today, encouraged by specific ongoing [Israeli] government policy."
– David Satterfield, US State Department Envoy to the Peace Process, quoted in *Ha'aretz*,
  January 13, 2004

When 2.5 million people live in a closed-off Gaza, it's going to be a human catastrophe. Those people will become even bigger animals than they are today, with the aid of an insane fundamentalist Islam. The pressure at the border will be awful. It's going to be a terrible war. So, if we want to remain alive, we will have to kill and kill and kill. All day, every day. If we don't kill, we will cease to exist. The only thing that concerns me is how to ensure that the boys and men who are going to have to do the killing will be able to return home to their families and be normal human beings.
– Arnon Sofer, professor of Geography at Haifa University, father of Sharon's "separation
  plan," quoted in *The Jerusalem Post* weekend supplement *Up Front*, May 21, 2004, p. 9)

When it comes to resolving conflicts such as that pitting Israeli Jews against Palestinian Arabs, framing is more important than the facts. Everyone agrees that around 3500 Palestinians and more than 1000 Israelis have been killed in the four years of the second Intifada (September 2000-late 2004). For most Israelis, however, the Israelis were victims of terror while the Palestinians were terrorists or unfortunate (but unavoidable) casualties, with no distinction made between combatants and civilians. For most Palestinians, their dead were casualties of a struggle for independence and victims of Israeli State Terror, while the Israeli dead were the unfortunate victims of their government's repressive policy of Occupation which left the Palestinians little choice. These are not minor differences. They embody fundamentally divergent perceptions and assumptions regarding the nature of the conflict, determining in the end which solutions are or are not possible.

All Israeli governments, be they Labor or Likud, have successfully promoted a framing based solely on security. Israel, the official framing goes, is a tiny, peace-loving country, a Western democracy besieged by a sea of Arabs intent on destroying it, embroiled in an existential fight for its survival in which it acts only out of self-defense. Missing from Israel's security framing is the very fact of occupation, which Israel both denies exists and excises from all its utterances. Instead, it casts itself as an innocent victim of "Arab terrorism." This framing, compelling and making great sense in the post-9/11 discourse of "security," nevertheless conceals other elements of the framing not related to security and not stated explicitly: that the entire country between the Mediterranean and the Jordan River "belongs" exclusively to the Jews, thus nullifying any Palestinian rights and claims -- indeed, even their even their existence as a people; that "security" requires Israel control over the entire country, thus eliminating the possibility of any truly viable and sovereign Palestinian state; that one side must win and the other lose, rendering impossible a just peace based on human rights, international law, reconciliation and regional integration; and a rejection of the Middle East in favor of integration – culturally, politically and economically, if not physically -- into the Western world.

1

While security is certainly a legitimate concern for Israel as it is for other countries, accepting its exclusively security-based framing means ruling out the possibility of a just and sustainable peace with the Palestinians. As Israelis who believe that Israel's security, survival and moral integrity depend upon reaching an accommodation with its neighbors, we do not find this an acceptable option. In fact, we reject the official framing altogether. Our reading of the history of the region, of Zionism, our understanding of how and why Israeli policy is made in regards to the Occupation and our experiences with our Palestinian partners and friends lead us to very different conclusions, to a very different framing.

The re-framing suggested here seeks to address the underlying causes of the conflict between Israel, the Palestinians ands the wider Arab world while offering ways out. It might be called a "post-Zionist" approach because the critical Israeli peace camp ("to the left of Peace Now," as we sometimes refer to ourselves) understands that an expanding Jewish state plumped in the middle of a country already inhabited by another people poses fundamental problems of co-existence, human and civil rights, self-determination and justice. It rests on the principle that two peoples live in Israel-Palestine, each possessing rights of self-determination yet capable of finding ways to co-exist. At a minimum it endorses a two-state solution, yet it is open to others as well: the creation of a common bi-national or democratic state encompassing both peoples, a regional confederation, or any other arrangement that respects the parties' human and national rights. Indeed, it argues that only a political solution conforming to human rights and international law will finally meet each people's concern for justice and security. Since it also recognizes the strong and vital cultures of both peoples, the alternative human rights framing relies less on attempts to carve out distinctive Jewish or Palestinian states – an impossible task in a country in which the peoples are so intertwined – as it does on finding a political configuration that affords each its national expression yet preserves the fluidity of residence and movement this shared space requires.

In the end, the reframing offered by the critical Israeli peace camp rejects the fundamental premise of the security paradigm: that Muslims and Arabs as a whole, and Palestinians in particular, are our enemies. We insist that the conflict be conceived as a political one that therefore has a solution. We reject all attempts to mystify it through claims that Jews and Arabs have been enemies "from time immemorial" or that we are involved in a "clash of civilizations." We also reject the notion that terrorism lies at the root of the conflict. While we condemn any attack on civilians, we recognize that such violence is a symptom of intolerable oppression that will end only when the peoples' underlying claims and grievances are resolved.

We also point out that significant gains have been made towards a just solution to the conflict even though they have been obscured by the violence of recent years. Both the Palestinians and the Arab League have recognized Israel within the "Green Line" (that is, on 78% of the shared country); Israel is at peace with Egypt and Jordan, has relations with many Arab countries and expanding ties throughout the Arab and Muslim worlds; a promising diplomatic Road Map has been formulated by the US, Europe, Russia and the UN; a majority of Israeli Jews have indicated a willingness to relinquish the Occupied Territories if their security could be assured; and Israelis and Palestinians have engaged in prolonged negotiations in the past. At the same time, as Israelis, we hold our country accountable for its actions. Security concerns aside, we reject the notion of Israel expanding into the Occupied Palestinian Territories, that 22% of the country that offers a displaced and battered Palestinian people its only hope for self-determination.

Our reframing, however, rejects the notion of "both sides." While we recognize that the Palestinians and the wider Arab and Muslim worlds possess their share of responsibility, we also recognize the fundamental asymmetry of power between the sides. Israel is an internationally recognized state possessing overwhelming military and economic might and allied to the world's dominant super-power. It is occupying the lands of a stateless people, impoverished, with no army and little political leverage.

Given that equation we contend that Israel possesses the ability to end the Occupation, the major obstacle to a just peace and regional security, and will do so only when it is brought into compliance with internationally accepted standards of human rights and international law – not to mention Jewish morality and values.

Our task in the critical Israeli peace movement is therefore four-fold. First, we must put into words Israel's official security framing, making it as explicit as possible so that people in Israel and abroad will understand where Israeli policies come from and where they lead. Second, we seek to show how the Israeli framing – and especially the element of exclusivity and Jewish victimhood – is used to justify expansion while laying the blame for the conflict on the Palestinian victims. We show how it deflects accountability from Israel as it pursues an ultimately futile win-lose policy. Third, we offer an alternative framing, a win-win approach, upon which a just peace can be built. Re-framing, we believe, opens possibilities for peace, security, self-determination and co-existence foreclosed by Israel's security paradigm. And finally, by presenting a framing that offers a clear and compelling way to a just peace, we aim to empower our partners to more effectively present our common case. In the end we offer a hope that permanent conflict need not be the lot of the suffering peoples of the Middle East.

The essential elements of two framings may be presented as follows:

REFRAMING THE ISRAELI-PALESTINIAN CONFLICT
Presented by Jeff Halper, ICAHD

The Israel i Security Framing concerns.	The Peace and Human Rights Framing
The Land of Israel belongs exclusively to the Jewish people; There is no other people that has legitimate rights or claims.	Two peoples reside in Israel/Palestine and each has rights of self-determination.
Israel's policies are based on concerns for security.	Israel pursues a pro-active policy of expansion into the Occupied Territories based on settlement and control.
● The Arabs don't want peace; the Palestinians are our enemies.	● The Palestinians recognize Israeli sovereignty over 78% of the country; the Arab world has offered Israel regional integration.
● There is no Occupation; the problem is Arab terrorism.	● The problem is Israel's Occupation; Palestinian violence is a symptom of oppression. In human rights language, all attacks on civilians are prohibited, whether from non-state or state actors.
● Since Israel is the victim fighting for its existence, it is exempt from accountability for its actions.	
● Any solution must leave Israel in control of the entire country.	● Israel is a major regional superpower that must be held accountable for its actions.
● Israel needs a Palestinian state, but only one that is truncated, non-viable and semi-sovereign.	● A Palestinian state has to be viable and truly sovereign, not merely a bantustan.
● The conflict is a win-lose proposition: either we "win" or "they" do.	● Only a solution based on human rights and international law ensures a win-win solution.
● The answer to anti-Semitism is a militarily strong Israel aligned with the United States.	● Anti-Semitism is a form of racism; only respect for human rights will effectively address anti-Semitism and Israel's security

THE ISRAELI FRAMING: SECURITY
AND A PRO-ACTIVE PROJECT OF CLAIMING THE LAND OF ISRAEL

More than anything else, Israel's success in presenting its case has been due to the clear and coherent narrative that underlies it. This simple, neat formula goes something like this:

> The Jews of ancient times (meaning the Hebrews, Israelites and Judeans, since the term "Jew" appears in the Bible only in the Book of Esther) constituted a nation with all the trappings of nationhood. They had a country that encompassed greater or lesser parts of the Land of Israel, a language, a religion, a national history, a literature and, above all, a tribal sense of identity based on ties of blood. After two abortive revolts against the Romans, the nation-tribe was exiled from its country. For two millennia it existed among the nations as a people apart – alien, persecuted, ghettoized, clinging to its national identity and longing for its return to Zion. In the late nineteenth century, spurred by nationalist movements throughout Europe, Zionism emerged as the national expression of Jews seeking a return to the Homeland from which they had been forcibly expelled so many centuries before. This right of return, of self-determination, conforms to that of all other nations who have sought political independence in the past two centuries. After a period of nation-building, the State of Israel arose triumphantly in 1948, defeating five Arab armies. Since then the tiny state has persevered despite constant Arab threats to its existence. Throughout, Israel has aspired to peace, only to be frustrated by its intractable enemies. All its actions against the Palestinians and other Arabs are merely reactions of self-defense foisted upon the small Jewish state. David and Goliath.

As a national narrative, the Zionist story is clear and compelling. As a narrative underlying the life of a modern country in which 30% of the population is not Jewish (inside Israel proper, rising to 60% if we include the Occupied Territories claimed by Israel), it is problematic at best. Four elements stand out as particularly troubling.

First, it's a completely Jewish story. A central slogan of the Zionist movement declared that the Land of Israel is "a land without people for a people without a land." If Palestinians appear at all, it is as mere background, an undifferentiated mass of "Arabs," romantic peasants at best, at worst intractable enemies whose only role is to kill innocent Jews. The narrative reveals the very core of the Israeli-Palestinian conflict, which is not a denial of Jewish ties to the country *per se* but of Jewish claims that are exclusive, that do not make room for the other people living there. In what can only be described as a kind of autistic nationalism, the Zionist movement saw a lot of "Arabs" living in the country but not a people with a distinctive national identity, legitimate claims to the land and a collective right of self-determination. The Arab presence was reduced to a non-issue or, as it was called in a 1906 Zionist tract, the "Hidden Question."

This was recognized by important members of the Zionist movement during the pre-state period. Judah Magnes, the founder and first Chancellor of the Hebrew University, wrote in 1930:

> What I am driving at is to distinguish between two policies. The one maintains that we can establish a Jewish home here through the suppression of the political aspirations of the Arabs, and therefore a home necessarily established on bayonets over a long period....The other policy holds that we can establish a home here only if we are true to ourselves as democrats and internationalists, thus being just and helpful to others....and intelligently and sincerely at work to find a *modus vivendi* with our neighbors.

Although Labor Zionism has always came across as more pragmatic if not actually progressive, it was the first policy described by Magnes that characterized the views of Ben Gurion and the mainstream

4

Labor movement, not to mention the Revisionist (later Likud) right. "From April 1948, Ben Gurion is projecting a message of transfer," says the prominent historian of the 1948 war Benny Morris in an interview in *Ha'aretz* magazine (January 9, 2004):

> There is no explicit order of his in writing, there is no orderly comprehensive policy, but there is an atmosphere of [population] transfer. The transfer idea is in the air. The entire leadership understands that this is the idea. The officer corps understands what is required of them. Under Ben Gurion, a consensus of transfer is created.

> *Ben Gurion was a "transferist?"*

> Of course. Ben Gurion was a transferist. If he had not done what he did, a state would not have come into being. That has to be clear. It is impossible to evade it. Without the uprooting of the Palestinians, a Jewish state would not have arisen here....

> *The term "cleanse" is terrible.*

> I know it doesn't sound nice but that is the term they used at the time. I adopted it from all the 1948 documents in which I am immersed.

In fact, over the years no Israeli government, Labor or Likud, has ever recognized the Palestinians as a distinct people with national or even individual rights. This was true even at the start of the Oslo process, surely the high point of Israeli-Palestinian relations. Rabin's government demanded, as a precondition for negotiation, "unconditional" Palestinian recognition of the State of Israel. "We demanded," writes Uri Savir, Israel's chief negotiator during the Oslo process, makes clear in his book *The Process*, "that the Palestinians accept Israel not just as a fact of life but as a legitimate political construct." Fair enough. But what did the Palestinians receive in return? Clear and explicit recognition of their existence as a people with the right of self-determination in their own country? Hardly. Israel only recognized the PLO as "the representative of the Palestinian people" with which it would negotiate. Nor did it promise that a Palestinian state would emerge at the end of the negotiations. "We were prepared to recognize the PLO as the representative of the Palestinian people," says Savir, "but not the PLO's version as leaders of a Palestinian state." Indeed, Rabin became agitated when Arafat, to bolster his position among his own people, "misrepresented" the Declaration of Principles as an Israeli agreement to a Palestinian state.

> Following a literal and legalistic interpretation of the declaration, this implied that Israel, as the official "source of authority," would grant the Palestinians limited powers...Israel tried to impose on them a security doctrine requiring everything Israel considered important to remain in its control (Savir 1998:98, 100).

The basic lack of symmetry is evident in the conditions imposed by Israel for its recognition of the PLO as a negotiating partner. While the Palestinians had to recognize Israel's right to exist in security and peace, accept UN Resolutions 242 and 338 [though, in Israel's reading, 242 does not obligate it to withdraw from *all* the occupied territories], renounce terrorism, halt the Intifada and rescinding the clauses of the Palestinian Covenant denying Israel's right to exist, Israel refused to accept the two most fundamental Palestinian demands: the rights of self-determination and the refugees' right of return. The Palestinians demanded a freeze on all settlement activity; Israel refused. The PLO wanted an Israeli commitment not to close Palestinian institutions in East Jerusalem; Israel agreed only to "non-PLO" institutions. On the contrary, Israel's "security" needs and interests became the overarching preoccupation of the peace process. After the signing of the initial Declaration of Principles, writes Savir (1998:81-82),

> Rabin chose a new team of negotiators...composed mostly of military officers. When the military grumbled bitterly at having been shut out of the Oslo talks, Rabin explained that the issues discussed in Oslo had been mainly ideological and political. But he did not reject the

5

criticism, led by Chief of Staff Ehud Barak….That Israel's approach was dictated by the army invariably made immediate security considerations the dominant ones, so that the fundamentally political process had been subordinated to short-term military needs…. The Foreign Ministry had strong misgivings about this military emphasis but did not express them publicly.

Oslo, then, became a trap for the Palestinians. It committed them to a "peace process" over whose content and priorities they had little influence, and one that left Israel free to strengthen its Occupation (during the seven years of negotiations it doubled its settler population) without violating any of its provisions. In fact, the Oslo process is the best case in point of the prevailing Israeli view, shared by Labor and Likud alike, that there is only one legitimate "side" to the conflict, that of the Jews. There is no other "side," only a mass of intractable "Arabs" with which we must deal in one way or another. This is the source of Israel's ferocity in suppressing the Intifada, the use of massive military force against a civilian population and a degree of destruction of property far disproportionate to the actual threat. The "Arabs" must be put in their place; they must be disabused of the notion that they are equal partners in a peace process; they must be made to accept the fact, as Jabotinsky, the intellectual father of the Likud, once put it, that the Land of Israel will never become Palestine. This explains the "unilateral steps" that Israel is considering in imposing its own "solution." It explains the "take-it-or-leave-it" manner of negotiating with the Palestinians, the underlying paternalism of Barak's "generous offer." And it explains the absolute impunity Israel displays towards Palestinian human rights: the systematic demolition of more than 4,000 Palestinian homes in the four years of the Intifada, unabashed violations of international humanitarian law, continued settlement construction and, of course, the construction of "separation barriers" so high, in the words of a prominent Israeli military historian, "that even the birds cannot fly over them."

What follows from all this is *the second missing element of the Israeli framing: the very fact of occupation.* It has become clear that no Israeli government has ever seriously considered relinquishing its control of the West Bank and East Jerusalem, certainly not in favor of a *viable* Palestinian state. With minor differences over the extent of possible Israeli withdrawal, all Israeli governments have shared a formula regarding a Palestinian state that was best stated by Netanyahu: autonomy plus-independence minus. A form of limited sovereignty that uses a Palestinian mini-state to relieve Israel of the Territories' 3.6 million Palestinians yet leaves it in *de facto* control of the entire country. This position rests on several principles and assumptions:

• The exclusive Jewish claim to the country, at whose heart lies Judea and Samaria (the "West Bank"). Unlike Western democracies whose civil societies are based on citizenship and are thus capable of incorporating people of different ethnic and religious backgrounds, Zionism adopted the tribal form of nationalism that privileges the group which "owns" the country at the expense of "intruders," the Palestinians. This, plus the fact that the Palestinians never enjoyed sovereignty over the West Bank or Gaza, gives rise to the Israeli contention that there is no "occupation," only Israeli "administration." After all, how can one occupy one's own country? No matter which ideological or practical direction one comes from – the religious claims of the settlers, the tribal claims of the secular right-wing or the security concerns of Labor Party generals – it is inconceivable that a truly sovereign and viable Palestinian state could arise in the very belly (or heart) of the Land of Israel. Since their own national claims have been deemed invalid, the Palestinians' presence is based on sufferance, not on right. This is true within Israel, defined as a "Jewish democracy," where "Israeli Arabs" are required to recognize Israel as a Jewish state before they are allowed to run in elections. As far as the Occupied Territories are concerned, Israel reserves for itself the right to rule over the Occupied Territories, notwithstanding international law prohibiting it from taking any unilateral steps that render its occupation permanent. It has made it clear that only if the Palestinians accept Israel's "generous offer" of a mini-state will the conflict end.

- A fundamental assumption that the "Arabs" are, and always will be, Israel's enemies. No one has reaffirmed this basic element of the Israeli paradigm more categorically than Ehud Barak, a Labor Party prime minister. When the Palestinians rejected his "generous offer" (for very good reasons, which we will discuss below), he decreed that they are not "partners for peace," that in fact they seek only to throw the Jews into the sea. It was Labor and not the Likud, we must recall, that initiated the construction of the Wall. This explains why neither Peres, Barak nor Mitzna offered the Israeli public any meaningful alternative to Netanyahu or Sharon, and why Labor sits so comfortably in "National Unity" governments with the Likud. For Labor as well as the Likud, any Arab gestures towards peace are to be interpreted as mere ploys. This is what gives the "self-defense" element of the Israeli story its particular authority.

- The necessity of grounding Jewish claims over the country on massive and irreversible "facts." This doctrine of the "Iron Wall," articulated already in the 1920s, became a central tenet of both the pre-state *Jewish* Yishuv and subsequent Israeli governments. It is still invoked frequently in Israeli political discussions.

In 1923, long before organized popular Palestinian resistance to Zionism emerged, Ze'ev Jabotinsky, the founder of Revisionist Zionist and the ideological father of today's Likud Party, formulated the seminal "Iron Wall" doctrine. "Every indigenous people," he wrote,

> will resist alien settlers as long as they see any hope of ridding themselves of the danger of foreign settlement. This is how the Arabs will behave and go on behaving so long as they possess a gleam of hope that they can prevent 'Palestine' from becoming the Land of Israel." [The sole way to an agreement, then,] is through the iron wall, that is to say, the establishment in Palestine of a force that will in no way be influenced by Arab pressure....A voluntary agreement is unattainable....We must either suspend our settlement efforts or continue them without paying attention to the mood of the natives. Settlement can thus develop under the protection of a force that is not dependent on the local population, behind an iron wall which they will be powerless to break down.

Looked at from this perspective, the Matrix of Control that Israel has lain over the Occupied Territories can as seen as part of the "Iron Wall," whether in its physical form (settlements, roadblocks, house demolitions, the "Separation Barrier"), in its use of policy to control every element of Palestinian life (closure into isolated enclaves, restrictions on freedom of movement, construction and economic activities, extensive legal and administrative constraints) or in its overwhelming military presence and frequent use of force. All this is intended to generate such despair among the "natives" that resistance will be broken and they will submit to a mini-state or less. The policy of despair was already articulated by Ben-Gurion after the outbreak of the Palestinian Revolt in 1936.

> A comprehensive agreement is undoubtedly out of the question now. For only after total despair on the part of the Arabs, despair that will come not only from the failure of the disturbances and the attempt at rebellion, but also as a consequence of our growth in the country, may the Arabs possible acquiesce to a Jewish Eretz Israel.

The "Iron Wall" doctrine has remained a central element in pre-state and Israeli policy for the past 80 years. "An iron wall is the most reasonable policy for the coming generation," says Morris approvingly.

> My colleague Avi Shlaim described this well: What Jabotinsky proposed is what Ben Gurion adopted....Ben Gurion argued that the Arabs understand only force and that ultimately force is the one

thing that will persuade them to accept our presence here. He was right. That's not to say that we don't need diplomacy....But in the end what will decide their readiness to accept us will be force alone. Only the recognition that they are not capable of defeating us.

The conviction that reconciliation with the Arabs is hopeless, going back to the early days of Zionism, has given rise to what the Israeli sociologist Baruch Kimmerling calls ""civilian militarism," a central component of Israeli culture. The danger is that any view which dismisses any opening to peace from the start risks disconnecting Israel from political events or processes that might actually resolve the historic conflict. Conflict and war, says Kimmerling (2001:109), became "a self-evident and routine part of everyday life."

> Civilian militarism is systematically internalized by most statesmen, politicians and the general public as a self-evident reality whose imperatives transcend partisan or social allegiances. The gist of civilian militarism is that military considerations, as well as matters that are defined as national security issues, almost always receive higher priority than political, economic or ideological problems. Thus, dialectically, making peace is also a military matter [the election slogans "Peace with Security" being prime examples]....

This certainly throws light on Israel's intransigence towards the Palestinians. No matter what, Israel aims to overwhelm, to defeat the Palestinians. Only when the "Arabs" are made to despair of ever having a truly viable and sovereign state of their own, only when they agree to the semblance of a state that leaves Israel in control of the entire country, will "peace" finally come. Whether through the Oslo peace process or in Sharon's "unilateral steps," Israel pursues a single-minded – and ultimately futile – win-lose approach intended to subjugate the Palestinians once and for all.

It also answers a question frequently asked by visitors when they view the suffering caused by the Separation Barrier, the house demolition policy, the wholesale destruction to cities and neighborhoods by Israeli incursions and Israeli instruments of control: "Why does the Israeli public allow this? Don't they care?" The combination of an exclusive claim to the land, an autism regarding the rights and even the existence of Palestinians, the entrenched notion that the "Arabs" are and always will be Israel's enemy and therefore the only "solution" is an imposed security one, all removes the Palestinians from the equation. They simply are not partners for negotiation, and even if we talk to them it is certainly not as equals in the country. All this also removes the Occupation from the discussion, since Israeli governments deny the very fact of occupation or deny it as a causal factor in the conflict. Lacking, then, any political formulation that might resolve the conflict, the Israeli public has given up on the notion that peace is possible. All it seeks is "peace and quiet." They support whatever initiative will bring them that. "Whatever works." If the creation of a Palestinian state "works" (be it bigger or smaller, viable or not), then do it. If we must put the Palestinians on trucks and ship them out of the country, do it. Whatever works. Whatever brings peace and quiet, the suffering and the fate of the Palestinians being of little concern to the average Israeli. "We offered them a state and they refused in violence," describes the mind-set of 80% of the Jewish public. "They deserve no sympathy. They deserve anything they get. The hell with them. They brought their suffering on themselves."

The third missing element in the Israeli framing is symmetry. Israel presents itself as the victim, the hapless little kid in what Netanyahu called "a tough neighborhood of bullies." But this has never been the case. Israel, and the Zionist *Yishuv* that preceded it, always enjoyed international support denied to the

Palestinians, as well as economic and military superiority. Israel is the regional super-power. It is a state recognized by the international community with an economy three times larger than Egypt, Palestine, Jordan, Syria and Lebanon put together, more than 40 times the size of the Palestinians' ($80+ billion compared to less than $2 billion). It has a formal military alliance with the world's largest superpower, from which it receives more than $3 billion in annual military assistance, despite being the third largest arms manufacturer (after the US and Russia). Israel is also the world's fourth largest nuclear power, possessing up to 500 nuclear warheads. And it is an occupying power. The Palestinians, by contrast, have no state, no functioning economy, no army, not even the ability to move freely from village to village within their own areas. This asymmetry of power, combined with Israel's determination to retain control over the entire country, thrusts upon Israel an asymmetry of responsibility. Without relieving the Palestinians of their share of the responsibility, we must take into account that only Israel can end its Occupation, the entire Arab League, in April 2002, offered Israel full regional integration. This represents the ultimate concession to Israel's security concerns. Yet Israel failed to even acknowledge the offer (in fact, it has demanded that it be removed as a term of reference in the Road Map). Instead, it launched "Operation Defensive Shield" which laid waste to vast stretches of the Occupied Territories, including almost all their cities, and began construction of the massive "Separation Barrier." Its declared aim of eliminating the "infrastructure of terror" ignores, in a supremely self-serving way, that its own Occupation, its own policy of State Terrorism, its own refusal to countenance a viable Palestinian state, constitutes the very ground of terror, of resistance. As successful as the Israeli story is in shifting the blame to the Palestinians, it only prolongs the conflict.

THE MATRIX OF CONTROL

If it is true that every Israeli government since 1967 has sought to maintain control over the Occupied Territories, Israel nevertheless faces two fundamental dilemmas. First, the international community, including the United States, Israel's patron and firmest supporter, expects a Palestinian state to eventually arise alongside Israel. So Israel cannot annex the Territories outright; it must even reserve some space for the semblance of a Palestinian state. And second, if Israel wants to preserve its "Jewish character," it must find a way of relieving itself of the 3.6 million Palestinians resident in the Occupied Territories. If it annexes the Territories and extends Israeli citizenship to the Palestinians, who today constitute half the population between the Mediterranean and the Jordan River, the result would be a bi-national state, the antithesis of Zionism and an anathema to Israeli Jews. If, on the other hand, Israel rules permanently over the Palestinians but denies them citizenship, the result would be outright apartheid, an untenable "solution." What to do? A truly independent and viable Palestinian state is out of the question. Assuming that mass transfer is ruled out, only one solution remains: Netanyahu's "autonomy plus-independence minus," a mini-state in parts of the West Bank and Gaza that liberates Israel of the Palestinian population yet leaves it firmly in control of the entire country.

All this requires a deft slight of hand, granting the Palestinians an independent state while actually keeping full control, and getting the international community to go along. Enter the "Matrix of Control," a maze of laws, military orders, planning procedures, limitations on movement, Kafkaesque bureaucracy, settlements and infrastructure that conceals Israeli control behind a façade of "proper administration," thereby causing the Occupation to disappear from public view. The Matrix resembles the East Asian game of "Go." Unlike chess, where two opponents try to "defeat" each other by eliminating one another's pieces, the aim of "Go" is completely different. You "win" not by defeating but by immobilizing your opponent, by controlling key points on the matrix. This strategy was used effectively in Vietnam, where small forces of Viet Cong were able to pin down and virtually paralyze a half-million American soldiers possessing overwhelming fire-power. Israel's Matrix of Control accomplishes the same with the Palestinians. Maintaining the image of a democratic country only trying to defend its citizens from Arab terror, Israel uses seemingly innocuous and even benevolent policies and procedures to hide its control and repression.

The Matrix operates on three interlocking levels:

1. *Military Controls and Military Strikes.* As much as Israel tries to present its Occupation as merely a benign "administration," the only way it is able to rule over another people while expanding its own territory is through military force. In particular, Israel employs:

   • *Outright military actions*, including attacks on civilian population centers and the Palestinian infrastructure. Although especially evident during the two Intifadas (December 1987-1993; September 2000-present), military actions are not Israel's preferred means of control. They are too visual and by their outward brutality generate international as well as internal opposition; witness "Operation Defensive Shield" which resulted in scores of Palestinian dead, ravaged urban landscapes the virtual destruction of the Palestinian infrastructure in March/April 2002, "Operation Rainbow" which saw the demolition of some 300 houses of Palestinian refugees in the Rafah section of Gaza during one week of May, 2004, or "Operation Days of Penitence," in October 2004, when over 160 Palestinian civilians were killed in northern Gaza (over 30 of them children) and over 500 injured and 90 homes were demolished *(Ha'aretz*, 1.11.04). Still, military force is used effectively and with impunity against civilian populations – in absolute contravention of international humanitarian law – to suppress resistance to the Occupation. It is useful as a deterrent, for "teaching the Palestinians a lesson" or "conveying a message." As such it constitutes State Terrorism.

• *Collaborators and undercover "mustarabi" army units.* Besides outright military rule, control of the local population rests upon thousands of Palestinians turned unwillingly (and occasionally willingly) into collaborators through threats, extortion, "incentives" offered by Israel's stifling administration. Simple things such as obtaining a driver's or business license, a work permit, a permit to build a house, a travel document or permission to receive hospital care in Israel or abroad is often conditioned on supplying information to the security services. Needless to say, collaboration undermines Palestinian society by diffusing fear and distrust.

• *Mass arrests and administrative detention* are common features of Israeli control. The latter is used to imprison people for months or years without charges or trial. In the reoccupation of West Bank cities, towns, villages and refugee camps during the year 2002, about 15,000 people were detained. 760 remain in prison without charge or trial as of December 2004 (B'tselem website).

2. *Creating "Facts on the Ground."* Already in 1977, when he was the head of the Begin government's Ministerial Committee on Settlements, Sharon sought to create "facts on the ground" which would render Israel's Occupation irreversible. No matter what changes occurred in the political situation – new geo-political constellations, new American administrations, even an Israeli government willing to relinquish land for peace – the settlement blocs had to made so massive, the West Bank so completely incorporated into the urban fabric of Israel proper, that the Occupation would be immune to outside forces. This policy has maent:

• *Massive expropriation of Palestinian land,* part of a systematic campaign designed to confine Palestinians to small and disconnected enclaves while expanding Israel's settlements. Since 1967 Israel has expropriated for settlements, highways, "by-pass roads," military installations, nature reserves and infrastructure. This represents some 24% of the West Bank, 89% of Arab East Jerusalem and 25% of Gaza. Because Israel does not recognize Ottoman or British-era deeds, 72% of the West Bank is considered Israeli "state lands."

• *More than 200 settlements have been constructed in the Occupied Territories.* According to the Israeli Central Bureau of Statistics, 450,000 Israelis have moved across the 1967 boundaries (220,000 in the West Bank, 225,000 in East Jerusalem and 7000 in Gaza). The major goal of the settlement enterprise, together with laying an exclusive Jewish claim to the entire country, is to preclude the establishment of a viable Palestinian state. The settlements, the infrastructure serving them and the security system necessary to protect them have carved the Occupied Territories into dozens of isolated enclaves. Palestinians are forbidden to travel among these enclaves without military permission, thus turning their own towns and villages into prisons. Under Barak, the settlement network was consolidated into seven settlement "blocs" that

11

ensured effective Israeli control over any Palestinianentity.

- *A massive system of 29 highways and by-pass roads,* funded entirely by the United States, has been constructed during the course of the Oslo peace process. These highways, lined on both sides with "sanitary" margins that eliminate all Palestinian homes, fields and orchards in their path, are 300 miles in length and three to four football fields wide. Incorporating the West Bank into Israel's national highway system, they make it impossible to detach the Palestinian territories from Israel proper. The highways and "by-pass roads" create ribbons of fluid movement for settlers in and out of Israel while presenting formidable barriers to Palestinian movement.

- *Carving the Occupied Territories into dozens of small, disconnected and impoverished enclaves.* With the signing of Oslo II in 1995, the Occupied Territories, which had been coherent areas and whose integrity Israel was bound to respect, were atomized into more than 70 enclaves. The West Bank was divided into 64 islands: Areas A, B and C, plus a large "nature preserve" in the Judean Desert. Tiny Gaza, one of the most densely packed places on earth, was severed into four areas – Yellow, Green, Blue and White – with Israel keeping control of 40%, especially along the coastline. Many other devices further dismembered the Palestinian territories. Hebron was divided into "H-1" and "H-2," with 30,000 Palestinians living in the Israeli-controlled section because of 400 settlers. In Jerusalem, most of the Palestinian lands in the eastern part of the city were declared "open green spaces" in which Palestinians were forbidden to build. Thus the Palestinians constitute a third of Jerusalem's population but only have access to just 7% of the urban land for residential and community purposes. "Nature preserves," closed military areas and security zones further locked Palestinians into islands encircled by the Israeli Matrix. Even seemingly innocuous holy places such as the Cave of the Patriarchs in Hebron, Joseph's Tomb in Nablus, a synagogue in Jericho and various sites around Jerusalem serve as pretexts for maintaining an Israeli "security presence," and hence military control reinforced by settlements. On the pretext of "securing" Rachel's Tomb in Bethlehem, Israel's Separation Barrier has incorporated it into Jerusalem proper.

- *The "Separation Barrier."* One of the most dramatic of recent developments in Israel's Matrix of Control is the construction of a massive barrier along almost the entire length of the western West Bank (Gaza was fenced in during the late 1980s), with a possible extension to the east as well (Map 7). Construction of the Barrier began in June 2002. Described as a "defensive fence," it will extend more than 670 kms (450 miles), encircling in a complex series of secondary barriers the Ariel, Modi'in, Greater Jerusalem and Hebron settlement blocs. It will de facto annex 10% of the West Bank, including some of its richest agricultural and olive-growing land. An electronic fence fortified by razor wire, watchtowers, sniper posts, mine fields, a ditch four meters deep, barbed wire, security perimeters, surveillance cameras, electronic warning devices and patrols of killer dogs along most of its length, the Barrier, upon approaching Palestinian cities, towns and neighborhoods, becomes a wall of solid concrete 8 meters/26 feet high. While 80% of the Israeli settlers fall on the Israeli side of the Barrier, some 800,000 Palestinians will be directly and adversely affected by it. 50,000 farmers will be trapped between the border and the wall, facing impoverishment, alienation from their land and water, and eventual transfer. Another 60,000 Palestinians holding Jerusalem residency will find themselves on the West Bank side of the Wall, which enters East Jerusalem by the Shuafat refugee camp, while the 230,000

Palestinian residents of East Jerusalem will be isolated from wider West Bank society. Entire cities such as Qalqiliya and Tul Karm, and large Palestinian neighborhoods in East Jerusalem, have been completely encircled. More than 500,000 Palestinians live within one kilometer of the Barrier. Described by Israel as a "temporary facility," the Knesset Finance Committee estimates that it will cost $3.4 billion (The UN Office for the Coordination of Humanitarian Affairs, Jerusalem, March 22, 2005).

The wall emerges directly from threats by Labor that it will pursue "unilateral separation" if the Palestinians object to Israeli dictates. In fact, constructing a larger wall was the central program of Mitzna's 2003 electoral campaign. The fruit of Barak's premiership, the "Separation Barrier," according to the "Security Separation Plan" published in October 2000, has four main objectives:

i. Providing physical security to Israeli citizens, including settlers;
ii. Preventing Palestinians from achieving any territorial, infrastructural or political gains outside of negotiations;
iii. Exacting from the Palestinians a high economic price, through closures, trade restrictions, sanctions and other means, as a way of pressuring them to submit;
iv. Keeping the door open for negotiations. Given the thrust of Israel's Matrix of Control, this means forcing the Palestinians to accept a kind of occupation-by-consent.

The Likud, fearful that "separation" might create a space in which a Palestinian state could emerge, reluctantly accepted the wall's construction on "security" grounds alone. It made it clear that the wall would not constitute a border, and that it had to serve the wider purpose of incorporating the West Bank and Jerusalem. For those reasons it is being built well within the Palestinian side of the "Green Line," including the main settlement "blocs."

- *Imposing a total "closure."* Since the start of the Oslo peace process, a permanent "closure" has been laid over the West Bank and Gaza, severely restricting the number of Palestinian workers allowed into Israel and impoverishing Palestinian society whose own infrastructure Israel has kept under-developed. The closure has many physical forms: 120 permanent checkpoints, hundreds of semi-permanent and "spontaneous" checkpoints which monitor and limit Palestinian movement, both between Israel and the Occupied Territories and among the 300 separate enclaves. The closure may be more porous one day (a "breathing closure") and, without warning or explanation, prevent any movement the next (a "strangling closure"). In different places it may be permanent, or it may be decreed for an indeterminate length of time or it may be "spontaneous." Whatever form it takes, closure prevents the development of a coherent Palestinian economy, wreaks havoc on family and community life and precludes the rational planning of one's individual life.

- *Construction of seven (of a planned twelve) industrial parks on the "seam" between the Occupied Terri*tories and Israel. At first glance this would seem a positive development. The industrial parks are intended, however, to blunt Palestinian aspirations for self-determination by giving the average worker employment and a living wage. By allowing some of its First World economy to trickle into the Palestinian areas, Israel can rob a Palestinian entity of its economic vitality, guaranteeing its continued dependence on Israel itself. The industrial parks allow Israel's most polluting and least profitable industries (aluminum factories, metalworks, plastic and chemical concerns, slaughterhouses and the like) to exploit cheap Palestinian labor while denying it access to Israel. Because of lax environmental standards in the Occupied Territories, they also afford continued opportunities to dump industrial wastes into the West Bank and Gaza. As economic anchors, the industrial parks breathe new life into isolated settlements, whose residents manage their plants.

- *Maintaining control over the main aquifers and other vital natural resources of the Occupied Territories.* Israel's Matrix of Control extends underground and into the air, as well as over the ground's surface. In spite of international law that forbids an Occupying Power to utilize the resources of an occupied territory, Israel takes about 30% of its water from the West Bank and Gazan aquifers located under its main settlements. In fact, 80% of the water coming from the West Bank goes to Israel and its settlements; only 20% to its 2.5 million Palestinians. Massive rock quarries, whose materials are used in Israeli settlement and road construction, scar the historic and fragile landscape. And Israel claims control of much of the West Bank and Gazan airspace, including its electro-magnetic communications fields. All this limits the viability and sovereignty of a future Palestinian state.

3. *Bureaucracy, Planning and Law as Tools of Occupation and Control.* In order to render its Occupation invisible, to cast it merely as a form of "proper administration," Israel's Matrix of Control relies on bureaucratic and legalistic mechanisms that entangle Palestinians in a tight web of restrictions, triggering sanctions whenever Palestinians try to expand their life space. These most subtle of control mechanisms include:

- *"Orders" issued by the Military Commanders of the West Bank and Gaza.* Because an Occupying Power is forbidden by international law to replace the local laws with those of its own, Israel has imposed on the Occupied Territories some 2000 "military orders" which, when supplemented by Civil Administration policies, effectively constitute a corpus of law hostile to the Palestinian population and designed to strengthen Israeli political control. Military Order 59 (1967), for example, grants the Israeli Custodian of Abandoned Properties the authority to declare uncultivated, unregistered land as Israeli "state land." Since Israel refuses to recognize Ottoman- or British-era deeds and Order 291 (1968) stopped the process of land registration, Israel was able to classify a full 72% of the West Bank as "state lands," making expropriation from their Palestinian owners an easy administrative matter. Order 270 (1968) designated a further million dunams (250,000 acres) of West Bank land as closed "combat zones," which could then be handed over to settlements or used for Israeli infrastructure. Order 363 (1969) imposed severe restrictions on construction and land use in yet other areas zoned as "nature reserves." Order 393 (1970) granted any military commander in Judea and Samaria the authority to prohibit Palestinian construction if he believes it necessary for the security of the Israeli army or to ensure "public order." Order 977 (1982) authorized the Israeli army or its agencies (such as the Civil Administration) to proceed with excavation and construction without a permit, providing an avenue for settlement construction that by-passed legal and planning systems. Hundreds of other military orders prohibit Palestinian building around army bases and

14

installations, around settlements and whole settlement areas, or within 200 meters on each side of main roads. They effectively curb the development of Arab communities and alienate tens of thousands of acres of land from their Palestinian owners.

- *Administrative measures which severely restrict Palestinian freedom of movement, and which induce emigration.* The Civil Administration has divided the West Bank into eight "security zones" and Gaza into three, between which Palestinians need permits to travel. All the major roads of the West Bank and Gaza are closed to private Palestinian vehicles, and access to virtually every city, town and village is blocked by earthen or military obstructions. Five crossings are being constructed between the West Bank and Israel, in addition to the two between Gaza and Israel, through which all Palestinian movement – workers allowed into Israel as well as commercial traffic – will be regulated. A system of magnetic cards issued to each Palestinian worker, already activated in Gaza, will be extended to the West Bank, thus tremendously enhancing Israel's ability to monitor or control Palestinian movement. Palestinian residents of Jerusalem who seek affordable housing outside the municipal borders lose their Jerusalem IDs, thus locking them out of the city (and by extension, the entire country of Israel). Thousands of spouses live apart because they cannot get permits for "family reunification."

- *"Transfer."* Because Palestinians will outnumber Jews in the area between the Jordan River and the Mediterranean by the end of the decade, Israel considers the "demographic bomb" the greatest threat to its hegemony. To counter this trend, Israel actively pursues policies of displacement: exile and deportation of Palestinians, the revoking of residency rights, economic impoverishment, land expropriation, house demolitions and other means of making life so unbearable as to induce "voluntary" Palestinian emigration. Schemes of "transfer" have become an acceptable part of Israeli political discourse. Some policies of transfer are straightforward: thousands of Palestinians lose their right to return to the country if they go abroad to study, work or live. The educated middle classes are targeted in particular, because their removal renders Palestinian society weak and leaderless. But often transfer is carried out in less visible ways. Take Jerusalem as an example, where Israel endeavors to maintain a 72% majority of Jews over Arabs. The municipality uses zoning and expropriation to severely restrict Palestinian construction, enforcing its policies with an aggressive policy of house demolitions. The result is an artificial housing shortage – 25,000 housing units lacking in the Palestinian sector – thereby raising the cost of scarce housing. Since 70% of Palestinians residing in Jerusalem live below the poverty line, they are forced to find affordable housing outside the city borders. Once they have shifted their "center of life" from Jerusalem, the Ministry of Interior revokes their Jerusalem residency, turning them into West Bank residents, thus bolstering the Jewish majority.

- *Discriminatory zoning and planning policies* are ideal vehicles for subtly obstructing the natural development of Palestinian towns and villages – and ultimately inducing emigration – because they hide Israel's political agenda behind a facade of technical maps, "neutral" professional jargon and seemingly innocuous administrative procedures. Thus Israel has taken two British Mandate planning documents – the Jerusalem Regional Planning Scheme RJ5 (1942) and Samaria Regional Planning Scheme RS15 (1945) – and uses them effectively to freeze Palestinian development in Jerusalem and the West Bank as it was in the 1940s. RS15, for example, zones the entire West Bank as "agricultural land." Since it severely limits the construction of houses on such land, Israel can effectively deny Palestinians building permits, and demolish their houses if they build "illegally." A little-noted provision of British planning law gave the District

Commission (now the Civil Administration) the "power to grant a relaxation of any restriction imposed by this scheme." This enables the Israeli authorities to construct hundreds of thousands of housing units for Jews on lands zoned for agriculture, while strictly enforcing the Regional Schemes in the case of the Palestinians. Thousands of Palestinian homes have been demolished by court order, with thousands of demolition orders outstanding.

- _Administrative restrictions that intrude into every corner of Palestinian life._ Control and restrictions penetrate into even the most intimate areas of personal life. Israel fears any kind of Palestinian self-sufficiency that would help the population weather its policies of impoverishment, collective punishment and intimidation. The planting and marketing of Palestinian crops, for example, is severely restricted; Palestinians need permits even to grow vegetable gardens next to their houses! The opening of banks and businesses is severely curtailed, and even seemingly routine practices such as licensing and inspection of Palestinian businesses are exploited as a way to harass businesspeople and stunt the local economy.

- _Manipulation of international humanitarian law._ How to protect the rights and well-being of people under occupation is a central concern of international humanitarian law, particularly addressed in the Fourth Geneva Convention which governs how an Occupying Power must conduct itself vis-à-vis the population and territory under its control, as well as the rules of engagement in warfare. Israel, which is in the process of making its occupation permanent in violation of international law, attempts to by-pass this responsibility in many ways. Among others, it denies the very fact of occupation in the West Bank and East Jerusalem (and Gaza, before "disengagement"), it unilaterally annexes occupied territory ("East" Jerusalem and the Golan Heights), and it openly violates the principles of the Fourth Geneva Convention (by transferring its population into the settlements and displacing the local population).

A new benchmark in the manipulation of international law came with the outbreak of the second Intifada. In order to avoid the constraints of international law in combating terrorism (the label applied to all forms of Palestinian resistance, which is considered by Israel as mere criminal activity), it declared "a conflict short of war," a state of "almost war" unknown in international law. This novel form of war conveniently removes any political context of the conflict. Although oppressed peoples have a right to resist -- even in an armed fashion, although not involving attacks on civilians – such a undifferentiated term as "conflict short of war" allows Israel to represent forms of resistance as "terrorism," thereby abrogating such basic Palestinian human rights as the right of self-determination and the right to a secure and decent existence, even under occupation. In this way Israel also relieves itself of all responsibility for state terrorism, attacks on civilian populations equally prohibited under international law. Israel thus enjoys the benefits of a protagonist in a declared war without the constraints and responsibilities. It can justify the killing civilians as a form of "collateral damage;" it can pursue a campaign of assassination against political leaders and those engaged in legitimate resistance; it does not have to grant Palestinian prisoners the status and rights of POWs; it does not have to compensate Palestinians for physical injury or material damage; nor does it have to meet other obligations required in a state of war. It is the best of both worlds: free to conduct a full-scale war on "criminals" among an essentially civilian population using all weapons of conventional warfare, yet also freed of legal constraints imposed by the rules of war.

16

The extent of the collateral damage" entailed in this strategy cannot be understated. According to figures gathered by B'tselem, the Palestine Monitor and the Palestinian Center for Human Rights for the four years of the second Intifada (Sept. 29, 2000-December 2004):

- More than 3,300 Palestinians have been killed, at least 85% of them civilians. Some 650 were children and youth, half under the age of 15. In 88% of the incidents in which children were killed, there was no direct confrontation with Israeli soldiers. 297 Palestinians have been killed by assassination or extra-judicial executions, some 180 intentionally targeted, the rest "collateral damage;" 86 have died as the result of delays at checkpoints; 34 were killed by settlers

- More than 50,000 Palestinians have been injured, 20% of whom are children and youth. Some 2500 civilians have been permanently disabled. Children in particular have been traumatized by the extreme violence to which they have been exposed: killings, military attacks, house demolitions, harassment, humiliation of their parents and teachers.

- According to the UN Conference on Trade and Development, as much as $2.4 billion has drained out of the economy of the West Bank and the Gaza Strip thanks to closures, mass unemployment, and the flattening of the Palestinians infrastructure by Israeli tanks and helicopters. More than $4 billion in income has been lost to the Palestinian economy. 70% of Palestinian firms have either closed or have severely reduced production. Unemployment runs to 67% in Gaza, 48% in the West Bank. 75% of Palestinians, including two-thirds of the children, live in poverty, on less than $2 a day. Half the Palestinian population requires external food assistance to meet their minimal daily food needs, with 30% of Palestinian children under five years of age suffering from malnutrition. 60% of the children in Gaza suffer from parasitic infections (Losing Ground, A report of Christian Aid, 2003).

- Out of a total of 12,000 Palestinian homes demolished since 1967, close to 5000 houses have been demolished during the second Intifada (September 2000-present) – 2800 in the West Bank, 2,400 in Gaza. 60% of the Palestinian homes demolished in the Occupied Territories were done so as part of military "clearing operations;" 25% were demolished as being "illegal," not having permits; and 15% for collective punishment (B'tselem Summary 2004:2). 15,000 houses have been damaged, 5000 of them in refugee camps. More than 75,000 people have been affected. In addition, some 30 mosques and 12 churches have been destroyed, 134 water wells sealed or destroyed, 180,000 olive and fruit trees uprooted or cleared (Palestine Monitor, B'tselem, ICAHD).

- Eighty per cent of the water resources of the West Bank and Gaza are under Israeli control. One third of Israel's water comes from the Occupied Territories, in violation of international law. Eighty per cent of the waters of the Mountain Aquifer, the only source of groundwater for the West Bank, go to Israel and its settlements. One third of Israel's water comes from the Jordan River; none goes to the Palestinians of the West Bank. Israeli settlers use six times more water per capita than Palestinians. Per capita water consumption in the West Bank for domestic, urban and domestic use is only 60 liters per person per day, below the minimum water intake of 100 liters per person per day recommended by the World Health Organization. Overall, Israelis consume 350 liters per person per day. Each settler is allocated 1,450 cubic meters of water per year, each Palestinian 83. 215,000 Palestinians in 270 West Bank villages have no running water. The destruction of Palestinian wells and water mains (which will intensify with the construction of the wall over the main aquifers) creates months of water shortages, while the need to purchase water from tankers is often beyond the financial resources of the impoverished population. Water purchased from a water network costs less than $1 per liter; water purchased from a tanker costs $3 during the rainy season and up to $8 in the dry months. Palestinians are forbidden to collect rainwater in open reservoirs (B'tselem 2001).

- 850 schools have been closed for varying periods; 185 have been shelled or shot at; 11 completely destroyed. 245 Palestinian pupils have been killed and 2600 injured on their way to or from school. More than 1000 school days have been lost since the start of the second Intifada (Palestine Monitor).

- Add to all this the harassment, humiliation, anger and frustration of life under occupation, as well as traumas suffered by tens of thousands of Palestinians (especially children) who have witnessed their homes being demolished, seen their loved ones beaten and humiliated, suffered from inadequate housing, and who have lost opportunities to actualize their life potentials.

The Matrix of Control, then, conceals behind a façade of seemingly innocuous administrative devices and ostensibly justified military and physical constraints a repressive regime intended to permanently deny the Palestinians self-determination, citizenship, and basic human and civil rights. It lowers the military profile of the army and its "Civil Administration," thereby giving the impression that the Palestinians are merely resisting "proper administration." By resorting to public displays of military control only when the Palestinians revolt against the Occupation, as in the two Intifadas, Israel is able to shift the blame for the "violence" onto the Palestinians. The Occupation disappears, the Palestinians are successfully portrayed as "terrorists," Israel's military repression comes off as "self-defense," and Israel preserves its image as the only peace-loving state in the region. The Matrix allows Israel to appear forthcoming – as in Barak's "generous offer" of 95% – whereas in reality Israel retains control, ensuring that a Palestinian state will be neither economically viable nor truly sovereign. The Matrix of Control represents the most sophisticated expression of the "Iron Wall," the Zionist doctrine that says the Arabs will submit to Jewish domination only when it has become so overwhelming, so permanent, that they will despair of ever having a viable state of their own. Laid out on a map (see Map 10), the Matrix clearly defines the outlines of a dependent mini-state, a bantustan.

Israel's manipulation of international law also poses a grave challenge to anyone concerned with achieving a just peace in the Middle East – or anywhere. Recognizing the increased importance of international law in global political life, an Israeli expert in international law, who curiously chose to remain anonymous, made this remarkably *candid comment* to the Jerusalem Post (Post magazine, April 15, 2005, p. 34):

> International law is the language of the world and it's more or less the yardstick by which we measure ourselves today. It's the lingua franca of international organizations. So you have to play the game if you want to be a member of the world community. And the game works like this. As long as you claim you are working within international law and you come up with a reasonable argument as to why what you are doing is within the context of international law, you're fine. That's how it goes. This is a very cynical view of how the world works. So, even if

you're being inventive, or even if you're being a bit radical, as long as you can explain it in that context, most countries will not say you're a war criminal.

BARAK'S "GENEROUS OFFER"

But what about Barak's "generous offer?" Didn't he offer to relinquish 95% (or 97% -- or 103% according to Shlomo Ben Ami, Barak's Foreign Minister) of the Territories at Taba in January 2001? Wasn't it the Palestinians who rejected Camp David and Taba with a violent Intifada, orchestrated by none other than Yassir Arafat himself? Didn't the Israelis do their part? They were forthcoming, they tried to "give them" a state, they were generous. Doesn't the fact that they rejected such an offer prove they really do not want peace, that they are not partners for peace? If that case, Israel is off the hook. The Palestinians are to blame for everything. The Israelis are not responsible; they needn't feel any guilt over the destruction of the Jenin refugee camp, the demolition of thousands of Palestinian homes during the Initfada, the deaths of almost 3000 people. Far from deserving sympathy, the Palestinians are getting what they deserve.

This has become the single most influential argument used to cast Israel as the forthcoming champion of peace, and the Palestinians as mere "terrorists." As a formula for framing the conflict, it effectively deflects public attention from the fact that Palestinians live under an occupation that is only getting stronger, an occupation that Israel presents as its justified and irreversible "claim" to the country that it will never renounce. The bulk of the Israeli public, joined by significant sectors of the Labor Party and even moderate members of the peace camp, blamed the Palestinians for "spoiling" the Oslo negotiations. In this way the Israeli public could grant its government a carte blanche to pursue the most oppressive of policies while relieving itself of any responsibility or even sympathy for the plight of the Palestinians. The "95%" line has also proven extremely effective to Israel's public relations abroad, especially since it has not been answered well by the Palestinians themselves. Without the complex Matrix of Control to explain Israel's subtle modes of domination, without reference to the "facts on the ground," it's difficult to argue that 95% is not a good deal. That simply defies common sense. Addressing the issue of Barak's "generous offer" is therefore critical to our ability to re-frame the dispute in a way that will lead to a just and sustainable solution, rather than to continued occupation and conflict.

What, then, of this "generous offer?" First of all, it never was. In an interview with the Israeli newspaper *Ha'aretz* (Shavit, 2002), Barak stated candidly: "It was plain to me that there was no chance of reaching a settlement at Taba. Therefore I said there would be no negotiations and there would be no delegation and there would be no official discussions and no documentation. Nor would Americans be present in the room. The only thing that took place at Taba were non-binding contacts between senior Israelis and senior Palestinians." The 95% figure comes from Clinton's proposal (of 96% concessions, excluding East Jerusalem), to which both sides felt the need to respond favorably, but with "reservations." According to Barak, Israel's reservations filled 20-pages.

What, then, were the Taba "non-negotiations?" Not much, at least in diplomatic terms. Barak would not even have entered into them had he not been pressured to do so by the "doves" in his government: Shimon Peres, Yossi Beilin and the head of the Meretz Party Yossi Sarid. When the talks were held in January 2001, Clinton had only a couple weeks left in his Presidency and Barak was facing certain defeat in the up-coming Israeli elections in March. Barak knew he had no mandate to enter into major negotiations, of which his own Attorney General Eliyakim Rubenstein reminded him. He had no functioning government; his coalition partners had already quit and he controlled only 42 of the 120 seats in the Knesset. Even if a breakthrough had been achieved, everyone knew an agreement would never be approved by the parliament. Still, Barak, who needed every vote and who had been elected on a platform of peace, was concerned over losing his liberal and left-wing voters if the "doves" made it known that he had abandoned the peace process. As Shlomo Ben-Ami, Barak's Foreign Minister put it, "there was a pistol on the table. The elections were a month away and there was a minister who told Ehud that if he did not go to Taba they would denounce him in public for evading his duty to make peace. He had no choice but to go to a meeting for something he himself no longer believed in" (quoted in Makovsky 2003).

If he had to go to Taba, Barak would at least seek some tangible benefit from it. That was a letter from the Palestinians telling the Israeli electorate that peace was in sight and could be achiev*ed* relatively quickly if Barak was re-elected. Barak intended to go to the electorate with that letter hoping it would change the tide of the election and allow him to defeat his rival, the Likud's Ariel Sharon. To speed up the process and to reach an agreement-in-principle, Barak did not send his team of negotiators to Taba, but rather three of the most "peace-oriented" members of the government, Peres, Sarid and Beilan. Neither had a mandate to actually negotiate, which is why Barak says that Taba represented only "non-binding contacts between senior Israelis and senior Palestinians." Their task was to produce the letter. To assist them Barak hinted at – but never actually tabled – the "generous offer," but it was more a kind of "best scenario" intended to elicit from the Palestinians a tentative agreement that would get Barak re-elected than an actual offer. At any rate it never had any guarantees or governmental authority behind it. When, after about two weeks of talks, it became clear that the letter would not be forthcoming, Barak broke off the TabThe ambiguous nature of the talks were reflected in the "non-paper" subsequently produced by Miguel Moratinos, the EU Special Representative to the Middle East Peace Process, which is considered an authoritative summary of the discussions. It is worth looking at Taba as the last bell-weather of Israeli and Palestinians intentions before Sharon's attempt to impose a *Pax Israeliana/Americana* on the Palestinians by military means plunged the entire area into hell. Taba is important for our re-framing because it demonstrates that the sides could talk, that considerable gaps existed but were not irrational or outwardly hostile or destructive to the other side, and that the Israeli framing of "security and terrorism" did not derive from the political facts on the ground, even if the Intifada had been re-ignited.

According to Moratinos, the talks floundered on predictable issues.

- *Territorial contiguity, viability and sovereignty versus Israeli expansion, control and hegemony.* While both sides accepted the principle, in accordance with the UN Security Council Resolution 242, the June 4 1967 lines would be the basis for the borders between Israel and the state of Palestine, and both accepted the "Clinton parameters" (with significant reservations), Israel insisted that the Clinton parameters permitted Israel to annex its major settlement blocs, including East Jerusalem (but excluding the Jordan Valley), presenting a map in which Israel annexes 6% of the West Bank and "leases" another 2% containing 80% of its settlers. Israel also insisted on maintaining contiguity between the settlements and Israel. The Palestinians rejected this position, offering instead 3.1 of the West Bank in return for a qualitative land swap. This was all left unresolved. It was agreed in spirit, however, that Israel would cede Gaza, although the nature of the two "safe passages" connecting Gaza to the West Bank was also left unresolved, the Palestinians insisting that the passages be extra-territorial and Israel refusing.

  Another dispute that remained unresolved stemmed from Israel's refusal to accept the Palestinian demand for a 1:1 ratio between the area of the West Bank annexed to Israel and the parts of Israel that would be given to the Palestinians in exchange. Israel proposed a ratio of 1:2, in its favor.

- *Jerusalem.* Both sides, according to Moratinos, accepted in principle the Clinton suggestion of having a Palestinian sovereignty over Arab neighborhoods and an Israeli sovereignty over Jewish neighborhoods. The Palestinian side affirmed that it was ready to discuss Israeli request to have sovereignty over those Jewish settlements in East Jerusalem that were constructed after 1967, but not Jebal Abu Ghneim [Har Homa] and Ras al-Amud. The Palestinian side rejected Israeli sovereignty over settlements in the Jerusalem Metropolitan Area, namely of Ma'ale Adumim and Givat Ze'ev. The Palestinian side understood that Israel was ready to accept Palestinian sovereignty over the Arab neighborhoods of East Jerusalem, including part of Jerusalem's Old City. The Israeli side understood that the Palestinians were ready to accept Israeli sovereignty over the Jewish Quarter of the Old City and part of the American Quarter. The Palestinian side understood that the Israeli side accepted to discuss Palestinian property claims in West Jerusalem.

  Both sides favored the idea of an Open City – though they did not agree to the borders between the "Open City," the territory that citizens of both countries can enter without passing through any checkpoints, and the surrounding Palestinian and Israeli areas. The Palestinians wanted it to encompass all of Jerusalem, while the Israelis wanted it limited to the Old City only.

  The Israeli side accepted that the City of Jerusalem would be the capital of the two states: Yerushalaim, capital of Israel and Al-Quds, capital of the state of Palestine. The Palestinian side expressed its only concern, namely that East Jerusalem is the capital of the state of Palestine. Both parties have accepted the principle of respective control over each side's respective holy sites (religious control and management). According to this principle, Israel's sovereignty over the Western Wall would be recognized.… Both sides agreed that the question of Haram al-Sharif/Temple Mount has not been resolved. However, both sides were close to accepting Clinton's ideas regarding Palestinian sovereignty over Haram al-Sharif notwithstanding Palestinian and Israeli reservations.

- *Dispute over Ma'aleh Adumim.* The importance of Israel's recognition of the June 4, 1967 border is that since 1967 (and even today), Israel's official position has been that UN Security Council Resolution 242 mandates withdrawal from "territories" conquered in the Six Day War. The Arab position, in contrast, is that the resolution requires withdrawal from "the territories."

  The dispute centered around the large stretch of territory between Ma'aleh Adumim and Givat Ze'ev, which contains both a fairly large Palestinian population and East Jerusalem's most important land reserves. The Palestinians retracted their earlier readiness to include these two settlements in the settlement blocs to be annexed to Israel after realizing that Israel also insisted on annexing the large tract that joins them – which would mean that Palestinian citizens would suddenly find themselves in sovereign Israeli territory.

- *Refugees.* Both sides stated that the issue of the Palestinian refugees is central to the Israeli-Palestinian relations and that a comprehensive and just solution is essential to creating a lasting and morally scrupulous peace.…Both sides suggested, as a basis, that the parties should agree that a just settlement of the refugee problem in accordance with the UN Security Council Resolution 242 must lead to the implementation of UN General Assembly Resolution 194. The Israeli side put forward a suggested joint narrative for the tragedy of the Palestinian refugees. The Palestinian side discussed the proposed narrative and there was much progress, although no agreement was reached in an attempt to develop and historical narrative in the general text. Both sides engaged in a discussion of the practicalities of resolving the refugee issue. The Palestinian side reiterated that the Palestinian refugees should have the right of return to their homes in accordance with the interpretation of UNGAR 194. The Israeli side expressed its understanding that the wish to return as per wording of UNGAR 194 shall be implemented within the framework of one of the following programs:

A. *Return and repatriation*

1. to Israel; 2. Israel swapped territory; 3. to the Palestine state.

B. *Rehabilitation and relocation*

1. Rehabilitation in host country; 2. Relocation to third country.

Preference in all these programs shall be accorded to the Palestinian refugee population in Lebanon. The Palestinian side stressed that the above shall be subject to the individual free choice of the refugees, and shall not prejudice their right to their homes in accordance with its interpretation of UNGAR 194.

The Israeli side, informally, suggested a three-track 15-year absorption program… Both sides agreed to the establishment of an International Commission and an International Fund as a mechanism for dealing with compensation in all its aspects.

- *Issues of Sovereignty.* The Israeli side maintained that the state of Palestine would be non-militarized as per the Clinton proposals. The Palestinian side was prepared to accept limitation on its acquisition of arms, and be defined as a state with limited arms. The two sides have not yet agreed on the scope of arms limitations.

The two sides recognized that the state of Palestine would have sovereignty over its airspace. The Israeli side agreed to accept and honor all of Palestine civil aviation rights according to international regulations, but sought a unified air control system under overriding Israel control. The Palestinian side was interested in exploring models for broad cooperation and coordination in the civil aviation sphere, but unwilling to cede overriding control to Israel.

Based on the Clinton proposal, the Israeli side agreed to a withdrawal from the West Bank over a 36-month period. The Palestinian side proposed an 18 months withdrawal under the supervision of international forces.

The Palestinian side was confident that Palestinian sovereignty over borders and international crossing points would be recognized in the agreement. The two sides had, however, not yet resolved this issue. The Israeli side recognized that the state of Palestine would have sovereignty over the electromagnetic sphere. but sought control over it for security purposes. The Palestinian side sought full sovereign rights over the electromagnetic sphere, but was prepared to accommodate reasonable Israeli needs within a cooperative framework.

- *Security and Terrorism:* Both sides were prepared to commit themselves to promoting security cooperation and fighting terror.
While they failed to get Barak re-elected, the Taba talks nevertheless had some promising elements, perhaps because they were "non-negotiations" among peace-minded interlocutors who

were not expected to "deliver." They therefore had the luxury of exploring promising avenues in a constructive spirit. In fact, they eventually led to the Geneva Initiative in which Yossi Beilan and Yasser Abed-Rabo, two of the more far-sighted Oslo negotiators, sought to show the Israeli public and the world that despite what Barak and Sharon said, Israelis and Palestinians were partners for peace. Taba, however, came too late in the process, and it is doubtful that Barak himself would have supported the eventual outcome (he certainly is not among the supporters of the Geneva Initiative). Just before his decisive defeat by Sharon in March, 2001, Barak declared all the tentative agreements reached at Taba "null and void."

If Taba had been useful in clarifying the positions of the sides, it was used by Israeli PR to obfuscate the issues in a cynical and self-serving way. It became the source of Barak's "generous offer," a mythical event that has played a destructive role in the public debate by laying the blame for the failed peace process squarely, exclusively and unfairly on the Palestinians. But let's say, for a moment, that the "Generous Offer" of 95% had been made. Would the Palestinians have been justified in rejecting it? Would it have led to a just and sustainable peace, or to a bantustan? If anything Taba reveals the extremely fine line between these two enormously contradictory outcomes. In our estimation, while offering territory, the "generous offer" conformed to Netanyahu's (and currently Sharon's) formula of "autonomy plus-independence minus."

- *Not Much Room for Maneuvering.* The attention paid to Barak's generous offer has obscured, if not eliminated from view altogether, Arafat's even more Generous Offer. On two occasions, that of the declaration of Palestinian independence in Algiers in 1988 and again at the start of the Oslo process in 1993, the PLO formally recognized Israel within the 1967 borders. That entailed a far-reaching concession that has never been appreciated. By so doing, the Palestinians relinquished political claim not only to the 54% of Mandatory Palestine partitioned to the Jews by the UN in 1947, but also to the additional 24% of Palestine, more than half the area granted to the Palestinians, conquered by Israel in the 1948 war. In Oslo the Palestinians offered a full peace to Israel in return for ending the Occupation and withdrawing to the 1967 boundaries – peace and recognition in return for only 22% of the country: the West Bank, East Jerusalem and Gaza. Whether that 22% is actually viable as a state is an open question, especially given the refugee issue. But it certainly cannot sustain Israeli settlements, roads or other forms of control that reduce the Palestinians' territory even further.

- *Control Versus Territory.* When we make corrections for East Jerusalem, the Latrun salient, No-Man's Land, the Palestinian area under the Dead Sea and various other "exceptions," then add in the settlement blocs and certain "security zones" claimed by Israel, plus land to be "leased," the territory Barak was willing to concede added up to about 80-85% of the West Bank (including non-contiguous enclaves in East Jerusalem) and all of Gaza. On paper, even this sounds "generous." But we must be careful not to equate territory with sovereignty or sustainability. Although gaining control of 85% of the territory would have been an achievement, it would not have provided the prerequisites of national self-determination: coherent territory, economic viability and genuine sovereignty.

Here is where the Matrix of Control comes into play. Israel could relinquish 85%, perhaps even 90%, of the Occupied Territories and still retain its main settlement blocs, still control the entire country, still preclude the rise of a viable and truly sovereign Palestinian state. Looked at through the Matrix of Control, these are what Barak's "generous offer" would allow Israel to reain:

24

- *Strategic Settlement Blocs.* In the mid-1990s Israel began a major strengthening and consolidation of its settlement presence (Map 5). In order to avoid international opposition to the establishment of new settlements, the government shifted to building new settlements within the expansive master plans around each settlement. In that way it was able to argue that it was simply "thickening" existing settlements to meet natural population growth (an outright falsification), not establishing new ones. It also began to merge discrete settlements into large settlement blocs. Although the fate of some of these blocs remains uncertain (the Jordan Valley settlements, for example, as well as the Kiryat Arba bloc near Hebron and settlements in heavily populated Palestinian areas), Israel is unmoving in this insistence on retaining seven large blocs comprising today some 150,000 Israeli settlers – or 80% of the West Bank settlers. (Barak has often said that he strove for a peace "that even the settlers would be happy with.")

- *The city of Ariel and its surrounding "Western Samaria" bloc* control a strategic area on the western side of the West Bank, seriously compromising territorial contiguity and the coherent flow of people and goods between the major Palestinian towns of Kalkilya, Nablus and Ramallah. It would also severely restrict the urban development of the Kalkilya area. No less important than its strategic location on the ground is Ariel's location vis-a-vis Palestinian resources under the ground: the Ariel bloc sits atop the major aquifer of the West Bank and would control the flow and distribution of water.

- *The central Givat Ze'ev-Pisgat Ze'ev-Ma'aleh Adumim-Beit El bloc* stretches across much of the central West Bank from the Modi'in area to within 20 kilometers of the Jordan River. It effectively divides the West Bank in two, compelling north-south Palestinian traffic (especially from Ramallah to Bethlehem and Hebron areas) to pass through Israeli territory – the funnel-like Eastern Ring Road. It also keeps the Palestinians of the West Bank far from Jerusalem, isolating the 200,000 Palestinians of East Jerusalem from their wider state and society, and cutting the natural urban link between Jerusalem and Ramallah. In terms of viability, this bloc, a main component of Israeli "Greater Jerusalem," constitutes the greatest threat to a coherent Palestinian state. In March, 2005, the Israeli government announced the construction of 3500 housing units in the E-1 corridor connecting Jerusalem to Ma'aleh Adumim.

- *The Efrat-Gush Etzion-Beitar Illit bloc* to the southwest of Jerusalem, connected the Ma'aleh Adumim bloc through Har Homa, Gilo and the newly-planned city of Givat Yael, is the other key component of "Greater Jerusalem." It also impacts seriously on the viability and sovereignty of any Palestinian state. The bloc severs any coherent connection between the major cities of Bethlehem and Hebron, as well as traffic using the "safe passage" from Gaza. It forces Palestinians moving between these areas to use Israeli-controlled "security" roads passing through dense areas of settlement, continually exposed to disruption and closure. It locks in Bethlehem to the extent of preventing its normal urban development. And, like the Ariel bloc, it sits astride and brings into Israeli control a major West Bank aquifer.

- *A "Greater [Israeli] Jerusalem."* The Givat Ze'ev-Adumim and Gush Etzion settlement blocs, 250 square kilometers containing some 80,000 settlers, when annexed to Israeli-controlled "Greater Jerusalem," will dominate the entire central region of the West Bank and obstruct the territorial contiguity necessary for a viable Palestinian state. They also function as a buffer, to separate Jerusalem from its wider West Bank surroundings, thus keeping the Palestinians at a considerable distance away. Because some 40% of the Palestinian economy revolves around Jerusalem in the form of tourism, commercial life and industry, removing Jerusalem from the Palestinian realm carries such serious economic consequences as to call the very viability of the Palestinian state into question. And in general the "Greater Jerusalem" concept neutralizes Jerusalem as a major Palestinian urban, religious and cultural center (see Map 15).

Greater Jerusalem is tremendously important to Israel. So important that Barak claims it was the issue that "broke" the Camp David negotiations. "Arafat's position on the issue of Jerusalem," he said in a taped interview in Hebrew immediately after the talks' collapse,

> is what prevented the reaching of an agreement. Ideas were raised more than once during the course of the negotiations [by the Israeli delegation] of the definition and growth of Jerusalem to dimensions that it never had at any stage of Jewish history, with extremely significant strengthening of its Jewish majority and a guarantee of a solid [Jewish] majority for generations through exchanging some of the cities surrounding Jerusalem – Ma'aleh Adumim, Givat Ze'ev, the Etzion Bloc – attaching them to Jerusalem and placing them under Israeli sovereignty, thus creating a situation in which the whole world recognizes this expanded and great Jerusalem as Israel's capital, at a price of transferring a few villages and neighborhoods situated within the municipal boundaries to Palestinian sovereignty. (Transcribed by the author).

• *An Israeli Metropolitan Jerusalem.* The ring roads and major highways being built through and around Jerusalem are intended to create a regional infrastructure of control, turning Jerusalem from a city into a metropolitan region. "Metropolitan" Jerusalem covers a huge area. Its boundaries, incorporating a full 10% of the West Bank (440 square kilometers), stretch from Beit Shemesh in the west up through Kiryat Sefer until and including Ramallah, then southeast through Ma'aleh Adumim almost to the Jordan River, then turning southwest to encompass Beit Sahour, Bethlehem, Efrat and the Etzion Bloc, then west again through Beitar Illit and Tsur Hadassah to Beit Shemesh. It also provides a crucial link to Kiryat Arba and the settlements in and around Hebron. In many ways "Metropolitan" Jerusalem is the Occupation. Within its limits are found 75% of the West Bank settlers and the major centers of Israeli construction.

By employing a regional approach to the planning of highways, industrial parks and urban settlements, an Israeli-controlled metropolis can emerge whose very power as a center of urban activity, employment and transportation will render political boundaries, such as those between Jerusalem and Ramallah or Jerusalem and Bethlehem, absolutely irrelevant. A good example of how this is already happening is the new industrial park, Sha'arei Binyamin, now being built at the "Eastern Gate" to metropolitan Jerusalem, southeast of Ramallah. In terms of Israeli control this industrial park provides an economic anchor to settlements – Kokhav Ya'akov, Tel Zion, Ma'aleh Mikhmas, Almon, Psagot, Adam, all the way to Beit El and Ofra – that otherwise would be isolated from the Israeli and Jerusalem economy. More to the point, it robs Ramallah of its economic dynamism, providing jobs and perhaps even sites for Palestinian industry that would otherwise be located in or around Ramallah. Again, looking at Israel's strategy from the point of view of control rather than territory, "Metropolitan Jerusalem" virtually empties a Palestinian state of its meaning in terms of viability and sovereignty (see map 15).

26

- *An East Jerusalem Patchwork.* Between the negotiations at Camp David and Taba, various options were explored to give the Palestinians more of a presence in East Jerusalem, which they claim as their capital. The peripheral villages and neighborhoods to the north and south of the city might have been ceded, although the Palestinians might receive less than full sovereignty over them – "functional autonomy," "administrative control" or "limited sovereignty." In Taba, Israel considered ceding some parts of the core areas as well: some of the "Holy Basin" between the Old City and the Mount of Olives, downtown East Jerusalem, the Sheikh Jarrah Quarter, and in the Old City the Muslim and Christian Quarters. The Temple Mount/Haram issue remained unresolved, with Israel prepared to cede "functional sovereignty" (though not official) to the "upper" area of the mosques, while retaining sole sovereignty over the "lower" Western Wall.

  Regardless of the size of the territorial compromises, Israel will not cede the entire area of East Jerusalem, where Israelis (about 225,000 in number) outnumber Palestinians. Since the settlements there were situated strategically for maximum control of territory and movement, and since they are today in the process of being connected, any Palestinian patches will become only tenuous connections to each other and to the Palestinian capital in Abu Dis. The Palestinian presence in Jerusalem will be fragmented and barely viable as an urban and economic center. Moreover, it would be entirely surrounded by the "outer ring" of Israeli "Greater Jerusalem," hemming it in and preventing East Jerusalem's normal urban and economic development. (Indeed, functionally ceding Palestinian areas of East Jerusalem to the Palestinians – relinquishing an "unwanted" population of some 200,000 people without relinquishing control – while incorporating the surrounding settlements into a "Greater Jerusalem" would increase the majority of Jews in the expanded city from the current 66% to 85%.) (See Map 14.)

- *Israeli Control over Highways and Movement.* Over the past decades (and especially during the Oslo process), Israel has been constructing a system of major highways and "by-pass roads" designed to link its settlements, to create barriers between Palestinian areas and to incorporate the West Bank into Israel proper. Even if physical control over the highways is relinquished, strategic parts will remain under Israeli control – the Eastern Ring Road, Jerusalem-Etzion Bloc highway, Road 45 from Tel Aviv to Ma'aleh Adumim, a section of Highway 60 from Jerusalem to Beit El and Ofra, and the western portion of the Trans-Samaria highway leading to the Ariel bloc. In terms of the movement of people and goods, this will effectively divide the Palestinian entity into at least four cantons: the northern West Bank, the southern portion, East Jerusalem and Gaza. There are other restrictions as well. Israel refuses to grant extra-territorial status to the "safe passages" from Gaza to the West Bank, crucial to the viability of a Palestinian state. It will only allow Palestinian administration of the passages, meaning that Palestinians traveling from Gaza to the West Bank could be detained, or arrested, arrested at any time. Israel also insists on retaining rights of "emergency deployment" to both the highway system and to the Jordan Valley, severely compromising Palestinian sovereignty. Indeed, the highways would retain the status of Israeli "security roads," meaning that Palestinian development along them would remain limited.

  To fully understand the role of the highway grid in completing the process of incorporation, one must link these West Bank developments to the ambitious Trans-Israel Highway project. Already in 1977, in his Master Plan for the settlement and incorporation of the West Bank, Sharon presented his "Seven Stars" plan calling for contiguous Israeli urban growth straddling both sides of the "Green Line." The Trans-Israel Highway, which hugs the border of the West Bank, provides a new "central spine" to the country. Hundreds of thousands of Israelis will be resettled in the many towns and cities planned along the length of the highway, especially along the "Green Line" and in areas of the Galilee heavily populated by Arabs. (In August 2003 the government published a map of 30 new settlements to be built inside Israel along the route of the Trans-Israel Highway.) New and expanded Israeli cities, towns and settlements on both sides of the Green Line will form a new "metropolitan core-region" in which Metropolitan Tel Aviv (including the Modi'in area settlements, Rosh Ha'Ayin and the Ariel bloc) meets Metropolitan Jerusalem (stretching from Modi'in, Kiryat Sefer, Beit Shemesh and the Etzion Bloc across most of the central West Bank to the settlements east of Ma'aleh Adumim. The Trans-Israel Highway, articulating as it does with the highways and settlement blocs of the West Bank, moves the entire population center of the country eastward, reconfiguring the entire country. It reconfigures the entire country from a north-south orientation in which two parallel states were possible to an east-west one in which each Palestinian canton is integrated independently into Israel, thus further weakening the viability of any future Palestinian state.

- *A "Secure" Israel Versus a Palestinian State of Limited Sovereignty.* "Security" is defined by Israel in such maximalist terms that it ensures Israeli political, military and economic control. Israel insists that a Palestinian state would be demilitarized and only semi-independent, unable to enter into pacts with other states without Israeli approval. Israel would continue to control Palestinian airspace and the electro-magnetic sphere crucial for communications. It would "supervise" the borders. It would reserve the right to unilaterally deploy forces in the Jordan Valley in the indeterminate event that it unilaterally perceives a "threat" of invasion. It would continue to control Palestinian labor and commercial movement through the imposition of "security borders," part of Israel's declared policy of "separation" that isolates the 20%-minus of Palestine that would be the state from the 80%-plus that is Israel.

All these sources of Israeli control can be contained within the 10-15% envisioned in Barak's "generous offer." In order to help people make the "switch" from the common sense view that 95% is indeed "generous" to the view that 5% is enough to frustrate Palestinian aspirations for self-determination, we might find a prison analogy helpful. If one looks at a blueprint of a planned prison, it appears as if the prisoners own the place. They have 95% of the territory: the living areas, the work areas, the exercise yard, the cafeteria, the visiting area. All the prison authorities have is 5%: the prison walls, the cell bars, the keys to the doors, some glass partitions. The prison authorities do not have to control 20-30% of the territory in order to control the inmates. Similarly, Israel only needs a few control points taking a limited amount of territory to completely neutralize a Palestinian state.

This was well illustrated by a comment of Netanyahu's when he was Prime Minister. During the Wye negotiations of 1998, the Americans were pressing for an Israeli withdrawal from the West Bank of "double figures" (around 11%), while Israel refused to go beyond 9% (and in the end withdrew from only 2%). As the negotiations teetered on the brink of crisis, Netanyahu was asked why he was quibbling over just a percent or two. Each percent of the West Bank, he answered, is equal to an area the size of Tel Aviv. Looked at in this way, relinquishing 95% would leave the equivalent of five Tel Avivs in the tiny, truncated territory of Palestine – ten Tel Avivs if we include East Jerusalem and various other areas Israel does not include in its calculations. Together the prison analogy and Netanyahu's comments on the significance of each percentage of land help us grasp how "ungenerous" was Barak's "generous offer" if the goal is a viable, sovereign Palestinian state.

28

THE PALESTINIANS REJECT AUTONOMY;
ISRAEL MOVES TOWARDS APARTHEID

While territory was offered at Camp David and Taba, the Matrix of Control remained intact. It had become obvious that Israel would never accede to a viable and truly sovereign Palestinian state – even on the mere 22% of Mandatory Palestine that the Palestinians claimed. Had Barak made a "generous offer" and had the Palestinians accepted it, they would have found themselves confined to a truncated, dependent mini-state with no territorial contiguity, no viable economy and no true sovereignty.

The ongoing conflict between Palestinian demands for full sovereignty in a viable state and Israel's desire to preserve its control over (and settlements in) the Occupied Territories came to a head with the outbreak of the second Intifada in September, 2000. Fearful that Israel and the US would succeed in pressuring Arafat to sign the Camp David "agreement" (in the three months following Camp David, the sides met 52 times), the Palestinian Street erupted into yet another uprising. Although Sharon's visit to the Haram/Temple Mount and the violent response of the Israeli police to non-violent Palestinian protests triggered the uprising, it was directed as much against Arafat as against the Occupation. The Street's central message to Arafat was: "You do not sign Camp David, since it will lead to nothing but a sophisticated form of apartheid." The second Intifada, which has turned into a full-scale war for independence, spelled the final rejection by the Palestinian people of the Oslo peace process.

The Final Push: Reoccupation and the Defeat of the Palestinians

Israel began its unrestrained onslaught on the Palestinian areas in October 2001, aided by post-9.11 American complicity and carefully framed in Bush's own words ("destroying the infrastructure of terrorism"). It reached its climax in the March 2002 invasion of the Jenin refugee camp, dubbed Operation Defensive Shield, which culminated in the reoccupation of the entire West Bank, as well as in massive attacks on Gaza. The Sharon government persuaded the Bush Administration that it could bring the Palestinian Authority to its knees within a matter of weeks, thereby achieving "industrial quiet" on the Israel/Palestine front that would enable the US to proceed with its plans against Iraq. Having received a green light from the US, Sharon's "National Unity" government developed a multi-pronged strategy to defeat the Palestinians once and for all. Israel, in return, played a key role in the invasion of Iraq: American troops trained for the invasion in mock Iraqi neighborhoods and villages built in the Negev; Israeli's security services played a major role in the disinformation campaign over weapons of mass destruction that preceded the invasion; and the US adopted from Israel its model of occupation, complete with a Civil Administration and a policy of demolishing Iraqi homes for "security reasons."

The campaign of suppression continues as of this writing in April 2005, despite some relaxation as a kind of cease-fire is implemented. Yet Israel's goal remains the same: to force the Palestinians to acquiesce to a bantustan. While tactical considerations emphasize one or another element at any particular time, the key elements of Sharon's final push to defeat the Palestinians remain in force:

- A campaign of attrition intended to erode the Palestinians' ability to resist the Occupation. The demolition of thousands of Palestinian homes and businesses (almost 5000 during the first four years of the Intifada), ongoing land expropriation and the clearing of thousands of acres of farmland and olive groves, an ever-tightening "closure" that has turned into a tight military siege of all Palestinian communities, prolonged curfews, starvation and the withholding of medical care, the induced emigration of thousands of middle-class families and an ever-expanding use of collaborators – these are just some of the draconian measures intended to break the Palestinians' will and drive them to submit to Israeli dictates.

- *Massive military* actions against the fragile Palestinian infrastructure and population centers using the most sophisticated and powerful of US conventional weapons – F-16s, tanks, artillery, Apache and Cobra helicopters equipped with laser-guided missiles, culminating in the current all-out invasion of Palestinian areas. Although presented as responses to Palestinian terrorist attacks, these military actions are pro-active, exploiting terrorist attacks to achieve political goals through military means.

- *Completing its program of creating irreversible "facts" on the ground.* While presenting itself as the peace-seeking victim of Palestinian aggression, Israel has never paused for a moment in expanding settlements and constructing its infrastructure in the Occupied Territories. By now Israel has all the land, settlements and settlers it needs; its highway and "by-pass" road system is almost complete. Still, it continues to add "security nails" in the coffin of a viable Palestinian state. The population of Ma'aleh Adumim will grow from its present 30,000 to more than 70,000 in the next five years. Israel is planning an entirely new city of 55,000 people, named Givat Yael, on the lands of Wallajeh between Jerusalem and Bethlehem. Three ultra-orthodox cities – Beitar Illit to the west of Bethlehem, Tel Zion near Ramallah and Modi'in Illit, an extension of the city of Modi'in to the west of Ramallah – represent the fastest growing settlements. And the construction of the Wall, accompanied by massive land expropriation and population transfer, continues apace. The most recent revelation of Israel's intentions to remain in permanent control of the West Bank is the plan unveiled in September, 2004, for an $80 million network of Palestinian highways, including sixteen "passages," bridges or tunnels that give the Palestinians "transportational" but not territorial contiguity, thus preserving Israel's own exclusive network of settler highways. With its hold on the Occupied Territories appearing unassailable, Sharon believes that his canton scheme, be it the outcome of negotiations or an imposed unilateral "solution," is within reach.

- *Reliance on the American Congress* to protect Israel from those forces – European, Arab, civil society – which would pressure it to dismantle its occupation and accede to a viable Palestinian state. The uncritical bipartisan support of Congress is Israel's trump card; it provides it with an impenetrable shelter from outside pressures. Even if the US Administration presses for a meaningful political process following Israel's suppression of the Intifada, Congress will ensure that it be an open-ended process, like Oslo, that will not endanger Israel's control. Thus, even before the Road Map was released by Bush in March, 2003, 91 out of 100 Senators sent the President a sharply worded message warning him not to place undue pressures on the Israeli government. Sharon's greatest victory on the political front was Congressional ratification in June, 2004, of the Bush-Sharon agreement that recognized the permanency of Israel's settlement blocs and undercut the Road Map as an effective means towards a just peace.

It is no wonder that former Israel Chief of Staff Moshe Ya'alon publicly declared Israel's "victory" over the Palestinians.

Towards a Bantustan

All this has given rise to a policy that Israeli military commanders call "constructive destruction." As reported in *Ha'aretz* (Oct. 25, 2002), this doctrine entails "laying waste to the Palestinian Authority, reinstating full Israeli control of the kind that existed before the first Intifada, and reaching an imposed settlement with obedient canton administrators." As the Matrix map indicates (see Map 9), the West

Bank will be divided into three separate cantons according to existing Israeli settlement blocs, highways and the wall. A northern canton would be created around the city of Nablus, defined by the Jordan Valley settlement bloc to the east, the Ariel settlement bloc to the south and the wall being constructed to the north and west. South of the Ariel settlement bloc, encircled by the wall, Israeli Greater Jerusalem and the Jordan Valley settlements, will be a central canton administered from Ramallah. A third canton to the south of Greater Jerusalem will center around Hebron. (A map presented on the Israeli TV news in the wake of Sharon's unveiling of his "Disengagement Plan" suggests that the West Bank will be divided by Israeli corridors into six cantons.) The Gaza Strip will become yet another canton. Once having established a "Greater Jerusalem" controlling the entire central portion of the West Bank, Israel could then cede isolated islands of Palestinian neighborhoods in East Jerusalem without jeopardizing its overall control of the city.

DEMOLISHING HOMES, DEMOLISHING FAMILIES, DEMOLISHING PEACE

Why the Focus on House Demolitions?

ICAHD has been working on the issue of house demolitions since 1997. Every time we think: "OK, we've exhausted the subject, let's go on to other, perhaps more pressing issues," the wholesale destruction of Palestinian homes returns to the center of the conflict with a vengeance. It happened in the Jenin refugee camp in March 2002. There, at the onset of Operation Defensive Shield, the indomitable drivers of the massive D-9 Caterpillar bulldozers, army reservists, labored for three days and nights without getting down from their cabs. More than 300 homes in the densely packed camp were razed. The once lowly bulldozer drivers became the heroes of the invasion, earning medals of valor from the army command. Said one driver, Moshe Nissim, who did not get down from the cab of his two-story D-9 Caterpillar bulldozer for 75 hours straight:

> For three days I just erased and erased. The entire area. I took down any house from which there was shooting. To take it down, I would take down several more. The soldiers warned with a speaker, that the tenants must leave before I come in, but I did not give anyone a chance. I did not wait. I didn't give one blow, and wait for them to come out. I would just ram the house with full power, to bring it down as fast as possible. I wanted to get to the other houses. To get as many as possible. Others may have restrained themselves, or so they say. Who are they kidding? Anyone who was there, and saw our soldiers in the houses, would understand they were in a death trap. I thought about saving them. I didn't give a damn about the Palestinians, but I didn't just ruin with no reason. It was all under orders.

> Many people where inside houses we set to demolish. They would come out of the houses we where working on. I didn't see, with my own eyes, people dying under the blade of the D-9. and I didn't see house falling down on live people. But if there were any, I wouldn't care at all. I am sure people died inside these houses, but it was difficult to see, there was lots of dust everywhere, and we worked a lot at night. I found joy with every house that came down, because I knew they didn't mind dying, but they cared for their homes. If you knocked down a house, you buried 40 or 50 people for generations. If I am sorry for anything, it is for not tearing the whole camp down.

> I didn't stop for a moment. Even when we had a two-hour break, I insisted on going on....I had plenty of satisfaction. I really enjoyed it. I remember pulling down a wall of a four-story building. It came crashing down on my D-9. My partner screamed at me to reverse, but I let the wall come down on us. We would go for the sides of the buildings, and then ram them. If the job was to hard, we would ask for a tank shell. I couldn't stop. I wanted to work and work. There was this officer who gave us orders by radio – I drove him mad. I kept begging for more and more missions. On Sunday, after the fighting was over, we got orders to pull our D-9's out of the area, and stop working on our 'football stadium', because the army didn't want the cameras and press to see us working. I was really upset, because I had plans to knock down the big sign at the entrance of Jenin – three poles with a picture of Arafat. But on Sunday, they pulled us away before I had time to do it.
> I had lots of satisfaction in Jenin, lots of satisfaction. I kept thinking of our soldiers. I didn't

feel sorry for all those Palestinians who were left homeless. I just felt sorry for their children, who were not guilty....(quoted in "7 Days," *Yedioth Ahronoth* Supplement, May 31, 2002)

(Amnesty International (2004:4) comments on this: "The largest single wave of destruction carried out by the Israeli army was in the Jenin refugee camp in April 2002. The army completely destroyed the al-Hawashin quarter and partially destroyed two additional quarters of the refugee camp, leaving more than 800 families, totaling some 4000 people, homeless. Aerial photographs and other evidence show that much of the house destruction was carried out after clashes between Israeli soldiers and Palestinian gunmen had ended and Palestinian gunmen had been arrested or had surrendered.")

House demolitions achieved prominence again in the spring and summer of 2003 when the Civil Administration demolished more than 180 shops and houses in the border village of Nazlat Issa, one of the few places where Israelis and Palestinians shopped together. It continues to happen on a more massive scale in Gaza, where almost 2000 houses have been demolished in the four years since the second Intifada began, the vast majority in the Rafah, Jabalyiah and Khan Yunis refugee camps. And it happened on December 1, 2004, when the house of the Sharaan family – a destitute family of nine, including an elderly grandmother, living in a concrete block shack on a lonely wind-swept hill in East Jerusalem – was demolished by the municipality. It was the 121st Palestinian home demolished in Jerusalem in 2004, one of the 12,000 houses demolished since 1967 in the territories occupied by Israel.

Palestinian homes are demolished for various and sundry reasons: the land they own has been declared by Israel "agricultural land" or "open green space;" they have no building permit (which the Israeli authorities refuse to grant Palestinians); the slope of their land is adjudged as "too steep;" their houses are too near settlements or Israeli-only highways (although the houses were there first); out of collective punishment for some action the punished people had nothing to do with; the "clearing" of vast tracts of land for military/security purposes; destruction for the sake of expanding roads, settlements and the "Separation Barrier;" houses "cleared" to make passage safe for settlers or for other security purposes; homes representing "collateral damage;" and more. The policy of house demolitions uses administration, planning, zoning and the law for overt political purposes: to quietly transfer Palestinians out of the country or, alternatively, to confine them to small enclaves, thereby leaving the land (*their* land) free for Israeli settlement and annexation. Most people think, of course, that Palestinians houses are demolished because their inhabitants performed some terrorist acts. This is not the case. In fully 95% of the cases the residents had absolutely nothing to do with security offenses: they neither committed illegal acts nor were even accused of doing so. (It should be noted, however, that demolishing homes belonging to families of terrorists is a form of collective punishment against innocent people that itself constitutes a war crime.)

The actual demolition of homes is only part of the story, of course. We must also take into account the tens of thousands of Palestinian families who own land and possess the financial resources to build modest homes who do not do so because they cannot obtain permits and do not want to risk demolition. In the Palestinian sector of East Jerusalem alone there are 25,000 "missing" housing units – a completely artificial and induced housing shortage that condemns thousands of families to crowded and inadequate living conditions. Again, this is part of what Israel calls "the quiet transfer," making life so difficult for the Palestinian population that it leaves the country altogether.

The vacuum created by halting Palestinian construction is filled, of course, by Israel itself. Amidst the demolitions, some 150,000 housing units have been built for the 450,000 Israeli Jews living across the 1967 border.

The Message of the Bulldozers

Israel's policy of house demolitions certainly plays a key role in maintaining the Occupation by confining the Palestinians to small islands, or driving them from the country altogether. But it goes beyond the Occupation, to the very heart of the conflict itself. This became clear to us when we began asking Why? Why does Israel pursue its house demolition policy so aggressively, even during times of negotiations when one would expect a more gracious approach towards its Palestinian interlocutors? Why does it remain at the center of the conflict?

To answer this question we must realize that the house demolition policy did not originate with the Occupation in 1967. The British Mandate authorities demolished Palestinian homes before 1948 as forms of "deterrence" against attacks, appreciative of the fact that this was the most painful punishment for Arabs (and, probably, for anyone). It was Israel, however, that applied the house demolition policy widely and systematically. House demolitions have stood at the center of Israel's approach to "the Arab problem" since the state's conception.

Although exact figures are impossible to arrive at, the stages in Israel's demolition campaign are as follows:

Stage 1: Inside Israel (1948-1960s)

- Between 1948 and into the 1960s Israel systematically demolished 418 Palestinian villages inside of what became the State of Israel, two-thirds of the villages of Palestine. This was not done in the heat of battle, but well after the residents fled or were driven out, so that the refugees could not return and their lands could be turned over to the Jewish population.

Stage 2: In the Occupied Territories (1967-present)

At the very start of the Occupation in 1967 the policy of demolition was carried across the "Green Line" into the West Bank, East Jerusalem and Gaza. As of 2005 approximately 12,000 Palestinian homes have been destroyed – homes, we must add, of people who had already lost their homes inside Israel in 1948 and after.

- At least 2,000 houses were demolished immediately following the 1967 war. Four entire villages were razed in the Latrun area (now known as "Canada Park"), while dozens of ancient homes were destroyed in the Mughrabi Quarter of Jerusalem's Old City to create a plaza for the Wailing Wall.

- In 1971, Ariel Sharon, then Commander of the Southern Command, cleared 2,000 houses in the Gaza refugee camps to facilitate military control. (Since he was elected Prime Minister in early 2001 he has overseen the demolition of another 1500 homes in Gaza.)

- At least 2,000 houses in the Occupied Territories were destroyed in the course of quelling the first Intifada in the late 1980s and early '90s.

- Almost 1,700 Palestinian homes in the Occupied Territories were demolished by the Civil Administration during the course of the Oslo peace process (1993–2000)

- Since the start of the second Intifada in September 2000, between 4000-5000 Palestinian homes have been destroyed in military operations, including hundreds in Jenin, Nablus, Ramallah, Bethlehem, Hebron and other cities of the West Bank, more than 2500 in Gaza alone. Tens of thousands of other homes have been left uninhabitable. Altogether around 50,000 people have been left homeless (Human Rights Watch, Razing Rafah, October 2004). Hundreds of shops, workshops, factories and public buildings, including all the Palestinian Authority ministry offices in all the West Bank cities, have also been destroyed or damaged beyond repair. According to Amnesty International more as than 3000 hectares of cultivated land – 10% of the agricultural land of Gaza – have been cleared during this time. Wells, water storage pools and water pumps which provided water for drinking, irrigation and other needs for thousands of people, have also been destroyed, along with tens of kilometers of irrigation networks.

- During the same period about 900 Palestinian homes have been demolished by the Civil Administration for lack of proper permits.

- More than 628 Palestinian homes have been demolished during the second Intifada as collective punishment and "deterrence" affecting families of people known or suspected of involvement in attacks on Israeli civilians. On average 12 innocent people lose their home for every person "punished" for a security offense – and in half of the cases the occupants had nothing whatsoever to do with the acts in question. To add to the Kafkaesque nature of this policy, the Israeli government insists it is pursued to "deter" potential terrorists, although 79% of the suspected offenders were either dead or in detention at the time of the demolition (B'tselem Summary 2004:1,3).

- In sum, during the second Intifada (September 2000-present), 60% of the Palestinian homes demolished in the Occupied Territories were done so as part of military "clearing operations;" 25% were demolished as being "illegal," not having permits; and 15% for collective punishment (B'tselem Summary 2004:2)

Stage 3: Back Inside Israel (1990s-present)

- Throughout Israel proper, in the "unrecognized" Palestinian and Bedouin villages, as well as in the Palestinian neighborhoods of Ramle, Lod and other Palestinian towns, houses continue to be demolished at an ever accelerating rate. Some 100,000 "internal refugees" from 1948 and their families still live in more than 100 "unrecognized villages" located in the vicinity of their now-destroyed villages, where they suffer from inadequate living conditions and constant threats of demolition. Entire Bedouin villages in the Negev, numbering some 60,000-70,000 residents, are threatened with demolition. Indeed, whereas Arabs comprise almost 20% of the population of Israel, they are confined by law and zoning policies to a mere 3.5% of the land. In mid-2004 the Israeli government announced the formation of a "Demolition Administration" in the Ministry of Interior to oversee the demolition of these homes of Israeli Arab citizens – between 20,000-40,000 in number.

The house demolition policy goes far beyond mere administrative and military means to contain or force out an entire population. In the aggregate, from 1948 till the present, it represents a policy of displacement, of one people dispossessing another, taking both their lands and their right to self-determination. Since people cannot survive or function without a house, the Message of the Bulldozers is clear: "Get out. You do not belong here. We uprooted you from your homes in 1948 and prevented your return, and now we will uproot you from all of the Land of Israel."

ICAHD resists demolitions of all kinds. As Israelis we block bulldozers coming to demolish, we chain ourselves in the houses, we conduct campaigns to mobilize opposition to the policy in Israel and abroad, we turn to the courts and, when demolitions finally occur, we rebuild demolished homes with the Palestinians as political acts of solidarity and resistance. We have come to see house demolitions as the very essence of the conflict between our two peoples: Israel's exclusive claim to the entire country in the name of the Jewish people at the expense of another people living in the country, a people being dispossessed by our own country. This is what gives the policy of house demolitions its special significance. When, as Israelis, we resist home demolitions and rebuild demolished homes as acts of civil disobedience, we are acknowledging the rights of both people to share the country. We are affirming our recognition that Palestinian claims carry equal authority to our own. And we are proclaiming loudly: We refuse to be enemies!

What is the Process of Demolition?

The motivation for demolishing Palestinian homes is purely political, although it employs an elaborate system of planning, laws and administrative procedures to lend it a proper facade. The goal is to confine the 3.6 million Palestinians of the Occupied Territories, together with the million Palestinian citizens of Israel, to small enclaves on only about 8% of the country – rising to 15% if a truncated Palestinian mini-state is established. In this way, Israel can effectively control the entire country, Palestinian state or not.

When homes are demolished in military actions or as acts of deterrence and collective punishment, there is no process. No formal demolition orders, no warning, no time to remove furniture or personal belongings, often barely time to escape the home falling down around your ears. This can happen to your home, or to the home of a neighbor whom the Israeli authorities have targeted. Nuha Maqqdmeh Sweidan, a Gazan mother of 10 and nine months pregnant, was killed when the house next to hers was dynamited by Israeli troops. "We were in bed, the children were asleep," her husband related to Amnesty. "There was an explosion and walls collapsed on top of us. I pulled myself from under the rubble....I started to dig in the rubble with my hands. First I found my two little boys and my three-year-old girl....One by one we found the other children, but my wife remained trapped under the rubble with our youngest daughter, who is two. She was holding her when the wall fell on her...." (Beit Arabiya is dedicated to the memories of Nuha and Rachel Corrie.) Writes Amnesty in its report *Under the Rubble* (2004:3):

> The Israeli authorities claim that these demolitions are not intended as punishment, but rather to "deter" Palestinians from getting involved in attacks. Israel has never destroyed the homes of Israeli Jews who committed serious attacks, such as the murder of Prime Minister Rabin, or bomb attacks against Palestinians or Israeli Arabs. These punitive forced evictions and house demolitions are a flagrant form of collective punishment and violate a fundamental principle of international law, which stipulates that collective punishment is never permissible under any circumstances.

On August 6, 2002, the Israeli High Court of Justice gave its consent to demolishing houses of families of people accused of terrorism without warning or a chance to appeal to the court; since then, 620 houses have been demolished outside of the legal system.

Demolitions are executed for "administrative" reasons (lack of a permit) by the Civil Administration in the West Bank and Gaza, by either the Ministry of Interior or the Jerusalem municipality in East Jerusalem. Regardless, the overall process is similar. Master plans and zoning regulations have been carefully prepared so as to limit Palestinian building, all carefully based on legal requirements. The entire West Bank has been designated "agricultural land," while most of the unbuilt-upon land owned by Palestinians in East Jerusalem has been zoned as "open green space." In both cases it is therefore possible to deny building permits to Palestinians on supposedly professional planning grounds and, if they nevertheless build on their own land (everyone must live somewhere), to demolish their "illegal" homes without appearing to discriminate. (While Jews may in rare cases receive a demolition order for an illegal porch or shed, there has never been a Jewish house demolished in either Jerusalem or the Occupied Territories, the removal of a few temporary trailers set up by settlers on remote hillsides excepted.) And the policy is explicit: "Our policy is not to approve building in Area C," an Israeli Army spokesperson said openly to Amnesty International delegates in 1999. "There are no more construction permits for Palestinians," reiterated Colonel Shlomo Politus, legal advisor to the Civil Administration, to the Israeli Parliament on 13 July 2003 (Amnesty 2004:4).

Since Palestinians do not have home mail delivery (including in East Jerusalem), demolition orders are distributed in a very haphazard manner. Occasionally a building inspector may knock on the door and hand the order to anyone who answers, including small children. More frequently the order is stuck into the doorframe or even left under a stone near the house. On many occasions Palestinians have complained that they never received the order before the bulldozers arrived, and thus were denied recourse to the courts. In Jerusalem a favored practice is to "deliver" an order at night by placing it somewhere near the targeted home, then arriving early in the morning to demolish. ICAHD has a case pending against David Schneider, the chief building inspector of the Ministry of Interior, who makes it a practice to keep lawyers or families who have obtained a last-minute injunction from the court from approaching him until the demolition has been completed.

If they do manage to reach the court in time, Palestinians may occasionally delay the order's execution (at considerable expense). We are not aware, however, of any order that has actually ever been overturned. Once it is affirmed, the bulldozers may arrive at any time – the same day, weeks or years later, or never. Palestinians, barred from any possibility of obtaining decent, affordable and legal housing, do a simple, cold arithmetic: thousands of demolition orders are outstanding, the various Israeli authorities destroy "only" 200-500 homes a year (military attacks and punitive demolitions aside), so if I build the chances are that I might buy a year or two or three before the bulldozers arrive. As in a perverse reverse lottery, I might even "win" and escape demolition altogether.

This gamble comes at a high emotional cost as well as financial. Imagine the anxiety families endure during the weeks, month and years of waiting for bulldozers to arrive. "My morning routine," says Huda Dandis, whose home in Anata was finally demolished in November 2004 after a wait of eight years, "consisted of getting out of bed, going to the window to see if the bulldozers were approaching, then going to the bathroom." Whether the home is demolished or not, the psychological tensions often lead to stress-related health problems, domestic violence and trauma, all aggravated by poor living conditions and financial strain. Men who fear for the safety of their homes and their families often quit their day jobs to be present if the bulldozers come. The Israeli authorities know all this and even incorporate it into the "planning" process. ICAHD members have been told explicitly by legal officials in the Civil Administration that fear and intimidation are effective in deterring Palestinians from building.

When the dreaded day finally arrives, it does so almost without warning. Though families know their homes are targeted, actual demolitions are carried out at random, without pattern, and can strike anywhere at any time. (Normally demolitions do not occur on Fridays or Saturdays due to the Jewish Sabbath, or on Jewish holidays. These are the only times Palestinians can truly relax – an ironic twist on the idea of the "Day of Rest.") Randomization is part of the generalized fear that underlies the policy of "deterrence." The wrecking crews, accompanied by tens of soldiers, police and Civil Administration officials, usually come in the early morning hours just after the men have left for work. The family is sometimes given a few minutes to remove their belongings before the bulldozers move in, but because family members and neighbors usually put up some kind of resistance – or at least protest – they are often removed forcibly from the house. Their possessions are then thrown out by the wrecking crews (often foreign guest workers). Amnesty's report Under the Rubble (2004:4) relates the story of As'ad Mu'yin and his cousin Ziad:

> On 21 August 2003, on the morning of his wedding, As'ad Mu'yin had his house demolished; the house of his cousin Ziad As'ad, who had married a week earlier, was demolished at the same time. The two adjacent houses were in the West Bank town of Nazla 'Issa. As'ad Mu'yin had been living on the ground floor of the house with his parents and three brothers and had furnished and prepared the second floor to move in with his wife. The house was demolished before he could do so. The new furniture and the wedding gifts disappeared under the rubble, along with the content of the family home on the ground floor. He told Amne*sty International: "The army came early in the morning, at about 7am. I was getting ready for the wedding, for a very happy day. They had bulldozers . They gave us 15 minutes to leave the house. We had no time to salvage anything. They said that we did not have building permits. But everyone knows that Israel does not give building permits to Palestinians in Area C."*

In addition to the emotional suffering of seeing their most personal possessions broken, ruined and thrown out in the rain, sun and dirt, demolitions constitute a serious financial blow, especially to the poor families who make up the vast majority of demolition victims. About 70% of Palestinians living in both Jerusalem and the West Bank/Gaza live below the poverty line. Families whose monthly income is around $500 are burdened by the Israeli courts with hefty fines in the range of $10-20,000, to be paid in monthly installments whether the house is demolished or not. In Jerusalem families must also pay for the demolition of their own homes; at the end of the demolition they are presented with the wrecking company's bill around $1500 When the bulldozer finally begins its systematic work of demolition, the whole process takes between five minutes (for a small home of concrete blocks) to six hours (for a five story apartment building). At times demolition is resisted amidst violence; people are beaten, jailed, sometimes killed, always humiliated. At other times the family and their neighbors watch sullenly as their home is reduced to rubble. One can only imagine their feelings and thoughts.

House Demolitions in Jerusalem

A key "front" in the struggle to contain or expel Palestinians is Jerusalem, and especially "East" Jerusalem where some 200,000 Palestinians reside. Although Israel insists that the city is now "united," deriving its legitimacy from its history as Israel's capital, "East" Jerusalem is in fact a fiction. During

Jordanian rule (1948-1967), the Arab city of Jerusalem consisted of only six square kilometers – the Old City and its immediate surroundings. To this, Israel added another 64 square kilometers of West Bank land, gerrymandered to include as much unbuilt upon land as possible for future Israeli settlements while excluding large Palestinian populations, calling the whole "united Jerusalem." Since that time all urban policy has been directed towards maintaining an artificial 72%-28% majority of Jews over Arabs, the proportion that existed when the two sides of the city were unilaterally "united" in 1967. A complex system involving the partisan use of planning and zoning mechanisms, of land expropriation and house demolitions, of bureaucratic means of revoking Jerusalem residency has been developed to ensure the "Jewish character" of the city. In Jerusalem, explains Amir Cheshin, the long-serving Advisor on Arab Affairs for the Jerusalem Municipality under Kollek and, for a time, under Olmert,

> Israel turned urban planning into a tool of the government, to be used to help prevent the expansion of the city's non-Jewish population. It was a ruthless policy, if only for the fact that the needs (to say nothing of the rights) of Palestinian residents were ignored. Israel saw the adoption of strict zoning plans as a way of limiting the number of new homes built in Arab neighborhoods, and thereby ensuring that the Arab percentage of the city's population - 28.8% in 1967 - did not grow beyond this level. Allowing "too many" new homes in Arab neighborhoods would mean "too many" Arab residents in the city. The idea was to move as many Jews as possible into east Jerusalem, and move as many Arabs as possible out of the city entirely. Israeli housing policy in east Jerusalem was all about this numbers game (Cheshin *et al.* 1999:10, 31-32).

(Despite this, the Jewish majority has dwindled to about 66%.)

Palestinian residents of "East" Jerusalem are confined to highly circumscribed parts of "East" Jerusalem. Since 1967, 35% of the Arab-owned land of "East" Jerusalem has been expropriated for Israeli settlements, roads and other facilities, while another 54% of Palestinian-owned land, designated as "open green space" reserved for "public purposes," is forbidden for Palestinian construction). Cheshin writes:

> Planners with the city engineer's office, when drawing the zoning boundaries for the Arab neighborhoods, limited them to already built-up areas. Adjoining open areas were either zoned "green," to signify they were off-limits to development, or left unzoned until they were needed for the construction of Jewish housing projects. The 1970 Kollek plan contains the principles upon which Israeli housing policy is based to this day - expropriation of Arab-owned land, development of large Jewish neighborhoods in east Jerusalem, and limitations on development in Arab neighborhoods (Cheshin 1999:37).

That leaves only 11% of East Jerusalem available for Palestinian housing and communal needs, only 7% of the city's total urban space.

This sets the stage for what in Israel is known as the "Quiet Transfer." The goal is to confine Palestinians to small enclaves of "East" Jerusalem, to remove them from the city altogether, and ultimately to induce their emigration from the country. The system works like this:

- Since Palestinian residents of Jerusalem cannot acquire permits to build on the 89% of "East" Jerusalem that they own, some 25,000 housing units are currently lacking in the Palestinian sector. Since the Palestinians own land and have the resources to build at least modest homes, the shortage is artificial and induced, a way to force Palestinians out of the city.

- The scarce stock of housing in "East" Jerusalem thereby raises the price of buying or renting to unaffordable levels. 70% of the Palestinian residents of "East" Jerusalem live below the poverty line. In order to secure affordable housing, they must cross the city's boundaries to less expensive accommodations found in the West Bank – in Palestinian areas that were cut out of the municipal borders in 1967.

- Unlike Jewish residents of the city, Palestinians wishing to retain their Jerusalem residency must continually prove to the Israeli Ministry of Interior that Jerusalem remains their "center of life." Moving to affordable housing just beyond the municipal border invalidates that status, leading the Interior Ministry to revoke the Jerusalem residency of those "emigrants." It is estimated that since 1967 about 6000 Jerusalem ID cards have been confiscated, forcing some 25,000 Palestinian Jerusalemites into exile or illegal residency in their own homes. Thousands of other Palestinian Jerusalemites cannot obtain permission for their spouses coming from other places to reside in the city.

According to B'tselem (1998), Israel's policy in East Jerusalem works as follows:

> The Jerusalem Municipality expropriates land, prevents preparation of a town planning scheme for Palestinian neighborhoods, and refuses to grant building permits, CAUSING a severe housing shortage, FORCING residents to build without a permit, AFTER WHICH the Ministry of Interior and the Municipality demolish the houses, SO the residents move into homes outside the city, AND THEN the Ministry of Interior revokes their residency and banishes them from the city forever.

- Refusal to issue building permits confines Palestinians to small patches of "East" Jerusalem. In order to give "teeth" to its hostile zoning practices, the Jerusalem Municipality, together with the Ministry of Interior, demolishes "illegal" Palestinian houses. (Except for an occasional porch or other minor addition, Jewish-Israeli homes are never demolished, although 80% of the building violations take place on the western side of the city.) Thus, despite an induced shortage of 25,000 units, the Municipality grants only between 150-350 permits a year for Arab housing and demolishes 20-50 homes a year. 8,000 Palestinian housing units have been declared "illegal;" some 2000 demolition orders are outstanding. According to the Jerusalem Municipality itself, 335 Palestinian houses have been demolished in "East" Jerusalem in the past decade; none in Israeli "West" Jerusalem.

- Because of the protests the house demolition policy arouses in Israel and abroad, the authorities cannot demolish the thousands of houses they would like to. They have therefore adopted a policy of "randomization." In order to diffuse the fear of demolition and deter Palestinians from building altogether, houses are demolished throughout "East" Jerusalem in a completely unpredictable way. Thus someone receiving a demolition order might have his or her home destroyed immediately, while a neighbor might live for a year, or five, or forever, in a home that received a demolition order long before. Besides the financial ruin of the demolition itself, Palestinian families are required to pay fines of up to $25,000 and even to pay for the cost of demolishing their own houses (some $1500). This "deterrence" factor requires us not only to look at the number of houses actually demolished or the houses built "illegally," but also at the thousands of needed houses not built by Palestinians on their own land out of fear of demolition.

- Permits , even when possible to acquire, are far too expensive for the average Palestinian resident. Because Jews do not own land privately in Israel, all construction is based on commercial considerations. Thus the government will release a certain amount of "state land" for a new neighborhood, and contractors bid on rights to build hundreds of apartment units. Costs involved in acquiring permits, often reaching $20,000-60,000 (fees, surveys, engineering plans, connection to infrastructure), are simply built into the price of the many units. In places where the government wishes to encourage construction (the large settlements in East Jerusalem), fees are often waived entirely and building costs are subsidized to make the housing units affordable. None of this exists in the Palestinian sector, where most building is done for private family needs. Palestinians must not only assume the astronomical costs of securing the permit and connecting to the infrastructure, but their costs are often higher, since their residences are far from the Israeli infrastructure, making connection to sewage, electricity, water and telephone lines prohibitive.

- Even securing a building permit does not guarantee adequate housing, however. While Israeli contractors are allowed to build hundreds of percent the size of the property (that is, two to six or more stories), Palestinian building is confined to just 25% of their land. Jewish-Israelis, then, are able to acquire roomy apartments in medium- or high-rise buildings, or are able to purchase spacious "villas," (some of them, ironically, marketed as "Arab-style" housing), while Palestinians with large families are forced to live in small single-story houses. Additional rooms added as the family grows – or because of the inability of married sons to obtain building permits for their own families – are often demolished. Palestinians thus suffer from overcrowded conditions: 2.2 persons per room on the average for Arabs; 0.8 person per room in the Jewish sector.

- Although Palestinians are confined to 7% of the city's urban area in inadequate housing, Jewish-Israelis have access to spacious accommodation on both the eastern and western sides of the city. Between 1967-2003, some 90,000 housing units were built in East Jerusalem for Jews, almost all with government subsidies. None were built for Palestinians with public financing. New settlements arise regularly, on confiscated Palestinian land: for the Har Homa project separating Jerusalem from Bethlehem; for expansion of existing settlements; for 17 new settlements to be established around the Old City (in Silwan, now named by the Israelis "the City of David;" in Sheikh Jarrah; in Ras el-Amud, in Kidmat Tzion (the "front-line of Zion) in Abu Dis, in "Nof Zahav" in Jabal Mukaber, among others); and in the Old City itself, where Ateret Cohanim, a religious-messianic-settler organization seeking to expel the Muslim population from the Old City altogether, has been given license and resources to carry out its program.

- Discrimination against Palestinians exists also in the provision of municipal services. The Palestinian population comprises some 30% of the city's population but receives only 8-11% of the municipality's budget. Much of East Jerusalem is lacking such basic services as sewage systems, roads, parks, lighting, post offices, schools and community services.

- The "neighborhoods" built on "East" Jerusalem serve to isolate Palestinian populations in small and disconnected enclaves, and to prevent the development and expansion of the Palestinian side of the city. Together with a new system of Israeli "ring roads" and the creation of a "Greater"

Jerusalem enveloped by a wall, Jerusalem is being transformed from a city into a region dominating the entire central portion of the West Bank.

What Does It Mean to a Palestinian Family to Have Its Home Demolished?

The human suffering entailed in the process of destroying a family's home is incalculable. A home is not only a physical structure; it is the center of our lives, the site of our most intimate personal life, an expression of our identity, tastes and social status. It is a refuge, a physical representation of the family, an extension of our very selves. It is "home." For Palestinians, homes carry additional meanings. Upon marriage, sons construct their homes close to that of their parents, thus maintaining not only a physical closeness but continuity on one's ancestral land. The latter aspect is especially important in the world of farmers, and even more so as Palestinians have faced massive displacement in the past half century. Land expropriation is another facet of home demolition, an attack on one's very being and identity.

Demolition is an experience different for men, women and children. Men are probably the most humiliated, since demolition means you can neither protect your family nor provide for their basic shelter and needs. It also means losing a living connection to your family land, your personal patrimony and that of your people. Men often cry at demolitions (and long after), but they are also angered, swear revenge and intend to build again (although some men withdraw emasculated from active family life). Since men usually have jobs and access to the world outside the home, they also have a certain outlet for their frustrations.

Demolitions alter, even destroy, a woman's entire persona and role in the family. Palestinian women generally do not have careers outside the home. Their identity and status as wives, mothers and, indeed, persons is wrapped up in their domestic life. When their homes are demolished, women often become disoriented, unable to function without that organizing domestic sphere. Some sink into a kind of mourning, although in some cases, especially if the husband has withdrawn, they take on more assertive roles in the family. Demolition represents a double tragedy for women. Not only do they lose their own domestic space, but they are forced to move into the homes of other women, their mothers- or sisters-in-law. The overcrowding and tension this generates is exacerbated by the fact that the "guest" woman has little control over the domestic sphere, over the care of her own husband and children, further diminishing her role and status. In many cases this results in severe tensions within the families, including domestic violence spawned by the wife's demands (even unspoken) for a home of her own, and the husband's inability to provide it. Eventually families may move into their own rented quarters – another expense – or even rebuild their home, having no choice but to risk another demolition. Whatever the case, for many women a demolished home, like a loved one, can never be replaced, and the wound never heals.

For children, the act of demolition – and the months and years leading up to it - is a time of trauma. To witness the fear and powerlessness of your parents, to feel constantly afraid and insecure, to see loved ones (relatives and neighbors) being beaten and losing their homes, to experience the harassment of Civil Administration field supervisors speeding around your village in their white Toyota jeeps - and then to endure the noise, violence, displacement and destruction of your home, your world, your toys - these mark children for life. Psychological services are largely absent in the Palestinian community and there are many signs of trauma and stress among children: bed-wetting, nightmares, fear to leave home lest one "abandon" parents and siblings to the army, dramatic drops in grades and school-leaving, as well the effects of exposure to domestic violence that occasionally follows impoverishment, displacement and humiliation. In the words of Salim Shawamreh, a resident of the village of Anata whose home has been demolished four times: "The demolition of a home is the demolition of a family." According to the research of Eyad Serraj, a Palestinian psychologist who heads the Gaza Community Mental Health Program, 55% or more of the kids who become suicide bombers have had their homes demolished.

Why, then, do Palestinian families decide to build without a permit? First, many of those facing demolition began building during the initial phase of the Oslo process when thousands of Palestinians, encouraged by the prospects of peace, returned to their home towns and villages and built homes, or when local people, suffering severe housing shortages since 1967, felt that demolitions would cease. Indeed, Israeli leaders encouraged this kind of thinking (Prime Minister Peres announced a freeze on demolitions towards the end of his term). Palestinians report that the Civil Administration, too, led them to believe that since most of the land was going to be handed back anyway, they would face no demolition problems - even if the process had not formally changed. This attitude is reflected in the wording of Article 27(2) ("Planning and Zoning") of the 1995 Interim Agreement (Oslo II): "In Area C, powers and responsibilities related to the sphere of Planning and Zoning will be transferred gradually to Palestinian jurisdiction that will cover West Bank and Gaza Strip territory, except for the issues that will be negotiated in the permanent status negotiations." After Netanyahu's election in 1996 (and thereafter), the rules of the game suddenly changed, and many Palestinians found themselves victims of the "peace process" and of bad faith.

Despite repeated inquiries to the various authorities, it is impossible to obtain accurate figures as to how many permits are granted, what percentage of applicants are turned down, how many families even apply. The Civil Administration claims it has granted 3,000 permits retroactively; a reliable source tells us that only two or three building permits a year are issued in the entire Hebron area, comprising a third of the West Bank. If the Civil Administration claims there are 5,000 "illegal" structures on the West Bank and has issued 2,000 demolition orders, and if the Jerusalem Municipality claims there are 10,000 "illegal" structures and has issued 2,000 orders (affecting 4,000 housing units), a major problem exists even if the planning and licensing procedures were non-political.

While every country has planning regulations, zoning and enforcement mechanisms, Israel is the only Western country that systematically denies permits and demolishes houses of a particular national group. Similarly, Jerusalem is the only city that systematically denies permits and demolishes houses of a particular national group. These actions, reminiscent of apartheid-era South Africa and the Serbs in Kosovo, other cases in which the homes of a particular ethnic group were destroyed for clearly racist or nationalistic reasons, violate the fundamental human rights of the Palestinian people. The Universal Declaration of Human Rights states that "Everyone has the right to a standard of living adequate for the health and well-being of himself and his family, including food, clothing, housing" (Article 25.1). The International Covenant on Economic, Social, and Cultural Rights "recognize[s] the right of everyone to an adequate standard of living...including adequate food, clothing, and housing" (Article 11.1). The International Convention on the Elimination of All Forms of Racial Discrimination obligates state parties "to guarantee the right of everyone, without distinction as to race, color, or national or ethnic origin, to equality before the law..., in particular the right to housing" (Article 5). Moreover, the Fourth Geneva Convention requires occupying powers such as Israel to protect the well-being of civilian populations under their control. Under the Hague Regulations of 1907 and the Fourth Geneva Convention of 1949, for example, Israel is enjoined as an occupying power to protect and ensure the needs of the Palestinian population. Human rights organizations agree that Israel's policy of house demolition constituGiven the massive scale and prolonged time period that the house demolition policy has characterized Israel's relationship with the Palestinians on both sides of the "Green Line," the bulldozer certainly deserves to take its rightful place alongside the tank. The Israeli public knows almost nothing about the cruel and Kafkaesque system the Palestinians live under. Uri Savir, the Director-General of the Foreign Ministry under Rabin and Peres, "discovered" this reality only after the Oslo process was well underway. He writes:

> The negotiations [with the Palestinians at Oslo, in 1995] over the powers Israel has exercised over a whole generation, opened an entire world before me. Over the years Israelis has cultivated a self-serving myth that ours was an 'enlightened occupation.' I knew this was a contradiction in terms, but I did not know -- and I think few other Israelis did – how thoroughly we had invaded the lives of our Palestinian neighbors. We repressed this knowledge as we may have been the first conquerors in history who felt themselves conquered. Our self-image as a humane society and history's eternal victim, as well as Arab antagonism, blinded us to what was going on in the territories. What I discovered [in Oslo] was that a Palestinian could not built, work, study, purchase land, grow produce, start a business, take a walk at night, enter Israel, go abroad, or visit his family in Gaza or Jordan without a permit from us. The apparatus for managing this octopus was huge.

> Some of these restrictions stemmed from legitimate security concerns. But many were the products of inertia and a burgeoning bureaucratic monster with a bottomless budget to feed on.. During the twenty-eight years of occupation [until 1995], about a third of the Palestinian population in the territories had, at one time or another, been detained or imprisoned by Israel. And the whole of the population had, at some time, been grossly humiliated by us.

> The personification of the occupation, according to many Palestinians, was an officer in the Civil Administration named Moskovitch. If Moskovitch approved, you could build. If Moskovitch didn't approve, you could not, and until Moskovitch approved you could tear your hair out. Moskovitch had become an institution in himself. When I finally met him – a thin, religiously-observant, amiable man – he in no way impressed me as tyrannical. 'Moskovitch is a good man,' one of his superior officers told me. And this was just the problem – a good man carrying out the orders of an unfeeling bureaucracy makes an impossible situation, for there is no way under such conditions for goodwill or common sense to function" (Savir 1999:207-208).

THE SAGA OF THE SHAWAMREH HOME:
Demolition and Rebuilding, Despair and Hope, Resistance and Solidarity

The following pictures help visualize the house demolition issue. It is far more than a political policy designed to confine Palestinians (on both sides of the Green Line) to tiny enclaves, even more than an overall process of collective displacement. It represents a human tragedy that cannot be conveyed in words or in political analysis.

The pictures here present the briefest glimpse into the demolition of the Shawamreh home in the village of Anata near Jerusalem in July, 1998, followed by another four demolitions as ICAHD and the Palestinian Land Defense Committee rebuilt each time – with the combined efforts of Israeli, Palestinian and international volunteers – as non-violent acts of civil disobedience, of political resistance. They are accompanied by the Salim and Arabiya's description of their experience.

Salim: *My family came from the village of Amishuaf near Beer Sheva, one of the 418 villages destroyed in 1948. After my grandfather's death in 1943, my father moved us to the Old City of Jerusalem, where he ran a coffee shop. I was born in the Old City of Jerusalem in 1956, one of 10 children.*

After the war in 1967, my family, like many others living in the Old City, were forced to move to the Shuafat refugee camp, leaving our three-story home and the coffee shop. There we were given a room 3 meters by 6 meters for the entire family. I studied to be a construction supervisor in the UNRWA vocational school in Kalandia, and in 1978 I left to find employment in Saudi Arabia. I worked there as a construction supervisor for nine years, during which time I married my cousin Arabia, who grew up in Jordan, and began a family.

In 1987 we returned home with a nest egg and the expectation of beginning a decent life for us and our children. I came back to the camp from Saudi Arabia a "hero:" a local boy made good, coming home with money in his pocket. And because our family home in the camp was so small and overcrowded with my parents, my brothers and sisters and my brother's families, I was the one who was expected to find another home for his family.

Arabiya: *I am Salim's cousin. My family came from Deir Asal in the West Bank and settled in Ramallah, where I was born in 1965. During the 1967 war, my family, remembering Deir Yassin and the destruction of the Palestinian villages by Israel in 1948, fled in fear to Jordan, where they still live. I finished the ninth grade there. At the age of 16 I married Salim and went to live with him in Saudi Arabia. When Salim wanted to return to Jerusalem, I was very scared. I had never lived in Israeli-controlled territory; I did not know the language. But I came, and was granted a Jerusalem ID.*

Picture 1: Salim and Arabiya's house before the first demolition.

I found a small plot of land on the periphery of the nearby town of Anata, just a few dozen meters into the West Bank. Why did I buy there, even if I might have a problem securing a building permit from the Civil Administration [Israel's military government in the Occupied Territories,]? Well, getting a permit from the Civil Administration, is no more difficult than getting one from the Jerusalem municipality. And land just outside the municipal borders is much cheaper than inside.

I then applied to the Civil Administration for a building permit. Each application costs about $5000 in application fees, surveying, lawyers and the like. The permit was turned down because the land is zoned as "agricultural land," although it is far too rocky to ever have been farmed. I was told that if I applied for a special permit to build on agricultural land I might receive it, so I did. Another $5000 – and this time I was turned down because the "slope" was too steep. Jerusalem is built on mountains, and all mountains have slopes. From my land I can see the Hebrew University and French Hill, both built on slopes. These were only reasons given to frustrate my application. I was also told that my land was too close to a by-pass road – although the road was only begun years later. Of course, I had no knowledge of the plans and, besides, my house was far more than the maximum 150 meter "security margin."

But the Civil Administration officials advised to apply once more. Another $5000, and another refusal, this time because they claimed I lacked two signatures of previous owners on the deed! Finally, my money running out and with nowhere to go with my growing family, I decided to build anyway. It was a cold calculation. There are thousands of Palestinian homes with demolition orders, but Israel only demolished a couple hundred a year – so I might buy a year or two, or maybe even "win" the lottery and not have my house demolished at all. And don't forget, the "peace process" had by then begun and everyone was sure that house demolitions would stop and that we would become part of the Palestinian state.

So in 1994, after four years of trying to get a permit, we finally built our modest home on our own small plot of land. I invested about $35,000 in the house and I brought in twenty truckloads of soil and planted a garden of 52 trees of all different kinds. If there was anything "agricultural" about my land, it was what I made of it.

We moved in, and soon after the demolition order arrived. I immediately hired a lawyer and began legal proceedings to counter it. Together with a number of other families in the same situation we went all the way to the Supreme Court, but our appeal was turned down in 1995.

Despite the prospect of demolition hanging over our heads, Arabia, our family and I lived quietly in our house for four years. The order was present in our lives, a vague source of anxiety, but we managed to put it into the background. After all, the mid-1990s was the time of the "peace process," the numbers of demolitions had dropped dramatically, and we hoped that the danger had passed, that our house had been saved by peace.

I couldn't find work here as a construction engineer, so I did various things. I secured employment as the driver of Bashir Bargouti, editor of the al-Ataliya *newspaper and later the Palestinian Minister of Industry. At night I worked for an Israeli catering business, perfecting my Hebrew and making a lot of Israeli friends.*

After the election of Netanyahu in 1996 and the dramatic rise in house demolitions, we began to fear once more for our house. One day – the black day in my life which I don't wish on anyone else in the world, July 9, 1998 – I was having lunch with my family when I heard some noise outside. I opened the door and saw my house surrounded by 200 soldiers. "Is this your house," their commander Rami asked me. ""Yes, this is my house." "No, it isn't," he replied. "This is our house now. You have fifteen minutes to get your family and belongings out of the home. We are going to demolish it."

Picture 2: Rami and Micha (behind), the Civil Administration officials responsible for executing demolition orders

These are the "Civil" Administration officials, Rami and Micha, that appeared at Salim and Arabiya's door. Do civil servants in your city look like this? The term "civil administration" was chosen by Israel to downplay the military character of the Occupation. Thus although officials such as Rami and Micha are technically civilian employees, they are armed and always accompanied by soldiers, the Border Police and the regular Israeli police. Another twist to the story: they are also settlers. Micha lives in the settlement adjacent to Anata, so in the Shawamreh case he is demolishing the home of his neighbors. At any rate, placing settlers in decision-making positions vis-à-vis the demolition of Palestinian homes represents a grotesque conflict of interest.

Pictures 3-4: Salim after he was beaten and thrown out of his house; Arabiya being carried unconscious from the home.

Salim: *"What are you saying?!" I answered back, not knowing what to do or say. Rami approached me very closely, clutching his rifle, and when I tried to push him back soldiers jumped on me, beat me all over my body, handcuffed me and threw me out of the house.*

My wife, panicking and not knowing what to do, closed the door and locked it to protect the house and our children inside. The soldiers starting kicking down the door. In order to force my wife and children out, they broke a window and threw a tear gas canister into the house. (I found the canister later. It was produced in the Federal Laboratories in Pennsylvania, the US, and had clearly written on the side: "For Outdoor Use Only.") My wife used the few minutes to frantically call for help on the phone [one of the calls was to ICAHD], but when the soldiers finally broke into the home they found my wife unconscious and the children screaming and crying. The kids ran through the open door and scattered.

Since 1967, 12,000 Palestinian homes have been demolished in the Occupied Territories - for lack of building permits, as "deterrence," as collective punishment and under the guise of military operations. Whether carried out by the Civil Administration and the army in the West Bank and Gaza, or by the Jerusalem Municipality and the Ministry of Interior in East Jerusalem, demolitions are violent acts against families innocent of any crime except wanting a modest home on their own land – land coveted by Israel.

Picture 5: Jeff Halper, ICAHD Coordinator, being arrested after resisting the demolition of the Shawamreh home.

Jeff: *The demolition of Salim and Arabia's house was a turning point for us. Israel has been systematically demolishing Palestinian houses for years, but this was the first time Israeli and media actually witnessed it. Because of the valiant struggle put up by the Shawamreh fsmily, we had time to bring dozens of protesters and reporters. It was the demolition of this house that put the entire issue of Israel's house demolition policy on the political map.*

In fact, our success in publicizing this demolition was due to a number of serendipitous circumstances. ICAHD, Bat Shalom, Rabbis for Human Rights, the Palestinian Land Defense Committee, the Palestinian human rights organization LAW, Christian Peacemakers and other groups had planned a demonstration that very day opposite the Civil Administration headquarters. We happened to be nearby, then, when we got word that the Shawamreh house was about to be destroyed, and were able to divert a busload of protesters – including Knesset Member Naomi Chazan and some journalists – to the site in Anata. This was about one in the afternoon, and it was very unusual for the Civil Administration to demolish so late in the day. Usually demolitions happen at 6 AM when the men have left for work and outsiders are not present. That day they had already demolished five houses and apparently felt they could fit in one more before the day's "work" was finished. After all, bringing out the army, the Border Police and a commercial wrecking crew is expensive. I guess they wanted to get their money's worth.

I managed to run through the troops surrounding the house – one soldier even asked to see my ID. Since this was the first demolition we had actually been to, the army wasn't prepared for protesters. Apparently they thought I was a journalist.

I reached the house just as Salim and Arabia were being removed. It was a surrealistic experience. As foreign workers employed by the wrecking company removed the Shawamreh's belongings from the house – tearing apart livingroom and bedroom sets and throwing everything in a pile outside – the Civil Administration inspector, Micha, who was overseeing the operation, began to explain to me why the house was being demolished. He showed me maps where the Shawamrehs could have built within Area B of Anata – not knowing or not caring that because Israel had drawn such tight boundaries around the Palestinian towns the price of land in them had skyrocketed, making it impossible for a family like Salim's to afford to buy inside, where it is "safe" from demolitions. Then, as the bulldozer approached, I was shunted aside. We had talked of resistance to the occupation before, but what that really meant was still vague. As the bulldozer approached the house, however, I just couldn't stand by and watch. I ran in front to block it and was immediately jumped upon by soldiers. Passively resisting but holding onto soldier's legs, rocks, whatever came to hand, I felt myself being pushed down the hill towards where Salim was lying. I tossed my pocket camera to another activist who continued to photograph. Sitting in the dust by Salim and his neighbors, I tried to comfort him. Words like "Don't worry, it will be OK" sounded so hollow. I promised him we would turn this event into one of political significance – though that, too, probably sounded pretty hollow to him.

Picture 6: The Shawamreh's furniture being removed from the home.

Once the family has been removed by force and resistance quelled, the Civil Administration officials ordered foreign workers employed by the commercial wrecking company they hired to quickly remove the family's belongings. Here you see entire living room and bedroom sets ripped out and the family's papers and pictures thrown outside. Imagine the feelings of humiliation, invasion and rage felt by the family members.

Picture 7: The first demolition (July 9, 1998).

The bulldozer demolishing the home as Micha looks on. In a tragic and ironic twist, it turns out that the bulldozer driver, who happens to be employed by the contractor, was a Palestinian hailing from another village that had been demolished in 1948. And he knew Salim.

Salim: *Some neighbors tried to intervene but were pushed, together with me, down the hill, away from the house. Then I saw the bulldozer coming up the hill, escorted by soldiers. After some time,* *it began to demolish the home. Imagine yourself lying helpless on the ground watching your house being demolished.... I was surrounded by neighbors trying to comfort me. I couldn't see my wife or children and had no idea what happened to them. Jeff Halper of the Israeli Committee Against House Demolitions, who tried to block the bulldozer and who was kicked and pushed as we all were, came to me and held my hand as the house was being demolished. "They won't get away with this," he told me. "We'll let the whole world know what has happened here."*

Jeff: *And then, together in the dust, Salim and I watched as the house was demolished. There were certain poignant moments when the meaning of what was happening broke through – like when the TV antenna collapsed. At one point, when the house was half-demolished, the bulldozer began backing away. I saw Micha run over to the driver and yell at him to go back and finish. Only later did I find out that the bulldozer driver was himself Palestinian, coming from a village near Jerusalem that had itself been demolished by Israel in 1948. He had tried to leave after the intial demolition when some of the house remained standing, but as he worked for the wrecking company he had no choice but to continue. That is part of the tragedy within tragedy of our situation. Within an hour or so it was over. The bulldozer left, the soldiers dispersed. Arabia had been taken to the hospital and most of the kids were eventually found. Only little Mohammed remained missing. He was found that evening sleeping under a rock in a nearby field.*

Picture 8: The demolished home.

Salim's neighbor Mohammad Dandis surveys the ruins of the Shawamreh home. After living in fear for years, his house was finally demolished in November, 2004, leaving him, his wife and their eight children homeless.

Arabiya: *In that demolition I lost everything. I lost all the memories of my life – pictures, documents, belongings from my childhood, my wedding, our years in Saudi Arabia. Everything that meant something to me personally. We lost all our possessions – our furniture, appliances. All our savings from all those years of work were gone. I wasn't even aware of what was happening to me after I was taken to the hospital. Salim sent me to Jordan to be near my family, but I couldn't tell them what happened, I couldn't speak of it all. I missed my children. All of a sudden I was completely alone in the world, with nowhere to go, no one to talk to. People tried to comfort me, but I couldn't hear them. It was like mourning. I was sunk into myself, disconnected, preoccupied with what would happen to us, the kids, worried about our future. Where would we live? Where would we get money to rebuild our lives?*

Picture 9: ICAHD and the Palestinian Land Defense Committee rebuild the home.

Salim: *As soon as our house was destroyed, people from the Palestinian Land Defense Committee and ICAHD came to me with the suggestion of rebuilding the home.*

Arabiya: *When I came back to the Red Cross tent where Salim and the kids were living, I supported the idea of rebuilding the house, even though I was scared about going through the trauma of demolition again. When the Israeli peace people came and we started to rebuild I was there, rebuilding, with Israelis. In the rented apartment where we now live we are not really in home. We go back to home to visit the home sometimes, watering the plants that survived (2 olive trees and fig tree), building a stone fence.* ICAHD and its Palestinian partners bring dozens of activists from Israel, Palestine and abroad to rebuild demolished homes as political acts of resistance to the Occupation. Pictured here is Issa Samandar of the Land Defense Committee at the rebuilding of the Shawamreh home.

Pictures 10-11: Arabiya rebuilding her home.

Arabiya, flanked by two Israeli women, participates in the rebuilding of her home. That very activity and the socializing and solidarity it involves over weeks also offers support and comfort to the traumatized families – even though it is an "illegal" activity and they realize that their homes could be demolished again. In fact, the Shawamreh home was demolished another three times, and each time rebuilt by ICAHD and its Palestinian partners.

Picture 12: Celebrating the rebuilding.

When the concrete roof of the second home was poured, Israeli and Palestinian activists celebrated. Salim and Uri Avneri of Gush Shalo, can be seen at the center. To their right is Issa Samandar, the historian Teddy Katz, long-time peace activists Latif Dori, Issam Aruri of the Palestinian Agricultural Relief Committee and, hold the Gush Shalom sign, Ata Jabar, whose home near the settlement of Kiryat Arba has been demolished three times. To Salim's left are Arabiya and Gila Swirsky, one of the leaders of the Women's Coalition for Peace.

Picture 13: The Second Demolition (August 3, 1998)

Jeff: Despite the festive pouring of concrete for the roof, we all had the feeling that the Civil Administration would return to demolish the home. A number of us, including several members of the Christian Peacemaker Team, decided to sleep over. Sure enough, at 4:40 AM the Civil Administration officials, accompanied by soldiers, arrived to demolish the house for the second time.

Picture 14: The third demolition (April 4, 2001).

The Shawamreh's home was to be demolished twice more – by American Caterpillar bulldozers. This time the Civil Administration also brought a Caterpillar jackhammer to dig up the foundations so the house cannot be constructed again. But we vowed not to let the Occupation prevail. The house was rebuilt, demolished yet again (on April 3, 2003).

Salim: *You know, the demolition of a house means the demolition of a family. Everything changes after that. Demolition is the violent violation of the very essence of a family and of every person in it. Do you know what a home is? Think about it. Even the word is one of the most intimate words we have, like "mother," "father," "family." The law defines it as "a man's castle," a place of special sanctity and meaning. It is the place where your most intimate life is carried out – where you live safely with your family, where you create your own world through the pictures on the wall, the furniture, the garden, where your kids live and have their toys and their basic sense of security. It's a place you can call your own, that you have built with the money you earned and where you provide for your family.*

And my wife, Arabia. For two months after the demolition she didn't speak. I sent her to the hospital in Jordan, to be near her family. Until now, four years after the first demolition, she has not returned to herself. She has lost the joy of living, and sometimes I can see she is leaving me; she drifts off and becomes very silent.

Ashraf, my oldest son, had to leave school at the age of 16 to help support the family in its financial distress. He is now a casual laborer on the Israeli job market. During the Intifada, when Israeli tanks drove up to the rented apartment where the Shawamreh's lived and pointed their turrets at our building, Lamia, my 14 year-old daughter, became terrified. So great was the trauma that she was struck blind. I rushed her to the hospital, where after two hours her sight returned. Imagine what is going on within a young girl to trigger such a reaction – and then, to grasp what Occupation does to Palestinian families, multiply it hundreds of thousands of times.

My fundamental human right of providing a shelter for my family was violated. But it goes much deeper than that. I have lost the role of protector of my children. We now live in a rented apartment in Kufr Aqab, the northernmost Jerusalem neighborhood bordering on Ramallah. When the Israeli warplanes and Apache helicopters flew low over our home to attack Ramallah, my kids became so scared they couldn't stand on their legs, and their stomachs hurt. I said to them: "Don't worry, I am here. I'll protect you." Do you know what my nine year-old daughter said to me? "You can't protect us. We saw what the soldiers did to you when they handcuffed you and threw you outside when they demolished our home. You can't protect us." [Tears come to Salim's eyes.] *Such words of a daughter to her father is like putting a knife in my heart.*

My kids are now scared all the time. They will not go to the bathroom in the night unless my wife comes and takes them by the hand. Before the demolition their grades in school were excellent. Now they get marks in the 50s, and they have trouble concentrating. The Israelis say they are demolishing only homes of terrorists, but that's not true. They demolish homes of ordinary people.

Pictures 15-16: Building Beit Arabiya ("Arabiya's House).

In August 2003, ICAHD, together with the local authorities of Anata, initiated a work camp for the rebuilding of the home for the fifth time. Because of the trauma of demolition and its cost on the family's mental health, the Shawamrehs decided to rebuild as an act of resistance, but to make the home a center for Palestinian-Israeli strategizing over ways to bring a just peace to the country. The center, named Beit Arabiya, the House of Arabiya, and dedicated to the memories of Rachel Corrie and Nuha Sweidan, two women killed in Gaza during demolition operations, will serve as an active place of peace-making until such a time as the family can move back in.

Pictures 17-18: The dedication of Beit Arabiya (August 2003).

Mike Alewitz, an American labour muralist, dedicates a mural depicting the common struggle of Palestinians, Israelis and internationals against the Occupation (it features, under the red lightening, a dead Caterpillar bulldozer; the figures of Nuha and Rachel float over the scene). Beit Arabiya is already being used as a meeting place where Palestinians, Israelis and internationals strategize over ending the Occupation.

Picture 19: The demolition of the Dandis home (November 28, 2003).

Picture 20: Salim and Mohammad Dandis during the demolition.

Picture 21: Salim and Jeff appear on CNN

A key piece of ICAHD's work is bringing the experience of house demolitions and other manifestations of the Occupation to world attention. Our messages are several. Israelis and Palestinians are not enemies ("We refuse to be enemies"). Israel's Occupation is not defensive or based on security, but is a pro-active attempt to take control of the entire country. The policy of house demolitions cannot be explained by "security." Salim and Arabiya are not terrorists. They have never been accused of anything nor charged with anything (except building an "illegal" home). The only explanation for Israel's behavior towards them is the desire to take their land and confine them to enclaves. ICAHD's advocacy among the Israeli and international publics complements its resistance efforts "on the ground."

Pictures 22-24: The Separation Barrier.

Israel's Separation Barrier, which passes just below Beit Arabiya, confines Palestinians to small enclaves while tearing apart the social fabric of their lives and humiliating them. In populated Palestinian areas the Barrier becomes a wall 26 feet/8 meters high (twice as high as the Berlin Wall). As can be seen in Picture 20, it does not separate Palestinians from Israelis (since Israel does not want to build the wall where Israelis will see it) but rather Palestinians from Palestinians, cutting through the heart of communities. In rural areas the Barrier becomes an electronic fence alienating farmers from their fields. More than a security device, the Barrier represents a land grab, a new political and demographic border for an expanding Israel.

picture 1

picture 2

picture 3

picture 4

picture 5

picture 6

picture 7

picture 8

picture 9

picture 10

picture 11

picture 12

picture 13

picture 14

picture 15

picture 16

picture 17

picture 18

picture 19

picture 20

picture 21

picture 22

picture 23

picture 24

THE "ROAD MAP"

Since the policy statement of President Bush in June 2002, the "Quartet" – Europe, the UN, Russia and the US – has formulated its "Road Map" for ending the Occupation and establishing, in its words, "an independent, democratic, and viable Palestinian state" by the year 2005. The Road Map was officially released in March, 2003. President Bush has declared his "personal commitment" to the Road Map initiative, backed up by a trip to the region in June 2003, one of many made by top Administration officials including Colin Powell and Condoleeza Rice.

For his part, Tony Blair has spoken passionately of an "even-handed" approach that places the Israel-Palestine conflict on a par with that of Iraq (a linkage Israel vehemently rejects). In a speech before Parliament at the outset of the war in Iraq, he invited the public to "hold me to [the Road Map]." Overall, Europe has expressed its strong support for the initiative; both senior civil servants in the various foreign ministries and Miguel Moratinos, the EU's special representative for the peace process, have played critical roles in the Road Map's formulation. So, too, has Terje Larsen, the UN Secretary General's representative to the region, a seasoned, "hands-on" diplomat with keen first-hand knowledge of the realities "on the ground." For their part, the Russians shepherded a resolution through the Security Council, in November, 2004, when the initiative appeared stalled and virtually dead, that unanimously reaffirmed its salience in international policy towards the Middle East. The Palestinians have accepted the document; Israel has accepted it "provisionally" with fourteen major reservations (see the Appendix for the Road Map and Israel's reservations). In the wake of Bush's re-election, motions have been made toward reviving the Road Map, but it remains to be seen whether the United States – which undermined the Road Map fundamentally when it recognized the settlement blocs – will indeed exert the political will necessary so that a viable Palestinian state may emerge.

If anything unites Israelis of all persuasions, it is skepticism regarding this latest of a long series of failed initiatives. Most Israelis do not relate to the Road Map at all, and those of the peace camp think, almost unanimously, that the Quartet lacks the resolve necessary to force Israel out of the Occupied Territories. Palestinians tend to agree. They have little objection to the plan's content, but consider it almost inconceivable that Israel could be made to withdraw to the 1967 borders.

Indeed, few have objections to the Road Map's goals or structure. The document was obviously written by people who know the "lay of the land." As a political process, its "end game" is far more concrete than was Oslo's:

- A negotiated agreement leading to a final and comprehensive settlement of the Israel-Palestinian conflict by 2005, including issues of borders, Jerusalem, refugees, settlements, and a comprehensive agreement among Israel, Lebanon and Syria;

- An end to the Occupation;

- The emergence of an independent, democratic Palestinian state living side by side in peace and security with Israel and its other neighbors; and

- Addressing Israel's strategic goals of security and regional integration.

The Road Map's "performance-based" phases, with specified timetables, are also much more structured than was Oslo. It does place far more demands on the Palestinians in the early stages than upon Israel, and leaves the resolution of the "final status issues" far too ambiguous. But most who actually read it admit it could be a useful mechanism for advancing the two-state solution – if the international will to truly end the Occupation can be mustered. Israeli journalist and activist Uri Avneri, who dismisses the Road Map completely as a workable process, has this to say about it:

> The objectives are very positive. They are identical with the aims of the Israeli peace movement: an end to the Occupation, the establishment of the independent State of Palestine side-by-side with the State of Israel, Israeli-Palestinian and Israeli-Syrian peace, the integration of Israel in the region. In this respect, the Road Map goes further than the Oslo agreement. In the Oslo "Declaration of Principles" there was a giant hole: it did not spell out what was to come after the long interim stages. Without a clear final aim, the interim stages had no clear purpose. Therefore the Oslo process died with Yitzhak Rabin. The Road Map confirms that there now exists a worldwide consensus about these objectives. This fact will remain even if nothing comes out of it. Those of us who remember that only 35 years ago there was hardly a handful of people in the world who believed in this vision can draw profound satisfaction from this Road Map. It shows that we have won the struggle for world public opinion (personal communication).

Shortcomings of the Road Map

Having said all this, the Road Map contains some serious shortcomings that could fatally compromise its usefulness as a political initiative.

1. *Terms and Goals.* Like the Oslo Accords, the Road Map does not mention human rights or international law as terms of reference. This is meaningful. So enormous are the power differentials between Israel and the Palestinians, including Israel's total military control of all Palestinian lands and the massive presence of its settlements, that any negotiations based on power alone virtually assures Israel's "victory." International humanitarian law – and in particular the Fourth Geneva Convention which prohibits unilateral steps that prejudice fair negotiations – levels the playing field. It also defines terms. Although the Road Map speaks of "ending the Occupation," it fails to define what is meant by "occupation," even though in international law it clearly refers to all the territories conquered by Israel in 1967. If the Road Map actually seeks to end the Occupation – and if settlements are patently illegal under the Fourth Geneva Convention and should be simply dismantled – why does Phase III call for negotiations over Jerusalem and the settlements? Shouldn't those issues have been resolved as Israel returns to its 1967 lines? Here is the Road Map's major loophole. If the Occupation is defined politically, that is, by whatever concessions the Israelis can force the Palestinians to make, then it will clearly lead to a bantustan. If Sharon can coerce Abu Mazen to sign off on an agreement giving the Palestinians, say, 50% or 70% of the West Bank, Israel can declare an "end the Occupation." The Road Map thereby becomes merely a mechanism for institutionalizing a new apartheid. If, on the other hand, the Road Map defines "occupation" geographically, that is, as meaning all the territories conquered by Israel in 1967, then "ending the Occupation" means Israeli withdrawal to the 1967 lines – and a good shot at achieving a workable two-state solution.

    In fact, the Quartet must withstand Israeli demands to remove reference to "occupation" altogether. Israel has always denied that it has an occupation (despite Sharon's "slip of the tongue"), arguing that it is merely "administering" the Palestinian territories until their status is resolved, in the meantime creating "facts on the ground" which obviate any resolution besides Israeli control. This is evident in Israel's response to the Road Map, in which it insisted that "The purpose of the Road Map should be an end to the conflict…rather than an end to the 'occupation.'" Agreeing to this would undermine the Road Map's terms of reference to the point that Israel would "win," reducing the initiative to merely another instrument for perpetuating Israeli control.

It must also be understood that Israel views its fourteen "reservations" as integral parts of the Road Map (see the Appendix).

2. *The Refugee Issue.* Israel has already publicly made it clear that unless the Palestinians renounce the Right of Return, it will not participate in the Road Map process. The conflict cannot be resolved unless a just and agreed-upon solution is found, yet this is a "hidden" issue over which Israeli peace groups have no clearly formulated position. While the refugee issue is mentioned as a final status issue, the need to find a just resolution should be stated explicitly and up-front as a major goal. Here three aspects of the issue seem crucial, each in its own right: adherence to the principle in international humanitarian law that refugees have an inalienable right to return to their homes and properties; acknowledgment on the part of Israel that it played an active and major role in creating the refugee situation; and negotiations over the just disposition of the issue which include representatives of refugee communities.

3. *Implementation.* The Road Map offers protection to the Palestinian and Israeli peoples during the negotiating process while acting to prevent Israel from expanding its occupation and, eventually, dismantling it. Although it anchors implementation in UN resolutions, Israel's ability to by-pass such mechanisms – as in its success to persuade the Americans to reclassify the Occupied Territories as "disputed" – must not be allowed to undercut the Palestinians' ability to negotiate from a position of parity, as it did in Oslo, or to delay implementation indefinitely. As Hanan Ashrawi argues, Israel's implementation of UN resolutions, not to mention its adherence to international law, should be matters of immediate compliance rather than of persuasion or negotiation.

These are matters of concern when we consider the gap between the specific goals, processes, benchmarks, phases and monitoring laid out in the Road Map and its vagueness on the final status issues: borders, Jerusalem, refugees and settlements. Phase III only calls for an international conference (reminiscent of the Madrid Conference) "to launch negotiations between Israel and Palestine toward a final, permanent status resolution in 2005." The terms of reference for such final status negotiations should be brought into conformity with the goals.

The fact that the Quartet as a group determines whether implementation has been achieved and whether the sides are ready to progress to the next phase is a great improvement on Oslo, when the Americans served as the sole arbiters (although there are worrying signs that the Americans are again assuming sole control of the process). In order to ensure the asymmetry between Palestinian requirements and vague Israeli concessions, Israel insists that the US be the only mediator empowered to determine the progress of the Road Map (and, indeed, the Americans have indicated that they will have veto power over the Quartet's decisions). "We believe that the U.S. has a dominant and leading role in this process and accordingly the supervision mechanism should be led by the Americans," read an Israeli government statement. "Furthermore, we must agree on the nature of the supervision mechanism. It is essential that it include clear and specific subjects, that the supervision mandate be limited in time and that the members will be experts only. The Quartet may assist the process by supporting the American effort, but it cannot judge on issues such as determining goals for progress, judging on the transition from one phase to the next or addressing security issues." This stands in stark contrast to the Road Map, which specifies that the Quartet collectively supervises the progress of the process.

The supervisory capacity of the Quartet is itself a subject of skepticism. Many Palestinians express fewer problems with the Road Map's goals and processes than with the prospects of its implementation. Says Palestinian legislator Hanan Ashrawi:

> By now, Israeli tactics have become all too familiar. After sabotaging the substance, Israel proceeds to raise procedural and technical objections with the aim of prolongation and obfuscation. Thus with the parties totally bogged down in micromanaging the most obscure detail and side issue, Israel buys more time to create more facts to render the whole exercise entirely irrelevant. In the meantime, the US would have bought the artificial 'calm' it needs to carry out its regional designs (beginning with Iraq) and placating the Arab world by creating the impression of 'engagement' and commitment to the implementation of the presidential 'vision' of a two-state solution. Meanwhile, Israel is off the hook, continuing its business-as-usual policy of studied cruelty against and systematic destruction of Palestinian reality and lives while voraciously gobbling up more land and feeding the settlers' insatiable appetite for intimidation, violence, and expansion (personal communication).

If the problem with the Road Map lies more in implementation than in content, this seems the very point where intervention by the progressive civil society can be most effective. Having a strong presence on the ground, yet, through our networks, possessing considerable global reach, we are in a unique position to critically monitor implementation, raising our voices when it appears that the Quartet is not doing its job, mobilizing our forces when implementation falls short of the Road Map's goals. We are the ones called upon to keep the process honest, to "hold them to it."

4. *Mutuality.* The success of the Road Map depends upon upholding the principles of mutuality and parallelism, rather than conditionality and "sequentialism." Israel rejects the concept of simultaneous, mutual performance as a benchmark of progress. Instead, in its reservations to the Road Map, Israel insists that progress will be "conditional upon the complete cessation of violence and terrorism, full disarmament of terrorist organizations, their capabilities and infrastructure, the complete collection of illegal weapons and the emergence of a new and different [Palestinian] leadership." This puts the onus on the Palestinians, requiring them to give up all resistance to the Occupation and even facilitate Israel's "security" interests without any assurance that Israel will reciprocate in any meaningful way. A "performance-based" process must be a mutual one involving parallel Israeli and Palestinian steps, not one conditional on Palestinian concessions and later Israeli steps that may or may not happen. Indeed, in addition to overtly rejecting the idea of a viable, independent Palestinian state, Israel also rejects the demand that it remove its illegal outposts in Phase I, that it cease expanding settlements in the name of "natural growth," that it complete further withdrawals from the West Bank as agreed upon in previous covenants or that

it grant territorial contiguity to any Palestinian state. Using the same vague and non-committing language that characterized its approach to the Oslo process, Israel says it will consider a limited freeze on settlement construction only "following a continuous and comprehensive security

The importance of this is evident in the announcement that Israel will build 3500 housing units in the E-1 section of the Ma'aleh Adumim settlement, closing the last functional north-south route from the northern to southern West Bank and choking East Jerusalem off from the rest of Palestinian society. This, plus the ongoing construction of neighborhoods and entire cities in the Occupied Territories, stands in stark contrast to the requirement that Israel cease settlement construction in the first phase of the Road Map (not to mention in conformity with international law). Rejection of the principle of mutuality permits Israel to expand its settlement presence with impunity while avoiding completely its responsibility to creating conditions suitable for a just peace.

Adherence to phases and internal timelines is as crucial to the success of the Road Map as mutuality. Given the express unwillingness of Israel to countenance a viable, independent Palestinian state despite its declared acceptance of the Road Map, implementation rather than goal-setting is the key. The issue of moving from phase to phase was left open-ended in Oslo, permitting permanent "delays" in implementation, a flaw that eventually destroyed not only the process itself but the faith of the two peoples in it. Benchmarks must be clear and binding. Thus the provision in the Road Map which states "Phase II…ends with possible creation of a Palestinian state with provisional borders by end of 2003" is so open-ended as to be meaningless. In its version of the Road Map, Israel adheres firmly to Bush's original "vision" of "a Palestinian state whose borders and certain aspects of its sovereignty will be provisional," very different from "a Palestinian state with provisional borders." By insisting that the US be the sole determiner of performance and progress, Israel is placing itself in a position of determining or halting the progress of the Road Map. In order to grant the Road Map legitimacy, the Quartet must work as a team. No partner should have veto power. Only a concerted effort by the Quartet as a unit stands a chance of success. Only that unit will display both the fairness and will necessary to achieve a just peace.

5. *Palestinian sovereignty.* The Road Map obviously interferes with internal Palestinian politics. It insists that the Palestinians adopt a constitution, even though Israel does not have one. Its insistence on an "empowered" prime minister is a transparent attempt to get rid of Arafat, since there is nothing inherently wrong with a presidential system of government (as the Americans should appreciate). And so on. Nevertheless, many of the changes have already been made, so if a Palestinian government is allowed to develop within the context of an emerging sovereign state, these are conditions with which the Palestinians can probably live. More problematic is the danger of a Palestinian Authority or government being required to do Israel's "security" bidding, undermining its own right to resist occupation even before Israeli occupation and control actually end. Even more perilous is the possibility that Israel and the US might acquire the power to install a collaborationist Palestinian leadership that will sign off on a bantustan. These are issues that require our close monitoring.

Related to issues of sovereignty is the proposal that an interim Palestinian state without borders be established in Phase II over a transitional period of six months. The rationale is that such an entity would strengthen the political position of the Palestinians in negotiations by according them the status of a state partner. But it is also a step fraught with perils. The Road Map only talks of a "possible" Palestinian state, thus leaving a large loophole to by-pass or neutralize the empowering effects of statehood. Of greatest danger is the possibility that such a transitional state may get stuck in the middle of the process. The Sharon government, after all, has openly expressed its preference for a long-term interim agreement that gives the Palestinians certain "attributes of sovereignty" yet leaves the Israeli presence in place. Still, since the Road Map shows little sign of progressing, it is unlikely that Sharon will have to worry about ever reaching a final settlement.

SHARON'S UNILATERAL SOLUTION: BY-PASSING EVERYONE

Israel began constructing its Matrix of Control immediately after the Six Day War. "The Six-Day War was forced upon us," says Michael Ben-Yair, Israel's former Attorney General,

> however, the war's seventh day, which began on June 12, 1967 and has continued to this day, is the product of our choice. We enthusiastically chose to become a colonial society, ignoring international treaties, expropriating lands, transferring settlers from Israel to the Occupied Territories, engaging in theft and finding justification for all these activities. Passionately desiring to keep the Occupied Territories, we developed two judicial systems: one progressive, liberal - in Israel; and the other, cruel, injurious - in the Occupied Territories. In effect, we established an apartheid regime in the Occupied Territories immediately following their capture. That oppressive regime exists to this day. This is the harsh reality that is causing us to lose the moral base of our existence as a free, just society and to jeopardize Israel's long-range survival (*Ha'aretz*, March 3, 2002).

For all the years of the Occupation, the settlement enterprise was a work in progress. When asked by the left: "Where are you going with this? What will happen when Israeli control becomes permanent, when a viable Palestinian state is rendered impossible?" successive Israeli governments avoided giving a clear answer. By mid-2003 it was becoming clear, however, that the campaign of establishing irreversible "facts on the ground" was nearing completion, an impression brought home to everyone by the construction of the Separation Barrier. Suddenly, the Matrix of Control has become a reality of six fundamental "facts" that have reconfigured the entire country and raised the possibility that a viable two-state solution is no longer possible.

Fact #1: Confining the Palestinians to Areas A and B of the West Bank

Since the Oslo II agreement of 1995, the West Bank was divided into three Areas: A, under full Palestinian Authority control (comprising just 18% of the West Bank); B, under Palestinian civil control but joint Israeli-Palestinian security (22%); and C, under full Israeli control (60%). Although Area A was intended to expand until it included all of the West Bank except Israel's settlements, its military facilities and East Jerusalem – whose status would then be negotiated – in fact the division became a permanent feature. Today they comprise the territory, fragmented into 64 tiny enclaves that shape the "cantons" Sharon has proposed as a Palestinian state (see Map 3). Taken together with Gaza (which Israel will probably relinquish), the emerging bantustan will consist of just 10% of the country, truncated by Israeli settlements, by-pass highways and checkpoints, though another 5-10% could be cosmetically added without compromising Israeli control.

Fact #2: The Closure

With the beginning of the Oslo peace process, Israel imposed a permanent "closure" over the Occupied Territories. Regardless of its security justification, the hundreds of permanent and "flying" checkposts erected around, between and throughout the Palestinian areas have confined the population to an extremely limited life space for the past decade. Restricted in their movement to one or two islands, Palestinians have adjusted to a situation where travel from Jenin to Tulkarm, Ramallah to Jerusalem, Jericho to Hebron, one's home to an airport, is virtually impossible. This has affected residential, marriage and commercial patterns; it has destroyed the fabric of Palestinian life, shredding it into tiny particles. After years of limited movement Palestinians have internalized the constricted space in which they live. Expectations of movement, let alone sovereignty, have been so reduced that, Israel hopes, the Palestinian public will accept with relief and gratitude a truncated mini-state in which the roadblocks have been removed and Palestinians can move freely within the cantons surrounded by Israel (see Map 4).

Fact #3: Israel's Settlement Blocs

When Ehud Barak proposed to "jump" to final status negotiations in 1999, he consolidated the settlements Israel sought to retain into "blocs," leaving the more isolated and less strategic ones liable to being dismantled. Thus, instead of dealing with 200 settlements, the Israeli government had only to negotiate the annexation of only seven settlement blocs: (1) the Jordan Valley Bloc; (2) the Ariel Bloc that divides the West Bank east to west and preserves Israeli control over the Territories' largest aquifer; (3) the Modi'in Bloc, connecting the Ariel settlements to Jerusalem and integrating the central West Bank into metropolitan Tel Aviv; a "Greater Jerusalem" consisting of (4) the Givat Ze'ev Bloc to the northwest of the city, (5) the expansive Ma'aleh Adumim bloc extending to the northeast and east of Jerusalem and (6) the Etzion Bloc to the southwest; and finally (7) a corridor extending from the settlements in the south to the Jewish community of Hebron. While these settlements blocs are somewhat flexible (Israel could conceivably relinquish the Jordan Valley and Hebron Blocs, with adjustments to others), their function is to further define, divide and control the Palestinian cantons (see Map 5).

Fact #4: Infrastructure

In order to incorporate the West Bank and East Jerusalem permanently into Israel proper, a massive system of highways and "by-pass roads" has been constructed that integrates the settlement blocs into the metropolitan areas of Tel Aviv, Modi'in and Jerusalem, while creating additional barriers to Palestinian movement. This ambitious project articulates with the Trans-Israeli Highway, now being built along the entire length of the country, hugging the West Bank in its central portion. Shifting Israel's population center eastward from the coast to the corridor separating Israel's major cities from the settlement blocs it seeks to incorporate, the Trans-Israel Highway will become the new spine of the country, upon which the by-pass road network can be hung. The result is the reconfiguration of the country from two parallel north-south units – Israel and the West Bank, the basis of the two-state idea – into one country integrated east-west. Besides ensuring Israeli control, the reorientation of traffic, residential and commercial patterns further weakens a truncated Palestinian mini-state; each Palestinian canton is integrated separately into Israel, with only tenuous connections one to the other (see Map 6). The plan to build an $80 million network of Palestinian highways, including sixteen "passages," bridges or tunnels that give the Palestinians "transportational" but not territorial contiguity, unveiled in September, 2004, provides the bantustan's own infrastructure.

Fact #5: The Separation Barrier/Wall

The final defining element of the bantustan on the ground is the Separation Barrier – or the Wall, as the International Court of Justice defines it in its advisory ruling of July 9, 2004. This complex system of concrete walls and deadly electronic fences, effectively defines the border between Israel (including the settlements blocs and East Jerusalem) and the Palestinian cantons. It follows not the Green Line, which is the natural "security line" if indeed the Barrier was a security device, but rather a tortuous route hugging the contours of Areas A and B, then swinging around settlement blocs in order to ensure they are on the "right" side of the Barrier. It is clear that the Barrier's logic is one of a border – demographic as well as geo-political – separating what Israel intends to annex from what it is willing to concede to the Palestinians (see Map 7).

There is no question that the Separation Barrier constitutes a grave violation of both fundamental human rights and international law. The fundamental issue revolves around the relationship between ""military necessity" and "proportionality." Israel certainly has an obligation to protect its citizens from violent attacks, but as an Occupying Power it also has a responsibility to protect the safety, well-being and rights of the Palestinian civilian population under its control. The route of the Barrier, extending into Palestinian territory even without the post-ICJ ruling corre3ctions, is obviously intended as a political and demographic border, not as a security barrier. Rather than a linear defensive barrier running along the border of the West Bank, the Wall is a complex matrix that literally imprisons thousands of Palestinians in enclaves encircled by 26-foot high walls, electronic fences, watchtowers manned by Israeli soldiers and military patrols. In a brief presented to the International Court, the Association of Civil Rights in Israel argues that Wall's route and its other mechanisms of control are not necessary, proportionate or legitimate security measures.

As a result, the Barrier violates the basic provisions of the Fourth Geneva Convention, a key component of international law which protects civilians living under occupation. It divides families, destroys communities, obstructs people's very freedom of movement and, ultimately, drives them from the country. It violates prohibitions on confiscating private property in Occupied Territories. By alienating farmers from their land, it prevents them from earning a livelihood. Overall, it violates Israel's legal obligations to ensure the well-being of the civilian population under its control, including its right to liberty, security of person, mental and physical health and freedom from cruel, inhuman and degrading treatment. As such the Barrier constitutes a form of collective punishment levied against civilians innocent of any crime.

The Wall also violates political provisions of international law which forbids the acquisition of territory by force and thus prohibits an Occupying Power from making its occupation permanent. The route of the Wall unlawfully exploits the security provisions of international law to protect and annex illegal settlements. By impinging on Palestinian territory it violates their right to self-determination. Indeed, it violates the international prohibition of apartheid as an aggravated form of racial discrimination.

Fact #6: "Disengagement": The Maneuver of the Century

With the "facts on the ground" in place, the next stage in creating the Palestinian bantustan was to transform the Occupation into a formally accepted political fact by the only international player Israel cares about: the United States. An Occupation is defined in international law as a temporary military situation that has no political legitimacy and can be resolved only through negotiations. Had Sharon left office with his physical "facts" in place but with no recognized political fact to counter-balance the transient nature of the Occupation itself, he would have left his enterprise of a quarter-century half-done, susceptible to international pressures that threatened to dismantle it all. In a brilliant move exploited the eager complicity of Congress and the Bush Administration, Sharon inaugurated what his supporters have called "the maneuver of the century."

In late December 2003, Sharon unveiled his full-blown plan of "disengagement" from the Palestinians, carefully framing it as a "security initiative" and not a political plan so as not to breach the Road Map and embarrass the Americans. Thus, while expressing support for the notion of a Palestinian state, Sharon blamed the Palestinians for the Road Map's failure and, taking a line so effectively pursued by Barak, accusing the Palestinians – and the demonized Arafat in particular – of eliminating themselves as "partners for peace." Having cleverly straddled the divide between accepting the Road Map and nullifying it, he could easily justify the unilateral steps he would take without accepting any of the responsibility as an Occupying Power. Indeed, he gleaned the fruits of Israel's having removed mention of the Occupation since 1967. Rather than seeking to perpetuate the Occupation, to legitimize an expanded Israel and to eliminate the possibility of any truly viable and sovereign Palestinian state, his initiative was presented as security-based: Israel would merely respond to what the intractable Palestinians had forced upon it: to define unilaterally its own "security borders."

While the term "disengagement" gave a positive spin to Sharon's initiative, it was fundamentally misleading. True, Israel would remove all its 7000 settlers from Gaza, but it would hardly "disengage." Israel would continue to control the borders, including the access of Gazan workers to the Israeli job market, the only meaningful source of income now that Gazan agriculture, industry and even fishing had been virtually destroyed. It would also maintain tight control of the Gazan economy through its blockade of the sea, the air and land routes to Israel and the Arab countries. So as to create an illusion that withdrawal from Gaza signified a willingness to withdraw from the West Bank – an illusion seized upon by Blair even though Dov Weisglass, Sharon's closest confidant, head of the Prime Minister's Office and architect of the disengagement scheme admitted publicly that the "withdrawal in Samaria is a token one; we agreed to it only so it wouldn't be said that we concluded our obligation in Gaza" – Sharon announced the relocation of four small and non-strategic West Bank settlements situated deep in Palestinian territory to the large Israeli settlement blocs "that will remain in Israel under any foreseen agreement." Any doubt that Israel intended to retain large swaths of the West Bank and a "greater" Jerusalem were laid to rest with the announcement that "disengagement" from Gaza would be accompanied by accelerated construction of the Separation Barrier, literally setting in concrete the country's new "security borders."

In the end, "disengagement" from Gaza meant merely neutralizing a chronic point of conflict over an area Israel had no interest in retaining while consolidating its hold over the West Bank. "Disengagement," then, might better be phrased as redeployment. The result would be a situation with which Israel could live indefinitely.

Needless to say, none of this could occur without the knowing complicity of the United States. Sharon himself is absolutely clear on this point: "The unilateral steps that Israel will take in the framework of the disengagement plan will be fully coordinated with the United States. We must not harm our strategic coordination with the United States." And coordination there was. The disengagement plan set the scene for what must be considered the most important political achievement of Sharon's long career – indeed, the most important political event since the founding of the State of Israel: the formal recognition by the United States of Israel's hegemony over the entire Land of Israel between the Mediterranean and the Jordan River. In their famous exchange of letters in April, 2004, President Bush wrote to Sharon:

> Thank you for your letter setting out your disengagement plan. I remain committed to my June 24, 2002 vision of two states living side by side in peace and security as the key to peace, and to the roadmap as the route to get there....

The United States appreciates the risks such an undertaking represents. I therefore want to reassure you on several points….As part of a final peace settlement, Israel must have secure and recognized borders, *which should emerge from negotiations* between the parties in accordance with UNSC Resolutions 242 and 338. *In light of new realities on the ground, including already existing major Israeli populations centers [i.e. Israel's major settlement blocs plus "greater" Jerusalem], it is unrealistic to expect that the outcome of final status negotiations will be a full and complete return to the armistice lines of 1949,* and all previous efforts to negotiate a two-state solution have reached the same conclusion. It is realistic to expect that any final status agreement will only be achieved on the basis of mutually agreed changes that reflect these realities…. As you know, the United States supports the establishment of a Palestinian state that is viable, contiguous, sovereign, and independent, so that the Palestinian people can build their own future in accordance with my vision set forth in June 2002 and with the path set forth in the roadmap.

The United States understands that after Israel withdraws from Gaza and/or parts of the West Bank, and pending agreements on other arrangements, existing arrangements regarding control of airspace, territorial waters, and land passages of the West Bank and Gaza will continue.

The United States is strongly committed to Israel's security and well-being as a Jewish state. It seems clear that an agreed, just, fair and realistic framework for a solution to the Palestinian refugee issue as part of any final status agreement will need to be found through the establishment of a Palestinian state, and *the settling of Palestinian refugees there, rather than in Israel.* [Italics added]

A little more than two months later, on June 23rd, the US House of Representatives, in an act that went almost unnoticed by the media and the public, passed Resolution 460 endorsing the Sharon-Bush exchange. Although Bush's letter gave only brief nods to Palestinian aspirations of independence, the Congressional resolution edited it in a way that expressed total support for Israel at the expense of the Palestinians, eliminating any reference to a negotiated settlement or to a "viable, contiguous, sovereign, and independent Palestinian state." The vote was almost unanimous, 407-9, revealing how deep the bi-partisan support for Israel was in Congress. (For the record, the nine who voted against were Democrats John Conyers (Mich.), Carolyn Kilpatrick (Mich.), Dennis Kucinich (Ohio), Pete Stark (Calif.), Maxine Waters (Calif.), Lynn Woolsey (Calif.) and Barbara Lee (Calif.); Ron Paul (Texas) was the only Republican who opposed it. Three other Democrats, Donald Payne (NJ), Diane Watson (Calif.) and Mel Watt (N.C.), voted "present.") In late March, 2005, Condoleeza Rice, now the American Secretary of State, reaffirmed the Bush Administration's commitment to the settlement blocs.

The next day the Senate passed a similar resolution (S Resolution 393) by a vote of 95-3. While demanding that the Palestinians stop "armed activity and all acts of violence against Israelis anywhere," it goes on to assert that "it is unrealistic" for any peace settlement between Israel and Palestinians to require Israel to return to the borders that existed before the 1967 Six Day War. The Senate Resolution nevertheless mentions the Road Map and Israel's obligation to "limit" settlement activity, omitted from the House version altogether. (The three lonely Senators voting against the resolution were Robert Byrd (D-W.Va), James Jeffords (I-Vt) and John Sununu (R-N.H). Richard Lugar (R-Ind), and John Kerry (D-Mass) did not vote, although Kerry, from the campaign trail, sent a strong message of support.)

Sharon, as might be expected, called the vote one of the biggest diplomatic achievements in Israel's history. "This is a great day in the history of Israel," he told a meeting at the ruling Likud Party headquarters in Tel Aviv. "The bi-partisan Congressional support for the President's letter and the State of Israel is without a doubt one of the most important diplomatic achievements for Israel since its creation."

In one bold diplomatic move, then, Sharon transformed the Occupation from a temporary military situation into a permanent political fact recognized by both the executive and legislative branches of its greatest benefactor, the United States. US policy towards the Israeli-Palestinian conflict now officially rejects a return to the 1949/1967 "Green Line," (contradicting the very principle of a mutually negotiated settlement). By recognizing the permanency of Israel's settlement blocs, it unilaterally reduces the area considered "occupied" and therefore subject to negotiations to only 70% of lands conquered in 1967 – and then has the audacity to decree that all the Palestinian refugees must crowd exclusively into that truncated mini-state. It places the onus for ending violence and terror exclusively upon the Palestinians, even though Israel is the Occupying Power that uses weapons of war (many of them US-made) against civilian populations, pursues repressive policies such as house demolitions and refuses to adhere to human rights and international law. And, in addressing Sharon's great fear that civil society initiatives such as the Geneva Initiative will demonstrate that the Israeli and Palestinian peoples can in fact reach a just peace agreement, US policy now declares that "the United States will do its utmost to prevent any attempt by anyone to impose any other plan."

The sharp turn in American foreign policy represented more than simply a strengthening of the traditional pro-Israel line or even a renunciation of the Road Map – supposedly Bush's own initiative. It constituted a renunciation of the very post-World War II international system based upon the premise of the illegitimacy of the expansion of a country's territory by military force (Zunes 2004). The Bush Administration, together with Congress, effectively eliminated UN Security Council resolutions 242 and 338 calling on Israel to withdraw from territories seized in the June 1967 war in return for security guarantees from its Arab neighbors. All previous U.S. administrations of both parties had considered these resolutions the only working basis for Arab-Israeli peace. So, too, did the wider international community. The radical departure from the diplomatic and legal architecture of the Road Map precipitated a joint condemnation by the other Quartet partners (Europe, Russia and the UN).

From Israel's point of view, the disengagement plan virtually concludes the process, pursued by all Israeli governments over the past 36 years and by Sharon himself since 1977, of creating a cantonized Palestinian entity that gets the Palestinians "off our hands" while leaving Israel firmly in control, it sovereignty extended over 85-90% of the entire country. So self-assured is the Sharon government that it has "won" (especially with the backing the Labor Party, that entered the government as a junior partner in late December, 2004) that it feels free to openly flaunt its strategy. In an extraordinarily candid interview with the Israeli newspaper *Ha'aretz* ("The Big Freeze," *Ha'aretz Magazine* Oct. 8, 2004), Dov Weisglass spelled out explicitly the meaning of "disengagement" and how it contributed to permanent Israeli hegemony. If only as a document affirming the analytical line of this book, it deserves to be quoted at length.

[Interviewer]: If you have American backing and you have the principle of the road map, why go to disengagement?

[Weisglass]: Because in the fall of 2003 we understood that everything is stuck. And even though according to the Americans' reading of the situation, the blame fell on the Palestinians and not on us, Arik [Sharon's nickname] grasped that this state of affairs would not last. That they wouldn't leave us alone, wouldn't get off our case. Time was not on our side. There was international erosion, internal erosion. Domestically, in the meantime, everything was collapsing. The economy was stagnant, and the Geneva Initiative garnered broad support. And then we were hit with letters of officers and letters of pilots and letters of commandos [letters of refusal to serve in the territories]. These were not weird kids with green ponytails and a ring in their nose who give off a strong odor of grass. These were people like Spector's group [Yiftah Spector, a renowned Air Force pilot who signed the pilot's refusenik letter]. Really our finest young people.

What was your main concern in those months, what was the main factor that pushed you to the disengagement idea?

The concern was the fact that President Bush's formula was stuck and this would lead to its ruin. That the international community would say: You wanted the president's formula and you got it; you wanted to try Abu Mazen and you tried. It didn't work. And when a formula doesn't work in reality, you don't change reality, you change the formula. Therefore, Arik's realistic viewpoint said that it was possible that the principle that was our historic policy achievement would be annulled - the principle that eradication of terrorism precedes a political process. And with the annulment of that principle, Israel would find itself negotiating with terrorism. And because once such negotiations start it's very difficult to stop them, the result would be a Palestinian state with terrorism. And all this within quite a short time. Not decades or even years, but a few months.

I still don't see how the disengagement plan helps here. What was the major importance of the plan from your point of view?

The disengagement plan is the preservative of the sequence principle. It is the bottle of formaldehyde within which you place the president's formula so that it will be preserved for a very lengthy period. The disengagement is actually formaldehyde. It supplies the amount of formaldehyde that's necessary so that there will not be a political process with the Palestinians.

Is what you are saying, then, is that you exchanged the strategy of a long-term interim agreement for a strategy of long-term interim situation?

The American term is to park conveniently. The disengagement plan makes it possible for Israel to park conveniently in an interim situation that distances us as far as possible from political pressure. It legitimizes our contention that there is no negotiating with the Palestinians. There is a decision here to do the minimum possible in order to maintain our political situation. The decision is proving itself. It is making it possible for the Americans to go to the seething and simmering international community and say to them, `What do you want.' It also transfers the initiative to our hands. It compels the world to deal with our idea, with the scenario we wrote. It places the Palestinians under tremendous pressure. It forces them into a corner that they hate to be in. It thrusts them into a situation in which they have to prove their seriousness. There are no more excuses. There are no more Israeli soldiers spoiling their day. And for the first time they have a slice of land with total continuity on which they can race from one end to the other in their Ferrari. And the whole world is watching them - them, not us. The whole world is asking what they intend to do with this slice of land.

I want to remind you that there will also be a withdrawal in the West Bank.

The withdrawal in Samaria is a token one. We agreed to it only so it wouldn't be said that we concluded our obligation in Gaza.

You gave up the Gaza Strip in order to save the West Bank? Is the Gaza disengagement meant to allow Israel to continue controlling the majority of the West Bank?
Arik doesn't see Gaza today as an area of national interest. He does see Judea and Samaria as an area of national interest. He thinks rightly that we are still very, very far from the time when we will be able to reach final-status settlements in Judea and Samaria.

Does the evacuation of the settlements in Gaza strengthen the settlements in the West Bank or weaken them?

It doesn't hurt the isolated, remote settlements; it's not relevant for them. Their future will be determined in many years. When we reach a final settlement. It's not certain that each and every one of them will be able to go on existing.

On the other hand, in regard to the large settlement blocs, thanks to the disengagement plan, we have in our hands a first-ever American statement that they will be part of Israel. In years to come, perhaps decades, when negotiations will be held between Israel and the Palestinians, the master of the world will pound on the table and say: We stated already ten years ago that the large blocs are part of Israel.

If so, Sharon can tell the leaders of the settlers that he is evacuating 10,000 settlers and in the future he will be compelled to evacuate another 10,000, but he is strengthening the other 200,000, strengthening their hold in the soil

Arik can say honestly that this is a serious move because of which, out of 240,000 settlers, 190,000 will not be moved from their place. Will not be moved.

Is he sacrificing a few of his children in order to ensure that the others remain permanently where they are?

At the moment he is not sacrificing anyone in Judea and Samaria. Until the land is quiet and until negotiations begin, nothing is happening. And the intention is to fight for every single place. That struggle can be conducted from a far more convenient point of departure. Because in regard to the isolated settlements there is an American commitment stating that we are not dealing with them at the moment, while for the large blocs there is genuine political insurance. There is an American commitment such as never existed before, with regard to 190,000 settlers.

If what you are saying is correct, the settlers themselves should organize demonstrations of support for Sharon, because he did a tremendous service to the settlement enterprise.

"They should have danced around and around the Prime Minister's Office....Arik is the first person who succeeded in taking the ideas of the national camp and turning them into a political reality that is accepted by the whole world. After all, when he declared six or seven years ago that we would never negotiate under fire, he only generated gales of laughter. Whereas today that today that same approach guides the president of the United States. It was passed in the House of Representative by a vote of 405 - 7, and in the Senate by 95 - 5.

From your point of view, then, your major achievement is to have frozen the political process legitimately?

That is exactly what happened. You know, the term 'political process' is a bundle of concepts and commitments. The political process is the establishment of a Palestinian state with all the security risks that entails. The political process is the evacuation of settlements, it's the return of refugees, it's the partition of Jerusalem. And all that has now been frozen.

So you have carried out the maneuver of the century? And all of it with authority and permission?

When you say 'maneuver,' it doesn't sound nice. It sounds like you said one thing and something else came out. But that's the whole point. After all, what have I been shouting for the past year? That I found a device, in cooperation with the management of the world, to ensure that there will be no stopwatch here. That there will be no timetable to implement the settlers' nightmare. I have postponed that nightmare indefinitely. Because what I effectively agreed to with the Americans was that part of the settlements would not be dealt with at all, and the rest will not be dealt with until the Palestinians turn into Finns. That is the significance of what we did. The significance is the freezing of the political process. And when you freeze that process you prevent the establishment of a Palestinian state and you prevent a discussion about the refugees, the borders and Jerusalem. Effectively, this whole package that is called the Palestinian state, with all that it entails, has been removed from our agenda indefinitely. And all this with authority and permission. All with a presidential blessing and the ratification of both houses of Congress. What more could have been anticipated? What more could have been given to the settlers?

I return to my previous question: In return for ceding Gaza, you obtained status quo in Judea and Samaria?

You keep insisting on the wrong definition. The right definition is that we created a status quo *vis-a-vis* the Palestinians. There was a very difficult package of commitments that Israel was expected to accept. That package is called a political process. It included elements we will never agree to accept and elements we cannot accept at this time. But we succeeded in taking that package and sending it beyond the hills of time. With the proper management we succeeded in removing the issue of the political process from the agenda. And we educated the world to understand that there is no one to talk to. And we received a no-one-to-talk-to certificate. That certificate says: (1) There is no one to talk to. (2) As long as there is no one to talk to, the geographic status quo remains intact. (3) The certificate will be revoked only when this-and-this happens - when Palestine becomes Finland. (4) See you then, and shalom.

THE BANTUSTAN TAKES ON URGENCY

"Disengagement" was a product of the Arafat era, the fruit of Israel's diplomatic isolation of the Palestinian President (or "Chairman," as the Israeli authorities and media called him) when all political processes that might lead to a resolution of the conflict were frozen. It stemmed from Sharon's great fear of the Road Map which threatened to internationalize the conflict, removing from exclusively American hands the ability to impose a solution to Israel's liking - or, better, to back a long-term "interim" agreement that would leave Israel in *de facto* control of the Occupied Territories indefinitely. There were other threats to the *status quo* as well. Growing opposition to policies of repression in the Occupied Territories with no "political horizon" was generating discontent, as Weisglass indicates, from the middle and upper ranks of the military reserves. The "Courage to Refuse" letter signed (as of this writing) by 635 reservist soldiers who refuse to serve in the Occupied Territories, begins with this self-presentation: "We, reserve combat officers and soldiers of the Israel Defense Forces, who were raised upon the principles of Zionism, sacrifice and giving to the people of Israel and to the State of Israel, who have always served in the front lines, and who were the first to carry out any mission, light or heavy, in order to protect the State of Israel and strengthen it." It goes on to state:

> We, combat officers and soldiers who have served the State of Israel for long weeks every year,
> in spite of the dear cost to our personal lives, have been on reserve duty all over the Occupied
> Territories, and were issued commands and directives that had nothing to do with the security
> of our country, and that had the sole purpose of perpetuating our control over the Palestinian
> people... The missions of occupation and oppression do not serve this purpose [of Israel's
> defense] - and we shall take no part in them.

In September 2003, 27 active and reserve pilots in the Israeli Air Force issued a statement saying that "aerial activity over the [Palestinian] territories is illegal and immoral" and declared: "We, for whom the Israeli Defense Forces (IDF) and the air force are an integral part of our being, refuse to continue to hit innocent civilians... the continued occupation is critically harming the country's security and moral fiber." In December 2003, members of the IDF's elite Special Operations Unit *Sayeret Matkal* issued a letter to the Prime Minister: "We say to you today, we will no longer give our hands to the oppressive reign in the territories and the denial of human rights to millions of Palestinians, and we will no longer serve as a defensive shield for the settlement enterprise." These were not marginal elements in Israeli society but the very core of the dominant, if until now quiescent, middle class mainstream. Moreover, as military figures, they carried great legitimacy among the public. They could conceivably create a grassroots mutiny against Sharon's policies. As Weisglass says candidly in the interview above: "Domestically everything was collapsing."

An even greater spur to unilateral disengagement was the spectre of a bi-national state. With the construction of the Separation Barrier, the Israeli right suddenly came face-to-face with the implications of its settlement policies, its "Greater Land of Israel" ideology. It had succeeded in its twin tasks of irreversibly incorporating major parts of the West Bank into Israel proper while foreclosing the possibility of a viable Palestinian state. In any reasonable criteria - demographic, infrastructural, economic, political - Israel had, by its own hand, constructed a single state over the entire country. The red flags were up. Unless Israel acted gingerly to avert this worst-case scenario, the "demographic bomb" might explode in its face. When we reach the point where Arabs outnumber Jews in areas under

Israeli control, warned Deputy Prime Minister Ehud Olmert (*Yediot Aharonot*, December 5, 2003), the Palestinians might demand the right to vote. "The day they get it, we will lose everything," he said. "The Land of Israel is ours and only ours. But my mother and father immigrated from far-away China in 1933 in order to live in a Jewish and democratic state, and not in a bi-national state."

Disengagement, then, is an Israeli attempt to coopt the Palestinians before they could shift from a rapidly disappearing "two-state" solution to a demand for a single democratic state. To the two cardinal principles shared by Likud and Labor which we have discussed - absolute Israeli security control over the entire country and a willingness to eventually hand over to the Palestinians only the minimum amount of territory possible, and that truncated into "cantons" - we can add a third principle, now assuming a political urgency: guaranteeing the demographic viability of Israel as a Jewish state. Ehud Olmert, the Deputy Prime Minister and a member of the *Likud's* right wing, raised the possibility of "the unilateral evacuation of most of the territories [about 60%] and parts of East Jerusalem, and the division of the land of Israel into two states." Coming from a political position that has always rejected the notion of a Palestinian state at all, this seeming shift is understandable only on the background of a mounting concern with the demographic viability of a Jewish Israel called into question by the completion of the Matrix of Control. "The border between [the two states]," Olmert continues, "will be determined not by politics, national sentiment or religious tradition, but by demography.

> Of course, my preferred option is a political settlement, but we cannot wait for it indefinitely. One must hope that the Palestinian government will succeed in gaining control of the state, but - failing that - Israel must undertake an immediate, grand one-sided move. The pain will, in any case, be great, which is why Israel should not turn to small moves, but must act at once... The "birth clock" is ticking, and we haven't got unlimited time. The move must be made quickly. The American response at this stage reflects the American desire to try and pursue the roadmap. They are likewise opposed to any one-sided move which does not rely on the Green Line.
>
> "I accept Ben-Gurion's decision for a Jewish, democratic state, while giving up on the dream of the complete land of Israel" (speech to Herzliyah Conference 16.12.03).

Defining Israel by demography, Olmert went on to assert that it should consist of 80% Jews and 20% Arabs, a ratio that would ensure a Jewish majority well into the future. Only "an inclusive unilateral move...where we define our borders that will in no way be similar to the Green Line" will save the Jewish state yet preserve its control over the entire country. Israel would keep the settlement blocs (including the Jewish neighborhoods of East Jerusalem) with their 400,000 Jewish settlers. Thus Weisglass's categorical declaration: "Out of 240,000 settlers [in the West Bank], 190,000 will not be moved from their place. Will not be moved."

The outlines of the Palestinian bantustan which have steadily emerged since the waning days of Oslo produce Map 11, a Palestinian mini-state consisting of Gaza, Areas A and B of the West Bank and isolated islands of East Jerusalem, defined largely by the route of the Separation Barrier, with the major settlement blocs and Greater Jerusalem incorporated into an expanded Israel proper. It is a concept shared by Likud and Labor, which is what made Labor's entrance into Sharon's government at the very end of 2004 easy and natural. (Indeed, it was explicitly precipitated by the need to protect the Disengagement Plan from its right-wing opponents among the settlers and the religious, as well as from Netanyahu and the other "rebels" within the Likud itself). The only minor disagreement between the Likud and Labor is over the size of the mini-state. Labor would like a larger bantustan which would look more credible and therefore be easier to "sell" to the international community. Something on the order of an 85%-15% solution, in which the Jordan Valley and the Judean Desert could be ceded to the Palestinians if Israel retained control of the borders. The Likud believes that the world will accept a Palestinian state with a minimum of cosmetic concessions, so why relinquish any more territory than Israel absolutely must? For them a 90%-10% solution seems sufficient, with the Palestinians receiving Gaza, 60% of the West Bank and a few isolated islands on the periphery of East Jerusalem. All the scenarios conform to the formula "autonomy plus-independence minus" (see Map 12)

All this is couched in fine language, of course. Having achieved all he set out to accomplish - an irreversible Matrix of Control now legitimized in American foreign policy - Sharon has no reason to come off as "hard-line." On the contrary, he is now basking in public acclaim as a man of peace and disengagement. Still, the "hard bottom line" is evident, no matter how elegantly it is inserted into reconciliatory, statesman-like language. Thus in his December 16, 2004, speech to the Herzliya Conference, Sharon said:

> Disengagement recognizes the demographic reality on the ground specifically, bravely and honestly. Of course it is clear to everyone that we will not be in the Gaza Strip in the final agreement. This recognition, that we will not be in Gaza, and that, even now, we have no reason to be there, does not divide the people and is not tearing us apart, as the opposing minority claim. Rather, the opposite is true. Disengagement from Gaza is uniting the people. It is uniting us in distinguishing between goals which deserve to be fought for, since they are truly in our souls - such as Jerusalem, the large settlement blocs, the security zones and maintaining Israel's character as a Jewish state - rather than goals where it is clear to all of us that they will not be realized, and that most of the public is not ready, justifiably, to sacrifice so much for.

Nailing Down the Bantustan Before the Return of the Road Map

Rather than taking the wind out of the sails of unilateral disengagement, two simultaneous events in early November, 2004, opened the way to the final phase of bantuization: Bush's re-election and the death of Yasser Arafat. After translating the Occupation into a political fact through American recognition of Israel's settlement blocs, all that remained was to find a Palestinian leader who would sign off on the bantustan. To be sure, the deal could be "sweetened;" in addition to Gaza, pieces of East Jerusalem and Areas A and B, Israel could offer the Palestinians much of the Jordan Valley (not including the Jordan River, however) and the Judean Desert (though without access to the Dead Sea) - say, 70% of the West Bank - without touching their settlement blocs.

Indeed, the significant challenge to the process of bantuization became evident even as Arafat was being laid in his grave. Meeting at the White House on the very day of the funeral, President Bush and Prime Minister Tony Blair announced that they would rededicate their efforts to achieving a viable Palestinian state through a revitalized Road Map process. (In March, 2005, Bush reiterated his commitment to a "truly viable" Palestinian state. While declaring emphatically that "a state of scattered territories will not work," he did not indicate how a viable Palestinian state could be reconciled with his recognition of Israel's settlement blocs.) Concerned lest the "post-Arafat era" reopen the possibility of a viable two-state solution envisioned by the Road Map, Sharon again took the initiative. Declaring 2005 "the year of great opportunity," he expressed hope that Arafat would be followed by a "moderate and pragmatic leader" with whom Israel could "do business." In Mahmoud Abbas (Abu Mazen) he has placed great hopes. After all, this was the man who, in secret agreement with Israel's former Justice Minister Yossi Beilin in October 1995, laid the foundations for Barak's "generous offer," the Clinton proposals and the Geneva Initiative - all leaving Israel's settlement blocs intact, if somewhat reduced. In the Beilin-Abu Mazen Agreement, Abbas also accepted the notion that the Palestinian capital should be located in far-away Abu Dis, as well as rejecting the refugees' Right of Return. On January 9, 2005, Abbas was elected President of the Palestinian Authority by a comfortable majority, fortunate his main opposition, Hamas, chose not to compete.

Sharon fears the Road Map initiative. It calls for an "end to the Occupation," a term and concept that Israel has always tried to deny. It call for a "viable Palestine state," which contradicts the bantustan concept. And it removes some of the political process from exclusive American hands and places it with the Quartet. This violates a cardinal principle of Israeli diplomacy: never allow any party besides the US to acquire a decision-making role in any peace process. So firm is this principle that it represents one of the fourteen "reservations" Israel presented to the Road Map. Reservation # 4 states: Monitoring the progress of the Road Map will be solely under American management.

Sharon is therefore in a race to nail down the Palestinian bantustan before the Road Map initiative puts paid to his plans. In order to coopt the Road Map process, he could conceivably set up Abbas for yet another "generous offer." With all the hype generated around the new "moderate and pragmatic" Palestinian leader, Abbas is being put in a corner. Once elections are held for the Palestinian Legislative Council in June and the settlements are removed from Gaza in July, Sharon - coordinated, as always, with the Americans - may well spring his own Generous Offer: Gaza plus 60-70% of the West Bank and a symbolic presence in East Jerusalem. If Abbas agrees, he will be the quisling leader Israel has hoped for; if he refuses, Sharon will pounce and say: "See?! The Palestinians have refused yet another Generous Offer! They obviously do not want peace!" And Israel, off the hook, will be able to rebuff any renewed Road Map initiative, freed to expand its control of the Occupied Territories for years to come.

TERRORISM "FROM BELOW," TERRORISM "FROM ABOVE"

"Neither Jewish ethics nor Jewish tradition can disqualify terrorism as a means of combat."
(Former Prime Minister Yitzhak Shamir, *Journal of the LEHI, the Stern Gang*, Summer, 1943)

"The battle against Palestinian terrorism" is the lynchpin of Israel's framing of its policies. And, indeed, terrorism is a frightful and immoral thing. It takes innocent lives and by its nature violates the most fundamental human right of all: the right to life. As Amnesty International notes: "A fundamental principle of international humanitarian law is that parties involved in a conflict must at all times distinguish between civilians and combatants, and between civilian objects and military objectives. It is not permitted to target civilians, that is, people who are not members of the armed forces of either side. This principle, known as the Principle of Distinction, is codified in the four Geneva Conventions of 1949 and their two Additional Protocols of 1977. The Principle of Distinction is a fundamental rule of customary international humanitarian law, binding on all parties to armed conflicts, whether international or non-international" (Amnesty, *Without Distinction* 2002). And it is unarguable that some Palestinian resistance groups have embarked on a prolonged campaign of terror against Israeli targets, although whether this is a strategy sponsored by the Palestinian Authority is questionable.

The issue of terrorism is more nuanced, however, than blanket (and usually self-serving) statements of condemnation imply. First of all, what is terrorism? Amnesty avoids the term, finding it far too loaded to be useful. After all, one person's terrorist is another person's freedom fighter. People suffering from oppression have a recognized right to resist. They cannot be expected to abrogate their own human rights, indeed, their very lives, without resistance. We often call upon oppressed people to adopt non-violent tactics (which, of course, they should do); here, however, is where the double standard becomes part of the system of oppression. Since only states can go to war and "legitimately" use massive military force, people accept their actions, even if they are critical of them. We seldom demand that oppressive states cease their violent means of repression. We might call for "peace" and we might condemn the excessive use of force, but for some reason states are not expected to adopt non-violent policies. Oppressed non-state peoples, by contrast, can only "resist," and since armed resistance on their part is illegitimate, it is easy for states to frame it as "terrorism." Regardless of how we feel about it, armed resistance to oppression is just as "legitimate" as the use of arms by countries.

Most useful would be to adopt Amnesty's blanket condemnation of "attacks against civilians," which are unacceptable in any context and by any party. "Attacks on civilians are not permitted under any internationally recognized standard of law, whether they are committed in the context of a struggle against military occupation or any other context," Amnesty argues. "Not only are they considered murder under general principles of law in every national legal system, they are contrary to fundamental principles of humanity which are reflected in international humanitarian law." What this does allow us to do is condemn all terror, whether "from above" by states or "from below" by non-state parties. It brings state terror into the picture and promotes efforts to hold countries accountable for their policies and actions. In fact, state terrorism is a much greater problem - though far less discussed - than non-state terror. In his book *Death By Government* (1994:13), R.J. Rummel writes: "In total, during the first eighty years of this century, almost one hundred and seventy million men, women and children Đ conceivably nearly three hundred and sixty million people Đ have been shot, beaten, tortured, knifed, burned, starved, frozen, crushed or worked to death; buried alive, drowned, hung, bombed or killed in any other of the myriad ways governments have inflicted death on unarmed helpless citizens and foreigners." And that doesn't include Bosnia, Somalia, Sudan and Rwanda. In fact, "terrorism from below" pales in comparison to the "terrorism from above" of states. Except for the year 2001, terrorists have claimed less than a thousand victims per year worldwide, while the killing of civilians by states reaches into the hundreds of thousands. This is why Bush, Sharon, Putin, the Burmese generals, the Chinese Politbureau, Third World generals and despots and other state actors frame their "war against terrorism" in moralistic terms (the "axis of evil") or as self-defense, rather than in terms of human rights. Able to distance themselves from their victims and hide behind the statesmen-like paraphernalia of their mahogany offices, moralism from on high allows them to evade responsibility. A human rights accounting does not distinguish between perpetrators of terror, and is therefore to be avoided.

There is no doubt, of course, that Palestinian organizations have resorted to terrorism in their struggle against the Occupation. But so has Israel in its attempt to suppress the Palestinians' struggle for freedom and perpetuate its control. Alongside more than 1000 Israelis that have been killed (including more than 113 children and youths) and approximately 6000 injured since the start of the second Intifada, some 3500 Palestinians have died in Israeli attacks (85% of them non-combatant civilians; 650 children or youth), with more than 29,000 injured (Palestinian Red Crescent Society; The Palestine Monitor). All are victims of terrorism, as the Israeli-Palestinian organization of bereaved families, The Parents' Circle, argues. If we accept Binyamin Netanyahu's definition of terrorism as "the deliberate and systematic murder, maiming and menacing of the innocent to inspire fear for political purposes," then the long list of attacks on Palestinian civilians - attacks that either cannot be justified on grounds of defense or security, or are so disproportionate as to constitute grave violations of human rights - places Israel squarely in the category of state terror. The demolition of thousands of homes of Palestinians for "administrative" and planning reasons, the wholesale destruction of homes in the Jenin and Rafah refugee camp, of businesses and infrastructure in Bethlehem and Ramallah, the disproportionate use of violence against non-combatant civilian populations, and the impoverishment and displacement of Palestinians through land expropriation and closure - all these clearly add up to a policy that conforms to Netanyahu's definition. The demand that Palestinians cease their terror campaign must be linked to the demand that Israel do the same. If terrorism is unjustifiable, then it must be unjustifiable across the board.

In all this the international community bears prime responsibility. The Palestinians have no history of terrorism; they have never been known as an especially fierce or belligerent people, Indeed, the turn to terrorism on the part of some Palestinian groups obscures the fundamentally non-violent nature of their resistance over the years, including during the two Intifadas. Thousands of acts of non-violent Palestinian resistance to the Occupation go unnoticed: rebuilding demolished homes, jumping over high "separation walls" to ("illegally") seek employment in Israel, demonstrating with Israeli and international peace activists against the Barrier, appealing to both Israeli and international courts against human rights violations, or simply remaining *sumud* ("steadfast") in one's house or farm despite threats, administrative policies and harassment - not to mention years of negotiations and diplomacy. If the international community demands that oppressed peoples renounce terrorism as a weapon of resistance, it must provide them with alternative legitimate means of achieving their freedom and rights. Equality before the law and the universality of human rights (including their obligations) must be enforced. The international community may condemn Palestinian terrorism only if the legitimate avenues for throwing off the Occupation and securing their rights to self-determination are made available to them.

Those "legitimate" avenues of redress are two. The Palestinians can either enter into a process of negotiations intended to resolve the conflict, or the Occupation can be made to collapse by the weight of its own illegality if the international community will only apply existing international law (such as the Fourth Geneva Convention). Both avenues have been closed to them, however. Israel and the United States refused to base the Oslo negotiations on international law because they knew that every element of the occupation was illegal and that Israel would lose. Instead, Oslo was based on power negotiations, in which case the Palestinians clearly lose. Not only was Israel allowed to strengthen its occupation during negotiations, prejudicing the very outcome of the talks, but its massive and blatant violation of human rights and international law were allowed to continue, including ever greater resort to violence, repression and state terror.

No one can justify terrorism, but moral outrage must be balanced by responsibility for the suffering of oppressed people. Instituting an international system of laws based on agreed-upon covenants of human rights will eliminate two of the worst forms of terrorism. Political terrorism, considered a legitimate form of resistance by groups like Hamas, will wither away as their adherents achieve the level of freedom, personal security and well-being guaranteed them by human rights conventions. State Terrorism, such as that waged by Israel against the Palestinian civilian population, will end as conflicts are resolved on the basis of each party's rights and the principles of international law. State Terrorism employed as a weapon of conquest, domination or exploitation will, in a world based on universal standards of civil behavior, be exposed as the illegitimate action it is. What's more, strengthening mechanisms of enforcement will end both forms of terrorism by holding offenders accountable for their actions. Only the third major form of terrorism, ideological terrorism of groups like al-Qaida, will remain intractable.

Accountability and justice based on universal human rights are not merely slogans, ideals or technicalities; they represent the most efficacious means of resolving conflicts in "win-win" ways that promote reconciliation and sustainable co-existence in a conflicted global reality.

In the meantime, if we are going to condemn terrorism, we would do well to employ the language of human rights that includes *all* forms of terror, state and non-state. It would raise issues concerning Israel's use of terror as a instrument of policy. As Weisglass disclosed candidly in the interview presented earlier, Israel's historic policy achievement was the principle that eradication of terrorism precedes any political process - what it calls the "sequence principle," although it contracts another fundamental principle of the Road Map, which "mutuality." Thus, Weisglass informs us, the Disengagement plan, which hinges on blaming the Palestinians exclusively for terror and thereby "forcing" Israel into taking unilateral steps is, we learn, nothing less than "the preservative of the sequence principle [which] supplies the amount of formaldehyde that's necessary so that there will not be a political process with the Palestinians." Putting this chain together, we are confronted with a calculated Israeli attempt to use terrorism to construct a political approach whose fundamental aim to freeze the peace process - and thereby the establishment in the near future of a Palestinian state. "This whole package that is called the Palestinian state," says Weisglass, "has been removed from our agenda indefinitely. And all this with... a presidential blessing and the ratification of both houses of Congress." If terrorism is so morally and legally unacceptable that is simply cannot be tolerated as a political or military tactic, why is Israel "permitted" to use it both in its military operations and as an effective instrument of policy?

ALTERNATIVE WAYS OUT OF THE CONFLICT (THAT ALSO HAPPEN TO BE JUST AND SUSTAINABLE)

For years the Israeli peace movement, together with the Palestinian people and leadership, has advocated a two-state solution to the conflict. That appears to be slipping away as Israel strengthens its grip over the Occupied Territories. Sharon's version of the two-state solution, a non-viable set of Palestinians cantons existing somewhere between autonomy and independence but completely under Israeli control, is as untenable as it is unjust. If both those options are eliminated, we are left with only two other possibilities: (1) an evolutionary "two-stage" conception in which two "real" states, Palestine and Israel, eventually join in a bi-national federation that in time will include Jordan, Syria, Lebanon and ultimately Egypt and other countries of the Middle East - a Middle East Union; or (2) a single democratic state encompassing all of Palestine/Israel. Which will prevail depends upon whether the Matrix of Control can be dismantled.

Option #1: The Two-Stage Solution

Stage 1: A "Real" Two-State Solution: The Option Favored by the Palestinians of the Occupied Territories, the Israeli Public and the International Community.

Based on the idea of partition, the two-state solution has been traditionally favored by Israel's peace camp, as in the recent Geneva Initiative, for example. It lies at the heart of the Oslo peace process and the Quartet's "Road Map," and has even been accepted, in principle, by Israel. It is also the only option being considered by the Palestinian leadership, since it alone addresses the Palestinians' demand for self-determination. Indeed, the strength of the "real" two-state solution derives from its recognition that self-determination for the two national groups sharing the same country necessitates separate states.

From this point of view, the two-state solution seems to be the most workable and just - although the justice and viability of this approach is diluted somewhat by the territorial imbalance between the two projected states. In the best-case scenario, with Israel abandoning its Occupation completely, the Palestinians get only 22% of the country. But the Palestinian leadership, in what can only be described as a "generous offer" towards Israel, has agreed to accept that imbalance, a position shared by most Palestinians of the Occupied Territories. The commitment to the two-state solution has withstood extreme provocation: constant expanding and strengthening of Israel's Occupation, an all-out war against the Palestinian civilian population, growing talk in Israel over the possibility of mass transfer of Palestinians out of the country and the unwillingness of even the most liberal Israelis to relinquish control of "greater" Jerusalem and some of the major settlements, not to mention Israel's insistence on imposing severe limitations on the sovereignty of any future Palestinian state. This reflects the overpowering desire on the part of the Palestinians of the Occupied Territories to achieve self-determination - even a modicum of self-determination - within a diminished state. Ultimately, however, a two-state solution must meet at least six fundamental conditions if it is to be even minimally acceptable:

- *Viability.* A Palestinian state, especially if it a diminished one, must be viable; it must be a "real" state. That means full sovereignty, control of its borders and its basic resources (such as water), territorial contiguity, freedom of movement for people and goods, the ability to develop a viable economy and the capacity to address the refugee issue.

- *An End to the Occupation*. The issue of viability depends not merely on the issue of territory but on whether Israel actually dismantles its Matrix of Control. We have seen how Barak's seemingly "generous" offer appeared more generous than it actually was. The fact that it left the Israeli public - including large sections of the peace camp - with the impression that the Palestinians rejected the offer because they did not genuinely desire peace should serve as a warning. Most people do not place much importance on the Occupation. Over the years Israeli governments have succeeded in "sanitizing" most of its settlements and certainly its rule over the Jerusalem area. Palestinian demands for a complete end of the Occupation, or even significant parts of it, are seen as "unreasonable" by most Israelis and many internationals. This is the basis of Israeli charges that the Palestinians did not negotiate seriously because they never came up with "counter-proposals" to Israel's various offers. The Palestinian position, fundamental and lacking room for maneuver, that the entire Occupation must end, was dismissed as "unreasonable" because the Israelis do not understand that a Palestinian state has certain minimal requirements. The link between the Occupation and crucial issues of viability and sovereignty, while self-evident to advocates of a just peace, must be clearly demonstrated to the wider public.

- *Evolutionary Potential*. One reason why many Palestinians consent to a diminished state is that they foresee a time when Palestine and Israel, having developed trust through a period of peaceful relations and joint economic growth, will evolve into a confederation conceivably including Jordan. This stands in stark contrast to the Israeli view which regards a signed agreement and the subsequent rise of a Palestinian state as the *end* of the process. Clauses inserted into the various Oslo texts - and repeated in *Article 1* of the Geneva Initiative - declare that the agreement resolves all the claims of the two sides, thus raising the ante considerably. It means that whatever the Palestinians sign is all they will receive; evolutionary developments are precluded (unless they are agreed upon by Israel and serve Israeli interests). Since the Geneva Initiative, concluded (in large part) in December, 2003, includes final borders, recognition of Israel as a Jewish state, Israeli veto power over the return of refugees, incorporation of settlement blocs and the majority of settlers into Israel, recognition of "Jewish Jerusalem" (including the massive settlements in East Jerusalem), limited Palestinian sovereignty (a demilitarized state with no army) and a Palestinian commitment to fight terrorism (but nothing reciprocal, although Israel has engaged in far greater acts of state terrorism), Article 1 threatens to lock the Palestinians into permanent non-viability.

- *Refugees.* Eighty percent of the Palestinians are refugees. A sustainable peace will not come merely from technical arrangements. Beyond the issue of viability, there is the issue of justice. As Jews well know, acknowledgement of injustice and the suffering it entails is no less important as any formal acts of reparation. A sustainable peace is dependent upon the just resolution of the refugee issue, and that, in turn, is dependent on three elements: Israel must recognize the refugees' *right* of return (and not frame it as a "humanitarian" problem to be addressed merely by symbolic gestures of "good will"); Israel must acknowledge its role in creating the refugee issue for a healing process to begin; and the issue of actual return must be addressed. Although the Palestinians have indicated that the process of return can be done in a way that does not compromise Israel's integrity, it must resolve, at a minimum, resolution of the unbearable Lebanon camps, repatriation of the remaining '48 generation that wishes to return and the option of choice whether to return or to accept compensation.

- *A Regional Dimension*. Despite our almost exclusive focus on the Israel/Palestine, the main issues facing both peoples of that country - refugees, security, water, economic development, democratization - are regional in scope and must be addressed as such.

- *Israel's Security.* Israel's legitimate security concerns must be addressed. A cardinal problem in negotiations until now has been an Israeli concept of security so broad and used to encompass so many elements of control that it leaves no breathing space for the Palestinians. That cannot be allowed, although the introduction of a meaningful time dimension in the peace process may assuage the basic fears while making it impossible to use "security" as an pretext for continuing occupation.

Stage 2: A Regional Confederation Leading to a Wider Middle East Union

Whether a one- or two-state solution prevails, the Middle East conflict cannot be resolved within the narrow confines of Israel/Palestine. The main issues facing both peoples are regional in scope - refugees, security, water, economic development, democratization and more - and they require a regional approach. The refugee issue must be confronted head-on and justly. Only half the Palestinians live in Palestine (three and a half million in the Occupied Territories, one million in Israel), and half of them are "internally displaced" refugees. The other half demands the choice between returning to their homeland or starting new lives in their countries of exile and diaspora. A confederation among the states of the region, beginning perhaps with Israel-Palestine-Jordan, then expanding to include Syria and Lebanon, then Egypt and other countries of the region, may seem like another pipe-dream, but it is actually the most do-able element of a Middle East peace process. It is a development that would likely take place fairly soon after a just conclusion to the Palestinian-Israeli conflict, once the Palestinian "gatekeepers" give the "green light." While taking into account issues of national self-determination, a regional confederation provides the strategic space necessary for wider accommodative processes to work.

In a Middle East Union, then, Palestinians would have the choice of either becoming citizens of the Palestinian state, retaining citizenship in their current countries of residence or applying for citizenship in one of the MEU member countries. Regardless, like all residents of the region, they would have the option of living and working anywhere in the MEU. Some may prefer to live in their own state, others to remain where they are, still others to "go home" to areas inside Israel, yet others may prefer emigration to other countries. Under such a confederation even a major influx of Palestinian refugees into Israel (under a viable two-state solution) would not endanger its sovereignty, since the refugees, as citizens of Palestine and the MEU, would not vote in Israeli elections. MEU laws and regulations, legislated by a confederal parliament, would protect their individual rights. In a regional confederation the Right of Return would no longer threaten Israel's sovereignty; after all, 350,000 foreign workers reside today in Israel without threatening its integrity. With their political identity realized by the existence of a Palestinian state, refugees could find substantive individual justice by living in any part of Palestine (or the wider MEU) they choose, including Israel, but would reside in the country as non-voting permanent residents. By the same token, Israeli Jews wishing to live in the settlements could continue to do so under Palestinian sovereignty. The settlements would be integrated and thereby cease to be settlements and sources of Israeli control.

A perspective of inter-communal harmony in Palestine-Israel within a context of a democratic and prosperous Middle East might sound utopian at the present moment. There is no doubt that decades of conflict, destruction, suffering, poverty, autocracy, religious intolerance and the domination of militaries have made the tasks of political and economic restructuring difficult and long-term. But, again, we must also note the positive concealed below these layers of strife. The PLO did recognize Israel within the 1949 Armistice Lines, Israel does recognize a Palestinian collectivity, Israelis do not adhere to the "Greater Land of Israel" ideology, and the Israelis and Palestinians have engaged in negotiations. The Geneva Initiative signed by representatives of Palestinian and Israeli civil societies demonstrates that the peoples have not given up the search for a just peace. Israel has formal peace treaties with Egypt and Jordan, and working relationships with countries in North Africa and the Gulf (not to mention a close alliance with Turkey, a major Muslim power in the region). Perhaps most hopeful of all is the Saudi Initiative announced by Prince Abdullah in April 2002 and supported by the Arab League. It offers Israel not only grudging recognition, not only a formal peace, but full regional integration in return for relinquishing its Occupation.

We must also recognize the Middle East's potential, the dynamic forces for change that, if released from autocracy and conflict - the Israeli/Palestinian conflict being the major constraint - would permit the region to assume its proper place in global affairs. Secretary of State Powell was correct when he noted that the Arab world contributes only 1% to international trade (aside from oil). This is not a "normal" situation." The peoples of the Middle East - Palestinians, Lebanese, Syrians, Bedouins, Egyptians, Israelis and others; Muslims, Jews and Christians - all have strong traditions of cosmopolitanism and commerce arising out of the centrality of the region to world culture and trade over the millennia. In terms of both development, stability and moderation the educated and affluent Palestinian and Arab diasporas, joined by a progressive Jewish diaspora, are also resources that should not be overlooked.

Option #2: A Single Democratic State

Until the autumn of 2003, only a tiny handful of Israeli ultra-leftists advocated the creation of a single state for the two peoples of Israel-Palestine. Yet no one familiar with Israel's campaign of creating "facts on the ground" can ignore the fact that, with the six elements described above virtually in place, the Occupation had reached - or passed - the point of no return. The Road Map is understood as the last gasp of the two-state solution. As it has faltered (the Security Council reaffirmed its unanimous support for it in mid-November, 2003, despite Israeli objections), it has led some Israelis to conclude that Israel, by its own hand, had made a just and viable two-state solution impossible. This growing sentiment was eloquently expressed by Meron Benveniste in an August 2003 interview in the Israeli daily *Ha'aretz*, where he declared that one state belonging to all the inhabitants of the Land of Israel/Palestine was the only possible option.

> In the past year, then, I reached the conclusion that there is no choice but to think in new terms. The seemingly rational solution of two states for two nations can't work here. The model of a division into two nation-states is inapplicable. You can erect all the walls in the world here but you won't be able to overcome the fact that there is only one aquifer here and the same air and that all the streams run into the same sea. You won't be able to overcome the fact that this country will not tolerate a border in its midst. This is a country in which the Arabs are the landscape, the natives. So I am not afraid of them. I don't see myself living here without them. In my eyes, without Arabs this is a barren land.There is no choice but to think about western Palestine [*Eretz Yisrael*, or the Land of Israel] as one geopolitical unit.

Although the establishment of a single democratic state had been the Palestinian position before they adopted the two-state approach in the 1980s, the Palestinian leadership resists advocating this line at the present time. Jumping to a single state endangers the very principle of self-determination. True, the Palestinians would have the majority, but they would be locked into a joint state with another people who are much stronger in terms of education, economy and institutions. The history of two national entities coexisting in one political framework has not been a happy one, especially when they have been locked into bitter conflict. For the immediate future, the Palestinians prefer to struggle for an end to the Occupation and the establishment of a state of their own alongside Israel. When, as could happen soon, they are finally forced by the facts on the ground to abandon all hopes of a viable state of their own, they could make a very effective case for a single democratic state. They could say, in effect: "OK, Sharon, you won. You have incorporated the Occupied Territories irreversibly into Israel proper, you have foreclosed the possibility of a viable Palestinian state, your settlements are here to stay. We concede. We accept that you have created a single state. All we want now are equal rights. One person, one vote."

While it is still too early to advocate for such a solution - the Palestinian Authority remains committed to the two-state solution as of this writing - the time is approaching when the one-state option becomes the only viable one. *Ha'aretz* reported (January 8, 2004) that in response to Sharon's threats to impose his unilateral "Disengagement Plan," Palestinian Prime Minister Abu Ala (Ahmed Qureia) warned that Palestinians would seek a bi-national state and demand the same rights as Israelis. "This is an apartheid solution to put the Palestinians in cantons. Who can accept this? We will go for a one-state solution...There's no other solution." Showing maps of the barrier, Qureia said it was an attempt to "put Palestinians like chickens in cages...The wall is to unilaterally mark the borders, this is the intention behind the wall. It will kill the Road Map and kill the two-state vision," he said.

Ha'aretz also notes that Palestinian officials say that calling for a bi-national state would be used only as a last resort since it would mean dropping longstanding aspirations for a state of their own. Having come so far in gaining international support for their claims of self-determination, the Palestinian leadership is loathe to jeopardize its efforts by introducing an entirely new program that entails the end of Israel as a Jewish state. Even raising the issue, many say, is counterproductive. Still, many Palestinians cling to the hope that whatever arrangement is reached, they will eventually find themselves in either a federation with Israel or merged into a single state.

From the Israeli point of view, of course, the single-state idea is absolutely a non-starter, despite Israeli government policies that are *de facto* turning the country into one integrated unit. Since a Jewish-Israeli state already exists, the threat of a single state to the *status quo* is much more tangible and immediate than the various future scenarios entertained by the Palestinians. For the transformation of Israel into a single state possessing a Palestinian majority means nothing less than the end of political Zionism, of Jewish claims to self-determination. The end of Israel as a Jewish state.

The two-state solution provides for both Palestinian and Israeli-Jewish aspirations for self-determination. It is also the least threatening to Israel. If, however, Sharon implements his unilateral "Disengagement Plan," the Iron Wall will crush a viable two-state solution. What remains, a "two-state solution" in which a Palestinian state exists within the Matrix of Control, is nothing more than a form of apartheid, replete with bantustans. Assuming that this is not acceptable to either the Palestinians or the international community (not to mention parts of the Israeli public), the end of a viable two-state option leaves but one other possibility: a single state in Palestine-Israel.

Is this an unthinkable option? Certainly the end of Israel as an ethnic state releases it from its primary preoccupation: maintaining a Jewish demographic edge over the Palestinians. This is a contest Israel cannot win. Palestinians make up almost half the population of the country between the Jordan and the Mediterranean, and will be a majority within less than a decade. Even without the Occupied Territories, however, a Jewish state is not demographically sustainable. The "blame," if we want to phrase it in this way, can only be placed on the doorstep of world Jewry. The vast majority of Jews - some 70% of them - never came to Israel or have permanently left. Indeed, wherever they had a choice, Jews preferred to migrate elsewhere. Today the Jewish majority in Israel stands at only 72% and dwindling. The Palestinian citizens of Israel make up almost 20% of the population; some 300-400,000 immigrants from the former Soviet Union are non-Jews; and today a half million Israeli Jews are estimated to live permanently abroad. Artificially maintaining a "Jewish" state on such a narrow base has become increasingly repressive. By law and zoning "non-Jews" are forbidden to buy, rent, lease or live on "state lands" - almost 93% of the country. In the fall of 2003 the Knesset enacted a law preventing Palestinian citizens of Israel from bringing their spouses from the Occupied Territories to live with them in Israel.

Cultural Zionism

Whatever political framework evolves in the future, political Zionism seems to have run its course. The sustainability of Israel as an ethnic state living in permanent fear, alienation and conflict with the very people with whom it shares its country is increasingly called into question. The time might be ripe for a return to what might be called a New Cultural Zionism. Between the 1920s and the establishment of Israel, some of the leading figures the Zionist movement questioned the viability, indeed, the very desirability, of a Jewish State. Their ranks included many of the leading thinkers and doers of the time: the essayist Ahad Ha-am; Eliezer Ben-Yehuda, the "father of modern Hebrew;" Arthur Ruppin, a member of the Zionist Executive responsible for land purchases in Palestine; philosophers Martin Buber, Gershom Scholem, Ernst Simon and Hugo Bermann; Henrietta Szold, the founder of Hadassah; Judah Magnes, the founder and first President of the Hebrew University; and the famous author Moshe Smilansky; as well as prominent Jews from Middle Eastern background such as the educator David Yellin. Opposed to Political Zionists who argued that Jews required a state and alarmed by the rise of Jabotinsky and his neo-fascist Revisionism, Cultural Zionists argued that the Jewish people needed only a cultural space where it could develop and flourish. They understood the pluralistic nature of pre-state Palestinian society and the necessity of acknowledging the Palestinian presence. In their efforts to revive Jewish culture and place it on a par with other contemporary cultures, the Land of Israel assumed a central importance, but as a national home, not yet a political state. Wrote Ahad Ha'am in 1921:

> [The historical right of the Jewish people] does not invalidate the right of the land's inhabitants, who have a genuine right to the land due to generations of residence and work upon it. For them this too is a national home and they have the right to develop their national potentialities to the utmost. This, therefore, makes Palestine into a common possession of different peoples, each endeavoring to establish here a national home, and under such circumstances it is impossible that either of them should be complete and contain everything included in this conception (quoted in Flapan 1979:164).

Political Zionism, they worried, might engender a state of the Jews but not a truly *Jewish* state. As a result, Cultural Zionists looked to bi-nationalism as the most workable arrangement that would give the Jews freedom to develop their cultural nationalism, institutions and Hebrew life, while forging a *modus vivendi* with the Palestinian majority. Indeed, before 1948, bi-nationalism offered the most rational, hopeful and workable scenario. The very success of Political Zionism in establishing a Jewish state would have seemed to vindicate its approach. But post-independence realities - Israel's inability to find accommodation with the Palestinians, not to mention its increasingly repressive and militaristic "non-Jewish" character - suggest that Cultural Zionism actually offers the best hope for the future, certainly if the two-state solution is gone.

The practicality of a single state rests on yet another aspect of Israeli life that is rarely taken into account, but which accords with the Cultural Zionists' view: the existence of Israeli society, culture, economy and institutions, all of which are vital and strong. The notion that Israel's survival as a Jewish state is essential to the survival of its Israeliness, the essence of Political Zionism, must be questioned. Just as the European sector of South African society survived the transition to black majority rule and even retained its position of influence, so, too, will the Israeli sector endure and even flourish, especially if it takes pro-active steps to end the conflict and get on with developing the country as a joint project with the Palestinians. The understandable aspirations of the Jews to control their destiny, to never again be dependent upon others, must give way to democratic procedures if only because the vast majority of Jews chose to settle abroad and not in Israel (including a considerable portion of Israeli Jews themselves).

Cultural Zionism would argue that the only source of security for Israeli Jews is a thoroughly democratic and economically prosperous state belonging to all its citizens. In fact, so strong is Israeli society and economy that many Palestinians fear becoming an underclass in a single state even if the Palestinians constitute the majority. It may be difficult to imagine Palestinian-Israeli harmony given the conflicts of the past century. Those who think such a development is impossible, however, should recall the euphoria and enthusiasm that accompanied the investment and joint economic ventures of Oslo's early years. If the envisioned state is integrated into a wider Middle East that is also democratic and prosperous - a process in which Israelis could play a major role - a secure and vibrant Jewish life in Israel/Palestine is further ensured. This line of thought may not reassure every Israeli, but the elimination of a viable two-state solution will leave it the only option available.

For the single state option to win Jewish supporters, two fundamental concerns must be addressed: the fear of coming under another people's rule (especially that of a current "enemy"), and the concern that a non-Jewish Israel/Palestine will not longer offer refuge to Jews in times of need. Here we might take a page out of the history of South Africa's resistance movement, the ANC. Even before the fall of apartheid it circulated a draft of a constitution for the future democratic state. That step alone lent a note of assurance to the European populations that feared a transition to majority black rule. It also gave an opportunity for people from all communities to contribute to the constitution-drafting process. That could be done in Israel-Palestine. Inserting an article guaranteeing the right of both Jews and Palestinians to return to the country, including the automatic acceptance of peoples of both communities in time of need, would go a long way towards assuring each people of the good intentions of the other. All this was suggested by Magnes back in the 1920s. "What is Zionism?" he asked. "What does Palestine mean to us?"

> I can answer for myself in almost the same terms that I have been in the habit of using for many years: Immigration; Settlement on the land; Hebrew life and culture. If you can guarantee these to me, I should be willing to yield the Jewish state and the Jewish majority; and on the other hand, I would agree to a legislative assembly, together with a democratic political regime so carefully planned and worked out that the above three fundamentals could not be infringed. Indeed, I should be willing to pay almost any price for these three, especially since this price would in my opinion also secure tranquility and mutual understanding (quoted in Flapan 1979:177).

Caught Between Two Impossibilities

In terms of the Israeli-Palestinian conflict, we find ourselves in a period of transition, with no clear direction. The "ground" tells us that a viable two-state solution is finished, that Israel has succeeded in creating such massive "facts" that it's presence in the Occupied Territories simply cannot be rolled back sufficient for a truly viable and independent Palestinian state to emerge. For anyone familiar with the lay of the land, it is clear that Israel has effectively transformed the entire country between the Mediterranean and the Jordan into one integrated territorial, legal and administrative unit - one state in all but name.

But other considerations still prevent a transition from a struggle for a viable Palestinian state alongside Israel to that of a single democratic or bi-national state. A single state means the end of two nationalisms: Zionism, Israel as a Jewish state, as well as Palestinian aspirations for self-determination in a state, even a small state, of their own. We are caught between two impossibilities. What is more impossible, to really end the Occupation or to dismantle Israel as a Jewish state in favor of a unitary state of all its citizens, Jewish and Arab alike?

The "ground" tells us the two-state solution is finished (unless we are prepared to accept Sharon's notion of a cantonized Palestinian mini-state); political realities tell us the time has not yet come to advocate for a single state. As we wrestle with possible solutions, the regional dimension assumes an ever increasing importance. If preserving Israel as a Jewish state is a rock-bottom requirement for both the Israeli Jewish public and most of the international community, a sustainable peace must then include Palestinian self-determination in a minimally-viable state of their own, plus the ability to address the refugee issue. The Occupied Territories are so small and truncated that the Palestinians are left with very little room to maneuver. If, however, a regional confedcration with Jordan (at a minimum) was a guaranteed part of the solution, then, as suggested earlier, the Palestinians could be more forthcoming in terms of territorial compromise. A regional confederation would expand the functionality of a Palestinian state. The state itself, too small and localized to deal with the entire refugee population, too limited to develop a strong economy, could nevertheless provide the dispersed Palestinian population with a political identity, national participation in the international community, and a modicum of self-determination. Other essential responsibilities too large for the small state - refugees, economic development and the like - could be dealt with on a regional basis. This would lighten the burden on the limited Palestinian state, thereby permitting the Palestinians to make territorial compromises they simply cannot make if a viable solution depends solely upon a separate state.

(It is interesting to note that a regional solution has long been seen by Israeli leaders as an integral part of any arrangement. Labor's "Jordanian Option" called for a "return" of Palestinian areas to Jordan, with Israel retaining half the West Bank as a "security zone." "Jordan is Palestine" has been Sharon's banner for years; it represented the essential component of his 1982 war against the PLO in Lebanon. In order to maintain control of the entire country yet keep Israel Jewish by relieving it of the Palestinian population - assuming that transfer is politically impossible and the establishment of a viable Palestinian state is politically undesirable - the right suggests making the Palestinians Jordanian citizens. Uzi Cohen, a prominent member of the Likud Central Committee, even proposes a Palestinian state in the Jordanian panhandle below Syria.)

Option #3? A Last Pro-Active Attempt at a Palestinian State

One last ditch play could yet shock the two-state solution back to life. If the Palestinian Authority grabbed the initiative and unilaterally declared a Palestinian state on all the territories conquered in 1967, blaming Israel for leaving them no choice, they could conceivably shift the focus of the conflict from Israeli security to their own national requirements made all the more urgent by Israel's continued construction of settlements and the Separation Barrier. Such a move would create a *fait accompli* - yet a reasonable one - that would galvanize world public opinion in favor of Palestinian statehood. Without such a bold move Sharon will succeed in keeping the focus on security, eventually smothering all chances for a viable two-state solution and leading to one of the more likely options set out above.

Regardless, advocating for a just solution to the Israeli-Palestinian conflict is not an easy task. Unlike apartheid South Africa where a single democratic state ("One Man, One Vote") was the clear and agreed upon end-goal, the Palestinian struggle is far more vague. Should we continue our efforts to end the Occupation or accept it as a permanent "fact on the ground" to be worked around? Do we advocate for a viable two-state solution in the hope that the Matrix of Control can be dismantled or do we draw the necessary conclusions and shift our struggle to that of attaining a single democratic state? What about bi-national federation or regional confederation? International activists cannot advocate without direction from their Israeli and Palestinian counterparts, which they lack, while Israelis must wait on a clear Palestinian program before advocating for any solution beyond that of two states, regardless of its feasibility.

What About the Geneva Initiative?

Despite the PR aroused by the Geneva Initiative signed by the Israeli liberal-left and Palestinians connected to the Palestinian Authority, there is little to suggest that it represents anything more than a simulation of what might have happened had the Taba talks continued another few weeks. The Israeli side made a great effort to be fair within the confines of a strict two-state solution. It agreed to complete withdrawal from 22% of the country - the Occupied Territories with the exception of certain settlements and settlement blocs, but with a one-to-one exchange of territory. Overall, however, Israel comes out on top. The Palestinians are held to 22% of the country, with Israel retaining its settlements in East Jerusalem, the Greater Jerusalem area and along an extended strip of the western West Bank. No viable or coherent Palestinian Jerusalem; no qualitative exchange of land. As in all other Israeli initiatives, the Palestinians get a state on more or less of the 22% but the country's developmental potential remains exclusively in Israeli hands. The Palestinians get their state, but without territorial congruity, control of borders and resources, and a Jerusalem organically integrated into it their state is little more than a Third World country living on a subsistence level from agriculture, casual labor, remittances and international relief. The Geneva Initiative also gibes a great deal of attention to the details of resettling (and compensating) the refugees *elsewhere*, but neither a recognition of the Right of Return nor an apology or acknowledgement of what happened in 1948 is offered. And it lacks any vision of an evolutionary potential. It is a cold technical document lacking elements that might lead to healing and reconciliation, or even hope and inspiration. Most important, it presents a certain picture of a possible political arrangement with no "road map" of how to get there. It remains a purely academic exercise. To be sure, Geneva represents a welcome civil society initiative. It demonstrates that there *is* a partner for peace. But it carries the air of something *passé*, a vision and a process that belongs to a past age, the Oslo process, but is no longer relevant.

Should the Geneva Initiative be supported? If the Palestinians feel it is a solution they can live with, there is no reason why not. If the Occupation can somehow be ended it might provide a basis for beginning discussion of a just solution. Most Israelis would certainly have no problem with it. But a viable two-state solution seems so remote that Geneva plays little role in efforts to reach a just peace, which may or may not involve two states at all.

SO WHAT SHOULD WE DO?

Any international effort to defeat Israeli apartheid needs a clear, compelling political vision accompanied by an aggressive and well-financed strategy of advocacy. Regardless of whether a new "hot" period of diplomatic activity thrusts the post-Arafat Palestinian leadership into new international initiatives and negotiations or we remain in prolonged periods of "cold" diplomatic inactivity, the reinvigoration of the international movement against the Occupation is crucial.

Towards A Pro-Active Campaign of Advocacy

An effective, pro-active, international campaign of advocacy involves at least three key elements: (1) a clear and compelling re-framing of the conflict, (2) mobilization of civil society forces, including close monitoring of international peace efforts and an assertive targeting of power, and (3) a focused and coordinated campaign of advocacy.

(1) An Alternative Human Rights Framing: A Just Peace And Regional Integration

We began this book by noting that the one who frames an argument usually wins the debate. We cannot confine our efforts to merely refuting Israeli claims, nor is the problem raw information. A fundamental starting point in our struggle to reach public opinion is to take control of how the conflict is presented. We must offer a re-framing of the conflict which highlights the overarching reality of the Occupation, advocates for a just and lasting solution that recognizes Palestinian claims and needs (including those of the refugees) while addressing Israel's security concerns, and ensures regional peace and development through regional integration. If we succeed in framing the public discussion in these terms, then the logic of a "win-win" solution will be compelling and self-evident.

In contrast to the Israeli framing presented at the start of this discussion, an alternative framing (although by no means the definitive one) may be tentatively put as follows:

> Two peoples defining themselves in national terms and claiming the right of self-determination are locked in a bloody contest over both fundamental claims to the country and ways in which they can share it. Both consider themselves the native inhabitants. Here the symmetry ends - and it is crucial to break the narrative of "both peoples" so as to see (1) the very different positions of each side and (2) the asymmetry of power between them.
>
> The Israeli Jews are the dominant party and have been since 1948, if not before. They have a state that has been recognized, by the Palestinian leadership, the Arab League and the international community alike, on 78% of the territory between the Mediterranean and the Jordan River. Since neither its national existence nor its right to live in security within the "Green Line" is challenged, the cause of Israel's continued war against the Palestinians is over control of the entire country, coveted by Israel for religious and national reasons, as well as security concerns. Israel's "bottom line" is a Jewish state existing within recognized borders, yet controlling Judea and Samaria (the West Bank). Israel's attempt to deny its occupation and to make its presence permanent flies in the face of international law which defines an occupation as a temporary situation of conquest that has to be resolved through negotiations, and is patently illegal. Israel has adopted a unilateral position, backed by its policy of creating "facts on the ground," that limits any Palestinian state to truncated parts of the Occupied Territories, even if Israel recognizes the Palestinians' right to self-determination. Similarly, the Palestinians refugees' Right of Return is guaranteed in international humanitarian law. Israeli insistence that Palestinian refugees may return only to a truncated Palestinian mini-state

93

(with some minor symbolic exceptions) also violates their rights and prevents a just resolution of the conflict. Compromise is possible only by mutual agreement, not by fiat.

The position of the Palestinian leadership, as represented by the Palestinian Authority, might not represent as clear and comprehensive a framing as the Israeli one, but it possesses political authority. In principle, it sees the entire country as Palestine, but recognizes the existence of Israel as a given. It is therefore a "two-state" position in which, for only minimal viability, the Palestinian state must encompass all the Occupied Territories, the 22% of the country conquered by Israel in 1967 (with some minor border adjustments). Israel must also recognize the refugees' Right of Return and acknowledge its role in creating the refugee problem, but the actual resolution of the issue can then be worked out. After that the Palestinians will support the Saudi offer of full integration of Israel into the region, including security guarantees. The two-state solution is not completely just (it leaves the Palestinians with less than a quarter of the country), but it is one they have indicated they could live with. It represents a compromise that could be "sold" to both peoples. If Israel's Matrix of Control proves too strong, we must be prepared for a transition to a one-state struggle. Only the Palestinians can signal that switch.

Re-framing rests on a number of key re-conceptualizations:

- *Israel as the strong party in the conflict.* Israel is able to avoid accountability by presenting itself as the victim. Since victims have no responsibility and enjoy the sympathy extended to the underdog, this permits it to act with impunity despite its obvious political, economic and military superiority over the Palestinians, not to mention its position as an occupying power. Re-casting Israel not only as the strong party in the local conflict with the Palestinian but a regional and even international superpower would enable us to demand accountability. It should be pointed out that Israel's economy is three times larger than Egypt, Palestine, Jordan, Syria and Lebanon put together, that it is the world's fourth largest nuclear power and the fifth largest producer of arms, that it possesses nuclear, chemical and biological weapons and has never signed a non-proliferation treaty or agreed to international inspection, that it is by treaty a "strategic ally" of the US and that it is the Occupying Power. This re-framing would serve to alter the public's perception of the conflict, laying the foundations, for example, for a campaign of sanctions. Highlighting human rights violations while disabusing the public of the notion that Israel is in an existential fight for its life opens the way for demands that international law - and in particular the Fourth Geneva Convention - be applied.

- *The Occupation as a pro-active policy.* Framing its policies as merely defensive responses to Palestinian terrorism while removing even the term "occupation" from the discourse represents one of Israel's great PR successes. A re-framing places the Occupation at the very center of the discussion and then goes on to make a telling point: that the Occupation represents a *pro-active* claim to the entire country. The major elements of what I call Israel's "Matrix of Control" - the settlements, the infra-structure of highways that incorporate the West Bank and East Jerusalem irreversibly into Israel, the closure, land expropriation and massive house demolitions, the invasive Wall-cum-border - cannot be explained in terms of security and defense. The contention, often stated by US policy-makers, that if only Palestinian "violence" ends and Israel's security can be ensured, then Israel would be willing to meet Palestinian demands for self-determination, is simply wrong. While more liberal Israeli parties are willing to entertain the notion of a Palestinian mini-state, as in the recent Geneva Initiative, no Israeli government will willingly consent to the establishment of a truly viable and sovereign Palestinian state. We must highlight the internal contradictions between Israel's security framing and its pro-active policies. The struggle should be recast pro-actively as the Palestinian people's seeking freedom from oppression.

- *The issue is not one of Israel's security, but its claim to the entire country and an unwillingness to countenance the emergence of a truly viable and independent Palestinian state.* While Israel has legitimate security concerns, its policies and actions in the West Bank, Gaza and East Jerusalem are not merely responses to terrorism, nor are they fundamentally motivated by genuine fears of terrorism. The issue is Israeli expansion, the refusal to dismantle settlement blocs; "dismantling the terrorist infrastructure" is actually the instrument for maintaining them. Even when security concerns are genuine, as in the case of Labor Party policies, the generals who dominate policy-making have such an exaggerated view of "security" - much of it relating to potential threats of other Middle Eastern countries, not of the Palestinians - that it simply leaves no room for Palestinian sovereignty. The Matrix of Control expresses security implications, of course, but if insisted upon it robs a Palestinian state of any genuine sovereignty. It offers only what Israel calls "certain characteristics of sovereignty."

- *Only a win-win scenario will secure a just and lasting peace.* Whatever the ideological claims or disparities of power, one thing is certain: neither the Israelis nor the Palestinians will defeat the other. The notion that Palestinians and Israelis are enemies, that they constitute two irreconcilable "sides," leads nowhere. It ignores the sources of the conflict and instead mystifies some sort of "primordial" antagonism that presumably exists "from time immemorial." It also contradicts the modern global dynamic of fluidity, intertwined economies, human rights - an emerging win-win (or lose-lose) reality. The fall of the Soviet Union, of apartheid South Africa, of the Shah, of Marcos, of the Latin American generals, of the Greek colonels, of Milosevic, all exemplify the ultimate inability of power to sustain an unjust situation over time. Only a win-win scenario will force the "sides" to ask what the other requires, thereby identifying both the fundamental elements underlying the conflict and suggesting areas of compromise.

- *The Israeli people do not support the settlements or seek a "Greater Israel."* The pro-active, expansionist policy of Occupation does not represent the will of the majority of Israelis and does not derive from any popular demand to expand settlements or confine Palestinians to a bantustan. On the contrary. Polls taken in Israel consistently show that two-thirds of the Jewish population of Israel desire "separation" from the Palestinians - "us here, them there" as Barak's election slogan had it - even if that means dismantling the settlements. True, the second Intidafa and the subsequent terrorist campaign strengthened Israeli distrust of the Palestinians, expressed in wide popular support for the construction of the Wall and Sharon's iron-fist policies, but it arises from a search for personal security rather than from any ideological aspiration to control the "Greater Land of Israel." Israel's unique system of proportional elections also tends to disenfranchise the public by granting tremendous autonomy to the political parties that make up all government coalitions. It gives far greater power to tiny single-issue groups, such as settlers, than to large but less organized sectors of society. Thus the "disconnect" between a populace desiring peace-with-separation and its governments' unilateral policies of territorial expansion and military "victory."

- *Both the Palestinians and the wider Arab and Muslims worlds support a just peace.* The contention that the "Arabs" do not want peace, a view that makes sense to people given Palestinian attacks

95

on Israeli civilians, not to mention the post-9.11 stereotype of Arabs and Muslims as supporters of terrorism, finds no empirical support. Hamas, Islamic Jihad, the al-Aqsa Martyrs Brigade and other extreme Palestinian groups that reject peace with Israel and have turned to violent means of resistance represent about the same proportion of Palestinian society in the Occupied Territories - say 15-20% - that extreme settler and other right - wing rejectionist groups represent in Israeli society. In the 1996 elections to the Palestinian Authority, Arafat and the supporters of the Oslo process, who conceded 78% of historic Palestine to Israel, won more than 90% of the vote. We must also be careful not to confuse resistance to Occupation and a struggle for liberation - even an armed struggle employing controversial tactics - with a rejection of peace itself. While Israel succeeds in framing Palestinian resistance as mere terrorism and uses it to argue that the "Arabs" are not "partners in peace," Palestinians cannot allow themselves to be imprisoned forever in a bantustan with no hope of any future for the coming generations. Thus is why the adjectives "just" and "viable" are integral parts of any sustainable "peace." The ability to balance peace and resistance depends on a framing that places the Occupation and its effects at its center. The fact that Israel has a long-standing peace treaty with Egypt and Jordan and functional ties with many other Arab and Muslim nations must also be factored in.

- *A just peace will come only with the intervention of the international community.* Israel will not relinquish its Occupation willingly, and the Palestinians are powerless to achieve a viable state on their own. As in the case of other protracted and immutable ethnic conflicts, outside intervention is needed. The Quartet's current Road Map initiative recognizes this and brings the US, Europe, Russia and the UN into direct involvement. So, too, does international humanitarian law require international intervention when universal justice, the guarantee of equal rights for all, is endangered. In the end, of course, only governments can negotiate. It falls on us, however, the international civil society of NGOs, faith-based organizations, political groups, trade unions and universities, together with activists and intellectuals, to prod them and keep them honest. We must articulate the elements of a win-win solution, raise our voices when the political leaders attempt to mislead us, engage with them when they adopt constructive positions, and mobilize our considerable clout, including initiating sanctions, when one side or the other attempts to impose a win-lose solution.

- *Terms of reference must be human rights and international law.* A major obstacle to addressing the Palestinian-Israeli conflict is the extreme partisanship and emotionalism it calls up. Employing a discourse of human rights and international humanitarian law avoids the emotional claims and counter-claims, the charges of anti-Semitism, the obfuscation in general. Because human rights are universal and internationally agreed-upon, they provide a useful basis for evaluating a situation and highlighting the sources of injustice and responsibility. And since Israel is the strong party pursuing a pro-active policy of expansionism in violation of international law, they provide the instruments by which Israel can be held accountable.

A rights-based approach is also valuable when addressing the issue of terrorism, a central elements of Israel's framing. It asserts the inadmissibility of attacks on civilians, thus highlighting not only on non-state "terrorism from below" but also the much more deadly state terrorism "from above." Indeed, in terms of the security needs of all the parties to the conflict, a re-framing of the solution that insists on conformity to the Fourth Geneva Convention, UN resolutions, international law and human rights conventions provides the most effective "road map" to a just - and ultimately win/win - resolution.

In Oslo, almost every protection and source of leverage the Palestinians possessed - including the Geneva Conventions and most UN resolutions -were set aside in favor of power-negotiations in which Israel had a tremendous advantage, even though virtually all the elements of the Occupation stand in violation of international law. Any solution, if it is to work, to enable a win-win solution, must be based on human rights and international law.

Palestinians carry a responsibility to adhere to international norms which prohibit terrorism, attacks on civilians and threats to Israeli integrity and security. Still, as the Occupying Power, Israel carries the primary burden. Virtually every element of Israel's Occupation violates human rights conventions - and especially the Fourth Geneva Convention that forbids an Occupying Power from making its presence a permanent one. Thus:

- Articles 50 and 51 of the "Protocols Additional to the 1949 Geneva Convention" emphasize the protection of civilians in time of war. "The civilian population comprises all persons who are civilians. The civilian population and individual civilians shall enjoy general protection against dangers arising from military operations."

- Article 3 prohibits "outrages upon personal dignity, in particular humiliating and degrading treatment," a routine element of Palestinian life under Israel's Occupation.

- Article 32 forbids assassinations, and any brutalization of the civilian population, including their treatment at checkpoints and in "security searches."

- Article 33 prohibiting pillage would obtain to Israel's extensive use of West Bank and Gazan water resources, especially as they are denied the local population. It also prohibits the use of collective punishment, as represented by the imposition of closure, curfew, house demolitions and many other routine actions of the Occupation authorities.

- Article 39 stipulates: "Protected persons [residents of occupied lands] who, as a result of the war, have lost their gainful employment, shall be granted the opportunity to find paid employment." It thereby prohibits the imposition of a permanent "closure" on the Occupied Territories, such as Israel has done since 1993.

- Article 49 forbids deportations and any "forcible transfers," which would include such common practices as revoking Jerusalem IDs or banning Palestinians from returning from work, study or travel abroad. It also stipulates that "The Occupying Power shall not transfer parts of its own civilian population into territories it occupies" - a clear ban on settlements.

- Article 53 reads: "Any destruction by the Occupying Power of real or personal property belonging individually or collectively to private persons is prohibited." Under this provision, the practice of demolishing Palestinian houses is banned, but so is the wholesale destruction of the Palestinian infrastructure (including its civil society institutions and records in Ramallah) destroyed in the reoccupation of March-April 2002.

- Article 64 forbids changes in the local legal system that, among other things, alienate the local population from its land and property, as Israel has done through massive land expropriations.

- Article 146 holds accountable individuals who have committed "grave breaches" of the

Convention. According to Article 147, this includes many acts routinely practiced under the Occupation, such as willful killing, torture or inhuman treatment, willfully causing great suffering or serious injury, unlawful deportation, taking of hostages and extensive destruction and appropriation of property. Israeli courts have thus far failed to charge or prosecute Israeli officials, military personnel or police who have committed such acts.

The PLO, it should be noted, also bears a measure of responsibility for the violations of its own people's rights under the Fourth Geneva Convention. According to Article 8, the PLO had no right in the Oslo Agreements to abrogate their rights and suspend the applicability of the Convention, since "Protected persons may in no circumstances renounce in part or in entirety the rights secured to them by the present Convention."

- *An emblematic conflict with global impact.* In terms of connecting to the wider public, one of the first questions we must address is: Why should I care at all about this conflict? My aim here is not to dictate a script, but I would only suggest a framing that brings the international public into the equation. Presenting the Israeli-Palestinian conflict as emblematic serves this purpose. Its significance as an arena in the struggle between American Empire and the incipient forces promoting human rights and international law should be highlighted. Here a fundamental question should be introduced: What if, in the glare of the mass media, on the southern border of Europe, as a direct consequence of American policy, the Occupation actually prevails? What if an entire people is literally imprisoned in a new bantustan and the world is confronted with a new apartheid? For American audiences in particular, this question should be supplemented by considerations of the conflict's negative impact on the global standing of the United States. How does the deep American involvement in sustaining the Occupation impact, for example, on "the war on terror" that so preoccupies the American public?

(2) Mobilizing International Civil Society

The Occupation poses a bold challenge to all of us. Progressive forces on both sides of the conflict work hard to resist the Occupation, to bridge essential differences, to bring a new vision of a just peace to our peoples. Palestinian and Israeli organizations meet and act together daily. The Geneva Initiative, the Ayalon-Nuseibeh and Gush Shalom Plans, human rights campaigns mounted by Palestinian and Israeli organizations, campaigns around issues such as house demolitions, olive harvesting, the Wall and the boycott of Caterpiller - these and many other important initiatives have arisen out of civil society.

But Israel and Palestinian civil societies are limited in what they can do, and their strategies of advocacy must take into consideration those limitations. By definition civil society groups are "out of the loop" in terms of policy-making, negotiations and concluding political agreements. This is especially true of the critical groups to which many advocates belong. Well-financed and mainstream organizations dealing with issues of conflict resolution often have think-tanks which give them a certain access to power; seldom is that true for advocacy groups - especially those advocating justice for the Palestinians. That does not mean that some form of engagement is not possible. Activist groups have met with decision-makers in Israel and abroad, and they do engage in limited lobbying. In fact, activist groups have managed to get their critical re-framing before the lower-to-middle levels of government officials, parliamentary members and the media. We can no longer say the problem is information: they, the decision-makers, know. The problem is actually influencing policy.

- **Monitoring the Road Map Process**

The passing of Arafat and election of Mahmoud Abbas has rekindled the moribund Road Map initiative. Although deficiencies in the Road Map are apparent - its lack of reference to international law, its thus-far one-sided application, the danger that it may get stuck in some interim stage that leaves the Palestinians in a kind of political limbo, problems of implementation given the disproportionate American role - it nevertheless has redeeming elements and, in the end, the only diplomatic show in town. If progressive civil society engagement is a key to prodding governments to "do the right thing," it is hard to see how advocates of a just peace between Israeli and Palestinians can simply sit it out. Engagement is called for both in terms of advocacy and monitoring. This is especially the case because Sharon believes that issues of viability, the fine distinction between a viable Palestinian state and a bantustan, is far too subtle for most people, political decision-makers included. Someone opening the morning newspaper seeing a map in which Israel "gives" the Palestinians Gaza, 60-70% of the West Bank and parts of East Jerusalem will say, "Well, that looks good enough to me," and will go on to the next topic of the day.

Precisely because viability and sovereignty are such complex issues, we grassroots advocates have a critical role to play as watchdogs. We who pay attention to the details, who have learned how critical the "facts" are on the ground, are in a unique position to offer a considered analysis, to ensure the transparency of any renewed peace process. We must clearly articulate the essential elements of any just peace, the "red lines," and hold them up to any proposed plan for resolving the conflict. We must ask the hard questions: Does this plan address fairly and effectively the key issues underlying the conflict? Does it really end the Occupation or is it merely a subtle cover for control? Does it offer a Palestinian state that is territorially, politically and economically viable, or merely a prison-state? Does it conform to human rights standards and international law? Does it lead to a true resolution of the conflict or is it a recipe for continued, if subtle, control and oppression? does it address the refugee issue? Beyond the local issues, Does this plan offer regional security and development? We have to be on top of developments, to anticipate what is coming and to have our reactions - negative, positive or qualified - ready. True, we run the risk of being dismissed as nay-sayers, but without our critical voice to prevent an "acceptable" solution (to Israel, the international community and perhaps elements of the Palestinian elite) from displacing a just one, the governments will seek the most convenient and self-serving ways out.

- **Targeting Power**

Lobbying is certainly an important form of engagement with the political establishment. Here NGOs tend to be spotty. Occasional letters are written to MPs or members of Congress, occasional meetings are held, but grassroots groups have nowhere the ongoing presence of the pro-Israel lobby: Israeli-sponsored lobbying organizations such as AIPAC in the US, Christian fundamentalist groups, the organized Jewish community, military lobbyists and others. Not every country is built for lobbying, but to the degree we can identify decision-makers and reach them with our message of a just peace, the more focused and effective we will be. Needless to say, decision-makers are not only elected officials; their staffs, advisors and even friends and family carry political clout that often out-weighs that of the politicians themselves. How to break into the circle of power-holders is a task that still awaits us.

Engagement has its limits, however. Governments will agree to occasional meetings with civil society groups but they do not consider them an integral part of policy formulation. Beyond monitoring and lobbying, pro-active advocacy involves a degree of assertiveness and, occasionally (or more), confrontation. Demonstrations have their effect, as do ceremonies held in religious contexts or marking particular political events. So, too, does holding political leaders accountable before their constituencies during election time for their votes and actions.

(3) Developing Strategic Campaigns of Advocacy

Once a structure of advocacy is set in place, an effective set of campaigns, focused on the most relevant issues and target populations, well coordinated, with the potential of turning into a global movement, may be launched. Here, not only does the question of the end-game enter in, but the very centrality of the Occupation itself as the focus of the resistance and advocacy efforts. Activist groups in Israel and abroad, lacking an over-arching campaign and strategy, pursue a myriad of issues of great importance, but not ones that will actually bring an end to the Occupation. The campaign against the Wall, resisting home demolitions, harvesting olives, boycotting Caterpillar, lobbying to suspend the EU-Israel Association Agreements, monitoring checkpoints, accompanying Palestinian children to school - all these and more justly highlight the sins of the Occupation but, collectively, do not constitute an effective and coherent campaign to resolve the conflict. On the contrary, they often come dangerously close to what Paulo Freire refers to as "dumb activism."

What is called for are strategic "meta-campaigns" that highlight the Occupation and the human rights violations it involves, Israeli accountability and the responsibility of the international community towards the Palestinians. Such meta-campaigns might include: a campaign to apply the Fourth Geneva Convention to the Occupied Territories; a campaign against apartheid; a campaign to freeze Israeli construction in the Occupied Territories; and a campaign to stop Israel's use of US weapons against Palestinian civilians. Given the current political situation, one of the most relevant meta-campaigns involves a campaign of divestment/sanctions.

- **A Campaign of Sanctions**

  Sanctions, divestment and boycotts are absolutely legitimate means at *everyone's* disposal for effectively opposing injustice. As penalties, protest, pressure and resistance to policies that violate fundamental human rights, international law and UN resolutions, they are directed at ending a *situation* of intolerable conflict, suffering and moral wrong-doing, *not* against a particular people or country. When the injustice ends, the sanctions end.

  Sanctions, divestment and boycotts represent powerful international responses that arise not only from opposition to an intolerable situation, but also to the complicity of every person in the international civil society that does nothing to resolve it. Because they are rooted in human rights, international law and the will of the international community, and because they are supremely non-violent responses to injustice, sanctions carry a potent moral force. A campaign of sanctions, even if it proves impossible to actually implement them, mobilizes what has been called "the politics of shame." No country wants to be cast as a major violator of human rights. Precisely because it is so difficult to enforce international humanitarian law, holding up its oppressive policy for all to see is often the only way of pressuring it to cease its oppressive policies. The moral and political condemnation conveyed by a campaign for sanctions and the international isolation it threatens sends a powerful, unmistakable message to the perpetrator: cease your unjust policies or suffer the consequences.

Rather than punishment, a campaign of sanctions rests upon the notion of accountability. A country threatened by sanctions stands in violation of the very principles underlying the international community as articulated in human rights covenants, international humanitarian law and UN resolutions. If we go by Amnesty's annual report, virtually every country could be "called on the carpet" for their human rights violations. A campaign of sanctions constitutes an extraordinary step, however. It is invoked when injustice and suffering have become so routinized, so institutionalized, so pervasive, so resistant to normal international diplomacy or pressures, that their very continuation compromises the very validity of the international system and the moral standing of its members, countries, corporations and citizens alike. And it targets the strong parties. The very basis of a call for sanctions is that the targeted country has the ability to end the intolerable situation. A campaign of sanctions embodies a fundamental principle of the international system: that each country must be held accountable for its policies and actions in light of accepted international norms. The message to all countries must be: Participation in the international community depends upon conformity to the "rules of the game."

Campaigns of sanctions are in essence educative, and that is part of their power. Since the reasons for taking such drastic action must be explicit, weighty and compelling, it forces those calling for sanctions to make a strong case for them. The very act of initiating such a campaign, then, raises awareness not only of the injustice itself, but of the principles it violates, thus strengthening the understanding of the international system itself. And since a campaign of sanctions must be accepted by the international community in order to succeed, it necessitates discussion and dialogue. The considerations behind the demand for sanctions are made transparent, and the targeted country given an opportunity to present its case. The likelihood, then, is that a campaign of sanctions initiated by civil society will express broad-based international consensus if it is to take hold.

Again, at issue is a serious violation of international law and norms. Just as in a case of an individual caught breaking the law, what is in question is what acts have been done, not _who_ the country or the individual is. To paraphrase Jefferson, who spoke of "a government of laws, not men," here we are speaking of "an international system of laws and not only countries that do whatever they want." Thus, when the violations end, the sanctions cease and the country in question rejoins the international community.

The Case for Sanctions Against Israel

In line with the principles just discussed, economic sanctions against Israel are not invoked against Israel _per se_, but against Israel _until the Occupation ends_. With this proviso it is Israel's policy of occupation that is targeted, its status as an Occupying Power, not Israel itself. When South Africa ended its system of apartheid, sanctions ceased and it fully rejoined the international community. When apartheid ended, so did the boycott of its sports teams, one of the most potent measures employed to impress on the South

African government its international isolation. The divestment campaign currently directed against Caterpillar has gained considerable momentum among the international public, effectively educating people about Israel's policy of demolishing Palestinian homes. It has generated calls for other sanctions, such as the Presbyterian Church's initiative to divest from companies profiting from the Occupation. The European Parliament has also called for trade sanctions on Israel given Israel's violation of the "Association Agreements" that prohibit the sale of settlement products under the "Made in Israel" label. The American Congress should take similar steps, since Israel's use of American weapons against civilian populations violates the human rights provisions of the Arms Control Exports Act. The boycott of California grapes in the 1960s played a key role in gaining employment rights for migrant workers. The current boycott of settlement products is intended to express moral opposition to the very presence of settlements while making it economically and politically difficult for Israel to maintain them.

Once it builds momentum, there is probably no more effective means for civil society to effectively pursue justice than a campaign of sanctions. Its power derives less from its economic impact - although, with time, that too can be decisive - than from the moral outrage that impels it. Sanctions themselves seriously affected the South African economy. Following massive protests inside South Africa and escalating international pressure in mid-1984, some 200 US companies and more than 60 British ones withdrew from the country and international lenders cut off Pretoria's access to foreign capital. US Congressional pressure played a crucial role as well, an element totally lacking *vis-^-vis* the Israel-Palestine conflict, which makes the possibility of actually imposing sanctions on Israel that more difficult. In 1986 Congress - *with a Republican-controlled Senate* - passed the Comprehensive Anti-Apartheid Act over the Reagan's veto. The Act banned new US investment in South Africa, sales to the police and military and new bank loans.

Although the Act was not strictly enforced by the Reagan and Bush Administrations, although European governments found ways of quietly doing business with Pretoria (while Israel, by the way, was helping South African businesses by-pass sanctions by peddling their products in the US and Europe under a "Made in Israel" label, as well as by continued involvement in military development in South Africa, including nuclear; Hunter 1986), it did generate a climate - moral and economic - that made it increasingly difficult to maintain business-as-usual with the apartheid regime. The moral dimension led to a delegitimization of the very apartheid system that left no room for "reform." Carried over to Israel's Occupation, the moral element in a larger political condemnation of Israel's policies could delegitimize the Occupation to the point where only its complete end is acceptable. A campaign of sanctions which highlights the moral unacceptability of Israel's Occupation could have a great impact, eventually impelling governments to impose economic sanctions while creating a climate difficult for businesses (beginning with Caterpillar) to continue function.

It is not only the political unacceptability of Israel's Occupation which makes the call for sanction urgent and obligatory, it is the massive violations of Palestinian human rights, of international law and of numerous UN resolutions that the Occupation entails. If Israel as the Occupying Power is not held accountable for the intolerable situation within its ability, indeed, within its *responsibility* to end, the entire international system of justice is rendered meaningless and empty. And that is what makes the Occupation an international issue. If Israel succeeds in defying the Fourth Geneva Convention and making its Occupation permanent, if an entire population is literally locked behind walls and its right of self-determination trampled, then the ability of human rights to win out over an international order founded on power politics and militarism is jeopardized. We all have a stake in ending the Occupation; the implications of occupation actually prevailing and a new apartheid regime emerging are chilling. Since the Palestinians do not have the power to shake off the Occupation on their own and the Israelis will not, only international pressure will effectively achieve a just peace. A campaign of sanctions represents one of the most efficacious measures.

ICAHD'S Position on Sanctions

Sanctions, divestment and boycott can be applied either totally or selectively, the decision involving a strategic mix of efficacy and moral stance. In the most successful case of sanctions, apartheid South Africa, the call was for total sanctions, since the entire system was considered illegitimate. In the case of Israel and the Occupation, it is the Occupation which is considered illegitimate, illegal and immoral, not Israel *per se*. Although there are those who would argue that a Zionist Israel whose ongoing policy is to displace Palestinians from the country or confine them to reservations is, indeed, as illegitimate as apartheid, this is a position from which it would be difficult to generate mass support. Most advocates of a just peace - including the Israeli peace movement, ICAHD included - support Israel's right as a recognized member state in the UN to rejoin the international community when the Occupation truly ends and a just peace is attained. Since governments must be induced to impose sanctions, on a purely pragmatic level it is difficult to imagine the international community, with the US at its head, actually agreeing to blanket sanctions.

More do-able would be a campaign for selective sanctions. This could be no less principled and focused than a call for total sanctions, but it targets Israel's Occupation rather than Israel itself. A campaign of selective sanctions can be effective if the choice of targets is strategic: refusing to sell arms to Israel that would be used to perpetuate the Occupation, especially in attacks on civilian populations, for example, or banning Israeli sports teams from competing in international tournaments, especially potent in the South African case. (Israel is currently the European basketball champion and is scheduled to play in the World Cup of football/soccer). These and other selected measures could have a great impact upon Israel, as well as the ability to mobilize international opposition to the Occupation. Yet, with strong civil society advocacy, they also have a reasonable chance, over time, of being adopted.

ICAHD, then, supports in principle a multi-tiered campaign of sanctions against Israel *until the Occupation ends*. We believe that a selective campaign is most effective and we would incorporate into that campaigns that other organizations have already launched. At this stage, ICAHD supports:

- *Sanctions:* Sales or transfer of arms to Israel, if they conform to international law and American law, should be made conditional upon their use in ways that do not perpetuate the Occupation or violate human rights and international humanitarian law, violations that would end if governments enforced existing laws and regulations regarding the use of weapons in contravention of human rights. Rather than adopting new policies of sanctions, ICAHD calls on the governments of North America, Europe and Asia to stop selling arms to Israel that are used in perpetuating the Occupation in accordance with their own laws prohibiting sales of weapons to countries engaged in serious human rights violations. No new policy of sanctions has to be adopted; the existing

103

laws prohibiting such sales must simply be enforced. In addition existing international law must be applied against Israel for using its weapons illegally: against civilian populations, for example, or in campaigns of extra-judicial executions, to name but two. Sanctions that comprise implementation of international and domestic laws should include a ban on purchasing Israeli weapons as well.

ICAHD is currently investigating Israel's involvement in the world's arms trade, including weapons development, joint production and coordinated sales with other countries. We believe this is a hidden element that underlies the broad support Israeli receives from governments, including those outwardly critical of its occupation policies. We hope that advocates for a just peace will use our information to expose their own country's complicity in policies that perpetuate the Occupation. We also call on activist groups to investigate and publicize the forms of aid their country - and especially the US - is giving Israel. Components of that aid that support occupation or settlement, whether military, technological or economic, should be opposed. We also call on Jewish communities to oppose the use of their donations to Israel - to the Jewish National Fund, for instance, or to the United Jewish Appeal, Israel Bonds and other channels of funding - in the Occupied Territories.

- *Trade sanctions on Israel.* Due to its violation of the "Association Agreements" it has signed with the European Union that prohibit the sale of settlement products under the "Made in Israel" label, as well as for violations of their human rights provisions, Europe should impose trade sanctions on Israel until its policies conform to the terms of the Agreements.

- *Divestment in companies that profit from involvement in the Occupation.* Here ICAHD supports the initiative of the Presbyterian Church of the US to divest in "multinational corporations that provide products or services to. The Israeli police or military to support and maintain the occupation, that have established facilities or operations on occupied land, that provide services or products for the establishment, expansion or maintenance of Israeli settlements, that provide products or services to Israeli *or Palestinian* organizations/groups that support or facilitate violent acts against innocent civilians, that provide products or services that support or facilitate the construction of the Separation Barrier." We certainly support the campaign against Caterpillar whose bulldozers demolish thousands of Palestinian homes.

We join with the Jewish Voice for Peace in the US whose statement in support of the Presbyterians says in part:

At JVP, we fully support selective divestment from companies that profit from Israel's occupation of the West Bank, Gaza, and East Jerusalem. This includes American companies like Caterpillar who profit from the wholesale destruction of Palestinian homes and orchards. It also includes Israeli companies who depend on settlements for materials or labor or who produce military equipment used to violate Palestinian human rights.

We believe that general divestment from Israel is an unwise strategy at this time. We believe that economic measures targeted specifically at the occupation and the Israeli military complex that sustains it are much more likely to produce results. However, we absolutely reject the accusation that general divestment or boycott campaigns are inherently anti-Semitic. The Israeli government is a government like any other, and condemning its abuse of state power, as many of its own citizens do quite vigorously, is in no way the same as attacking the Jewish people. Further, it is crucial not only to criticize the immoral and illegal acts of the Israeli government, but to back up that criticism with action. We also note with satisfaction the many Jewish and Israeli organizations who support the idea of selective sanctions on Israel: European Jews for a Just Peace (a coalition of 16 Jewish groups from eight European countries); New Profile (Israel); Not in My Name (US); Matzpun (Israel/International); Jews Against the Occupation (NYC Chapter); the petition of South African government minister Ronnie Kasrils and legislator Max Ozinsky, which has gathered more than 500 signatories from South African Jews; Jewish Voices Against the Occupation (US); Jewish Women for Justice in Israel and Palestine (US); Gush Shalom (Israel); Jews for Global Justice (US); and Visions of Peace With Justice (US), among others.

- *Boycott of settlement products* and of companies that provide housing to the settlements or which play a major role in perpetuating the Occupation, a campaign initiated several years ago by Gush Shalom.

These campaigns, it seems to us, build on existing initiatives. They are capable of garnering broad international support, are focused, raise public consciousness over the economic aspects of the Occupation and expose the complicity of the international community in it. They bring significant moral pressure to bear on Israel, while moving towards effective forms of economic sanctions designed to end the Occupation.

We believe that Israel as a powerful state occupying the territory of another people should be held accountable for its policies and actions. We would therefore add to the list of sanctions the following element:

- *Holding individuals, be they policy-makers, military personnel carrying out orders or others, personally accountable for human rights violations,* including trial before international courts and bans on travel to other countries.

Since sanctions are a powerful non-violent means of resisting the Occupation, ICAHD supports this burgeoning movement and calls on the international community - civil society as well as governments - to do all that is possible to bring a swift end to Israel's terrible Occupation so that all the peoples of the region, and especially Israelis and Palestinians, can enjoy the benefits of a just and lasting peace for the generations to come. The time has come; sanctions seem the next logical step in a global campaign to end the Occupation.

_____

APPENDIX

The Road Map (with Israel's 14 "Reservations")

Letter from Prime Minister Ariel Sharon to US President George W. Bush

Letter from US President George W. Bush to Prime Minister Ariel Sharon

Bush-Sharon Agreement: Congressional Approval

Advisory Opinion Of The International Court Of Justice

THE ROAD MAP

Reorganized for discussion by Jeff Halper

This abridged version of the Road Map sets out the initiative's goals and what is required of each of the parties.

Goals

Quartet

1. To resolve the Israel-Palestinian conflict through a negotiated settlement leading to a final and comprehensive settlement of the Israel-Palestinian conflict by 2005;

2. To end the occupation;

3. To see the emergence of an independent, democratic Palestinian state side by side in peace and security with Israel and its other neighbors;

4. To address Israel's strategic goals of security and regional integration.

Mechanisms

Quartet

- Goals and process based on terms of reference of the Madrid Conference and the principle of land for peace, UNSCRs 242, 338 and 1397, agreements previously reached by the parties, and the Arab initiative proposed by Saudi Crown Prince Abdullah, as endorsed by the Arab Summit in Beirut

- A performance-based plan with clear phases and benchmarks to be agreed upon (including their interpretation) in advance of the process.

- Supervision by the Quartet -- although the United States is bidding for a leadership role. According to the American plan, the U.S. will head the supervising mechanism of the road map's implementation, helped by the other members of the Quartet. (The American government recently announced that a special unit would be set up in the CIA to monitor the implementation process.) The supervising mechanism will further include four committees: a Security Committee that will deal with reforms in the PA security apparatus, renewed security coordination and monitoring of Palestinian activity against terror, as well as the Israeli withdrawals from PA areas. A Special Operations Committee will deal with the settlement freeze, evacuation of the illegal outposts, a cessation of the incitement and the reopening of Palestinian institutions in East Jerusalem. A Humanitarian Committee will try to alleviate the suffering of the Palestinian residents of the Occupied Territories and address the policies behind it (such as the closure). A fourth committee will deal with reforms in the Palestinian Authority

Phases of Implementation

Phase I: October 2002-May 2003 (Transformation/Elections);

First Stage: October-December, 2002 (3 months)

Quartet Requirements

- Quartet develops detailed roadmap, in consultation with the parties, to be adopted at December Quartet/AHLC meeting.

- Ad Hoc Liaison Committee (AHLC) Ministerial launches major donor assistance effort.

- In coordination with Quartet, implementation of U.S. rebuilding, training and resumed security cooperation plan in collaboration with outside oversight board. (US-Egypt-Jordan).

Palestinian Requirements

- Appointment of new Palestinian cabinet, establishment of empowered Prime Minister, including any necessary Palestinian legal reforms for this purpose.

- PLC appoints Commission charged with drafting of Palestinian constitution for Palestinian statehood.

- PA establishes independent Election Commission. PLC reviews and revises election law.

- Palestinian leadership issues unequivocal statement reiterating Israel's right to exist in peace and security and calling for an immediate end to the armed Intifada and all acts of violence against Israelis anywhere. All Palestinian institutions end incitement against Israel.

- Palestinian security organizations are consolidated into three services reporting to an empowered Interior Minister.

Israeli Requirements

- Government of Israel (GOI) facilitates travel of Palestinian officials for PLC sessions, internationally supervised security retraining, and other PA business without restriction.

- GOI implements recommendations of the Bertini report to improve humanitarian conditions, including lifting curfews and easing movement between Palestinian areas.

- GOI ends actions undermining trust, including attacks in civilian areas, and confiscation/demolition of Palestinian homes/property, deportations, as a punitive measure or to facilitate Israeli construction.

- GOI immediately resumes monthly revenue clearance process in accordance with agreed transparency monitoring mechanism. GOI transfers all arrears of withheld revenues to Palestinian Ministry of Finance by end of December 2002, according to specific timeline.

- GOI dismantles settlement outposts erected since establishment of the present Israeli government and in contravention of current Israeli government guidelines.

Joint Palestinian-Israeli Requirements

- Restructured/retrained Palestinian security forces and IDF counterparts begin phased resumption of security cooperation and other undertakings as agreed in the Tenet work plan, including regular senior-level meetings, with the participation of U.S. security officials.

Requirements of Arab States
- Arab states move decisively to cut off public/private funding of extremist groups, channel financial support for Palestinians through Palestinian Ministry of Finance.

Phase I: Second Stage: January-May 2003 (5 months)

(Goals: For the next five months: An end to terror and violence, normalization of Palestinian life and establishment of Palestinian institutions. Israel withdraws from the PA areas, and the status quo from before the Intifada is restored, in accordance with progress in the security cooperation, according to the Tenet work plan. A settlement freeze is announced, according to the Mitchell plan.)

Quartet Requirements

- Quartet monitoring mechanism established.

Palestinian Requirements

- Continued Palestinian political reform to ensure powers of PLC, Prime Minister, and Cabinet.

- Independent Commission circulates draft Palestinian constitution, based on strong parliamentary democracy, for public comment/debate.

- Devolution of power to local authorities through revised Municipalities Law.

- Palestinian performance on agreed judicial, administrative, and economic benchmarks, as determined by Task Force.

- Constitution drafting Commission proposes draft document for submission after elections to new PLC for approval.

- Palestinians hold free, open, and fair elections for PLC.

- The Palestinians begin focused efforts to dismantle the terrorist infrastructure, implement security cooperation, collect illegal weapons and disarm militant groups in the first stage of the program.

Israeli Requirements

- As comprehensive security performance moves forward, IDF withdraws progressively from areas occupied since September 28, 2000. Withdrawal to be completed before holding of Palestinian elections. Palestinian security forces redeploy to areas vacated by IDF.

- GOI facilitates Task Force election assistance, registration of voters, movement of candidates and voting officials.

- GOI reopens East Jerusalem Chamber of Commerce and other closed Palestinian economic institutions in East Jerusalem.

- GOI freezes all settlement activity consistent with the Mitchell report, including natural growth of settlements. Israel is required to make a top priority out of freezing projects that disrupt

Palestinian territorial contiguity, including in the Jerusalem area.

Joint Palestinian-Israeli Requirements

- Palestinians and Israelis conclude a new security agreement building upon Tenet work plan, including an effective security mechanism and an end to violence, terrorism, and incitement implemented through a restructured and effective Palestinian security service.

Requirements of Arab States

- Regional support: Upon completion of security steps and IDF withdrawal to September 28, 2000 positions, Egypt and Jordan return ambassadors to Israel.

Phase II: June 2003-December 2003 (Transition) (6 months)

(Goal: A transition phase, for the purpose of establishing a Palestinian state inside temporary borders according to a new constitution. The Quartet will convene an international conference, in consultation with the parties (in the early draft it required their consent), to be followed by the start of Israeli-Palestinian dialogue about the establishment of the interim state. Still under discussion is to what extent the Quartet will act to win the new Palestinian state acceptance in the UN.)

- Progress into Phase II will be based upon the consensus judgment of the Quartet of whether conditions are appropriate to proceed, taking into account performance of both parties." That judgment is facilitated by establishment of a permanent monitoring mechanism on the ground.

Phase II starts after Palestinian elections and ends with possible creation of a Palestinian state with provisional borders by end of *2003*.

Quartet Requirements

- International Conference: Convened by the Quartet, in agreement with the parties, immediately after the successful conclusion of Palestinian elections to support Palestinian economic recovery and launch negotiations between Israelis and Palestinians on the possibility of a state with provisional borders. Such a meeting would be inclusive, based on the goal of a comprehensive Middle East peace (including between Israel and Syria, and Israel and Lebanon), and based on the principles described in the preamble to this document.

- Conclusion of transitional understanding and creation of state with provisional borders by end of 2003. Enhanced international role in monitoring transition.

Palestinian Requirements

- Newly elected PLC finalizes and approves new constitution for democratic, independent Palestinian state.

- Continued implementation of security cooperation, complete collection of illegal weapons, disarm militant groups, according to Phase I security agreement.

Israeli Requirements

- Further action on settlements simultaneous with establishment of Palestinian state with provisional borders.

Joint Palestinian-Israeli Requirements

- Israeli-Palestinian negotiations aimed at creation of a state with provisional borders.

- Implementation of prior agreements, to enhance maximum territorial contiguity.

- Conclusion of transitional understanding and creation of state with provisional borders by end of 2003.

Requirements of Arab States

- Other pre-Intifada Arab links to Israel restored (trade offices, etc.).

- Revival of "multilateral talks" (regional water, environmental, economic development, refugee, arms control issues).

Phase III: 2004-2005 (Statehood)

(Goals: A permanent arrangement. The purpose of the agreement is an end to the Israeli-Palestinian conflict. In early 2004, a second international conference is convened, to welcome the new state with its temporary borders and to formally launch the negotiations for a final status agreement.)

- Progress into Phase III is based on the judgment of Quartet, taking into account actions of all parties and Quartet monitoring.

Quartet Requirements

- Second International Conference: Convened by the Quartet, with agreement of the parties, at beginning of 2004 to endorse agreement reached on state with provisional borders and to launch negotiations between Israel and Palestine toward a final, permanent status resolution in 2005, including on borders, Jerusalem, refugees and settlements; and, to support progress toward a comprehensive Middle East settlement between Israel and Lebanon and Syria, to be achieved as soon as possible.

Palestinian Requirements

- Continued comprehensive, effective progress on the reform agenda laid out by the Task Force in preparation for final status agreement.

Israeli Requirements

- None

Joint Palestinian-Israeli Requirements

- Continued sustained, effective security cooperation based on security agreements reached by end of Phase I and other prior agreements.

- The text also has a special section on Jerusalem. It says that a negotiated settlement of Jerusalem's status will take into account "the political and religious concerns of both sides and will protect the religious interests of Jews, Christians and Muslims throughout the world."

Requirements of Arab States

- Arab state acceptance of normal relations with Israel and security for all the states of the region, consistent with Beirut Arab Summit initiative.

ISRAEL'S 14 "RESERVATIONS"

1. The maintenance of "calm" is a condition for the commencement and continuation of the process. The Palestinians must disarm and dismantle the existing security organizations and "terrorist organizations" (Hamas, Islamic Jihad, the Popular Front, the Democratic Front, and the al-Aqsa Brigades), implement new security reforms and act to combat terror, violence and incitement. (Israel is not required to crease violence or end incitement against Palestinians.)

2. Progress between phases will be conditional on the full implementation of the previous phase. Performance benchmarks and not time-lines will be the only reference points.

3. The emergence of a new leadership in the Palestinian Authority.

4. Monitoring progress will be solely under American management.

5. The character of the provisional Palestinian state will be determined through negotiations between the Palestinian Authority and Israel. The provisional state will have provisional borders and "certain aspects of sovereignty." It will be fully demilitarized without the authority to undertake defense alliances or military cooperation. Israel will control the entry and exit of all persons and cargo, as well as its air space and electromagnetic space.

6. The Palestinians must declare Israel's right to exist as a Jewish state and waive the refugees' Right of Return.

7. The end of the process will end all claims and not only end the conflict.

8. A settlement will be reached through agreement between the two parties in accordance to Bush's June 24 address.

9. Neither the road map nor the Quartet will enter into final status issues. Among the issues *not* to be discussed are settlement, the status of the PA, and all other issues relating to the final settlement.

10. Removal of all terms of reference except UN resolutions 242 and 338, and those only as an "outline" of a settlement, which will be arrived at autonomously between the parties.

11. Continued reform in the Palestinian Authority, including a transitional Constitution. (Israel has no Constitution.)

12. Redeployment of Israel forces to the September 2000 lines will be subject to security considerations and calm.

13. Subject to security concerns, Israel will work towards the restoration of normalcy to Palestinian life - without reference to US Bertini Report.

14. Arab states will condemn terrorism. No link will be made between the Palestinian track and negotiating tracks with other Arab states.

LETTER FROM PRIME MINISTER ARIEL SHARON
TO US PRESIDENT GEORGE W. BUSH (April 14, 2004)

The Honorable George W. Bush
President of the United States of America
The White House
Washington, D.C.

Dear Mr. President,

The vision that you articulated in your 24 June 2002 address constitutes one of the most significant contributions toward ensuring a bright future for the Middle East. Accordingly, the State of Israel has accepted the Roadmap, as adopted by our government. For the first time, a practical and just formula was presented for the achievement of peace, opening a genuine window of opportunity for progress toward a settlement between Israel and the Palestinians, involving two states living side-by-side in peace and security.

This formula sets forth the correct sequence and principles for the attainment of peace. Its full implementation represents the sole means to make genuine progress. As you have stated, a Palestinian state will never be created by terror, and Palestinians must engage in a sustained fight against the terrorists and dismantle their infrastructure. Moreover, there must be serious efforts to institute true reform and real democracy and liberty, including new leaders not compromised by terror. We are committed to this formula as the only avenue through which an agreement can be reached. We believe that this formula is the only viable one.

The Palestinian Authority under its current leadership has taken no action to meet its responsibilities under the Roadmap. Terror has not ceased, reform of the Palestinian security services has not been undertaken, and real institutional reforms have not taken place. The State of Israel continues to pay the heavy cost of constant terror. Israel must preserve its capability to protect itself and deter its enemies, and we thus retain our right to defend ourselves against terrorism and to take actions against terrorist organizations.

Having reached the conclusion that, for the time being, there exists no Palestinian partner with whom to advance peacefully toward a settlement and since the current impasse is unhelpful to the achievement of our shared goals, I have decided to initiate a process of gradual disengagement with the hope of reducing friction between Israelis and Palestinians. The Disengagement Plan is designed to improve security for Israel and stabilize our political and economic situation. It will enable us to deploy our forces more effectively until such time that conditions in the Palestinian Authority allow for the full implementation of the Roadmap to resume.

I attach, for your review, the main principles of the Disengagement Plan. This initiative, which we are not undertaking under the roadmap, represents an independent Israeli plan, yet is not inconsistent with the roadmap. According to this plan, the State of Israel intends to relocate military installations and all Israeli villages and towns in the Gaza Strip, as well as other military installations and a small number of villages in Samaria.

In this context, we also plan to accelerate construction of the Security Fence, whose completion is essential in order to ensure the security of the citizens of Israel. The fence is a security rather than political barrier, temporary rather than permanent, and therefore will not prejudice any final status issues including final borders. The route of the Fence, as approved by our Government's decisions, will take into account, consistent with security needs, its impact on Palestinians not engaged in terrorist activities.

Upon my return from Washington, I expect to submit this Plan for the approval of the Cabinet and the Knesset, and I firmly believe that it will win such approval.

The Disengagement Plan will create a new and better reality for the State of Israel, enhance its security and economy, and strengthen the fortitude of its people. In this context, I believe it is important to bring new opportunities to the Negev and the Galilee. Additionally, the Plan will entail a series of measures with the inherent potential to improve the lot of the Palestinian Authority, providing that it demonstrates the wisdom to take advantage of this opportunity. The execution of the Disengagement Plan holds the prospect of stimulating positive changes within the Palestinian Authority that might create the necessary conditions for the resumption of direct negotiations.

We view the achievement of a settlement between Israel and the Palestinians as our central focus and are committed to realizing this objective. Progress toward this goal must be anchored exclusively in the Roadmap and we will oppose any other plan.

In this regard, we are fully aware of the responsibilities facing the State of Israel. These include limitations on the growth of settlements; removal of unauthorized outposts; and steps to increase, to the extent permitted by security needs, freedom of movement for Palestinians not engaged in terrorism. Under separate cover we are sending to you a full description of the steps the State of Israel is taking to meet all its responsibilities.

The government of Israel supports the United States efforts to reform the Palestinian security services to meet their roadmap obligations to fight terror. Israel also supports the American's efforts, working with the International Community, to promote the reform process, build institutions and improve the economy of the Palestinian Authority and to enhance the welfare of its people, in the hope that a new Palestinian leadership will prove able to fulfill its obligations under the roadmap.

I want to again express my appreciation for your courageous leadership in the war against global terror, your important initiative to revitalize the Middle East as a more fitting home for its people and, primarily, your personal friendship and profound support for the State of Israel.

Sincerely,

Ariel Sharon

LETTER FROM US PRESIDENT GEORGE W. BUSH
TO PRIME MINISTER ARIEL SHARON (April 14, 2004)

His Excellency
Ariel Sharon
Prime Minister of Israel

Dear Mr. Prime Minister,

Thank you for your letter setting out your disengagement plan.

The United States remains hopeful and determined to find a way forward toward a resolution of the Israeli-Palestinian dispute. I remain committed to my June 24, 2002 vision of two states living side by side in peace and security as the key to peace, and to the roadmap as the route to get there.

We welcome the disengagement plan you have prepared, under which Israel would withdraw certain military installations and all settlements from Gaza, and withdraw certain military installations and settlements in the West Bank. These steps described in the plan will mark real progress toward realizing my June 24, 2002 vision, and make a real contribution towards peace. We also understand that, in this context, Israel believes it is important to bring new opportunities to the Negev and the Galilee. We are hopeful that steps pursuant to this plan, consistent with my vision, will remind all states and parties of their own obligations under the roadmap.

The United States appreciates the risks such an undertaking represents. I therefore want to reassure you on several points.

First, the United States remains committed to my vision and to its implementation as described in the roadmap. The United States will do its utmost to prevent any attempt by anyone to impose any other plan. Under the roadmap, Palestinians must undertake an immediate cessation of armed activity and all acts of violence against Israelis anywhere, and all official Palestinian institutions must end incitement against Israel. The Palestinian leadership must act decisively against terror, including sustained, targeted, and effective operations to stop terrorism and dismantle terrorist capabilities and infrastructure. Palestinians must undertake a comprehensive and fundamental political reform that includes a strong parliamentary democracy and an empowered prime minister.

Second, there will be no security for Israelis or Palestinians until they and all states, in the region and beyond, join together to fight terrorism and dismantle terrorist organizations. The United States reiterates its steadfast commitment to Israel's security, including secure, defensible borders, and to preserve and strengthen Israel's capability to deter and defend itself, by itself, against any threat or possible combination of threats.

Third, Israel will retain its right to defend itself against terrorism, including to take actions against terrorist organizations. The United States will lead efforts, working together with Jordan, Egypt, and others in the international community, to build the capacity and will of Palestinian institutions to fight terrorism, dismantle terrorist organizations, and prevent the areas from which Israel has withdrawn from posing a threat that would have to be addressed by any other means. The United States understands that after Israel withdraws from Gaza and/or parts of the West Bank, and pending agreements on other arrangements, existing arrangements regarding control of airspace, territorial waters, and land passages of the West Bank and Gaza will continue.

The United States is strongly committed to Israel's security and well-being as a Jewish state. It seems clear that an agreed, just, fair and realistic framework for a solution to the Palestinian refugee issue as part of any final status agreement will need to be found through the establishment of a Palestinian state, and the settling of Palestinian refugees there, rather than in Israel.

As part of a final peace settlement, Israel must have secure and recognized borders, which should emerge from negotiations between the parties in accordance with UNSC Resolutions 242 and 338. In light of new realities on the ground, including already existing major Israeli populations centers, it is unrealistic to expect that the outcome of final status negotiations will be a full and complete return to the armistice lines of 1949, and all previous efforts to negotiate a two-state solution have reached the same conclusion. It is realistic to expect that any final status agreement will only be achieved on the basis of mutually agreed changes that reflect these realities.

I know that, as you state in your letter, you are aware that certain responsibilities face the State of Israel. Among these, your government has stated that the barrier being erected by Israel should be a security rather than political barrier, should be temporary rather than permanent, and therefore not prejudice any final status issues including final borders, and its route should take into account, consistent with security needs, its impact on Palestinians not engaged in terrorist activities.

As you know, the United States supports the establishment of a Palestinian state that is viable, contiguous, sovereign, and independent, so that the Palestinian people can build their own future in accordance with my vision set forth in June 2002 and with the path set forth in the roadmap. The United States will join with others in the international community to foster the development of democratic political institutions and new leadership committed to those institutions, the reconstruction of civic institutions, the growth of a free and prosperous economy, and the building of capable security institutions dedicated to maintaining law and order and dismantling terrorist organizations.

A peace settlement negotiated between Israelis and Palestinians would be a great boon not only to those peoples but to the peoples of the entire region. Accordingly, the United States believes that all states in the region have special responsibilities: to support the building of the institutions of a Palestinian state; to fight terrorism, and cut off all forms of assistance to individuals and groups engaged in terrorism; and to begin now to move toward more normal relations with the State of Israel. These actions would be true contributions to building peace in the region.

Mr. Prime Minister, you have described a bold and historic initiative that can make an important contribution to peace. I commend your efforts and your courageous decision which I support. As a close friend and ally, the United States intends to work closely with you to help make it a success.

Sincerely,

George W. Bush

BUSH-SHARON AGREEMENT: CONGRESSIONAL APPROVAL

108TH Congress, 2d Session, H. CON. RES. 460

CONCURRENT RESOLUTION

Whereas the United States is hopeful that a peaceful resolution of the Israeli-Palestinian conflict can be achieved;

Whereas the United States is strongly committed to the security of Israel and its well-being as a Jewish state;

Whereas Israeli Prime Minister Ariel Sharon has proposed an initiative intended to enhance the security of Israel and further the cause of peace in the Middle East;

Whereas President George W. Bush and Prime Minister Sharon have subsequently engaged in a dialogue with respect to this initiative;

Whereas President Bush, as part of that dialogue, expressed the support of the United States for Prime Minister Sharon's initiative in a letter dated April 14, 2004;

Whereas in the April 14, 2004, letter the President stated that in light of new realities on the ground in Israel, including already existing major Israeli population centers, it is unrealistic to expect that the outcome of final status negotiations between Israel and the Palestinians will be a full and complete return to the armistice lines of 1949, but realistic to expect that any final status agreement will only be achieved on the basis of mutually agreed changes that reflect these realities;

Whereas the President acknowledged that any agreed, just, fair, and realistic framework for a solution to the Palestinian refugee issue as part of any final status agreement will need to be found through the establishment of a permanent alternative and the settling of Palestinian refugees there rather than in Israel:

Whereas the principles expressed in President Bush's letter will enhance the security of Israel and advance the cause of peace in the Middle East;

Whereas there will be no security for Israelis or Palestinians until Israel and the Palestinians, and all countries in the region and throughout the world, join together to fight terrorism and dismantle terrorist organizations;

Whereas the United States remains committed to the security of Israel , including secure, recognized, and defensible borders, and to preserving and strengthening the capability of Israel to deter enemies and defend itself against any threat;

Whereas Israel has the right to defend itself against terrorism, including the right to take actions against terrorist organizations that threaten the citizens of Israel;

Whereas the President stated on June 24, 2002, his vision of two states, Israel and Palestine, living side-by-side in peace and security and that vision can only be fully realized when terrorism is defeated, so that a new state may be created based on rule of law and respect for human rights; and

Whereas President Bush announced on March 14, 2003, that in order to promote a lasting peace, all Arab states must oppose terrorism, support the emergence of a peaceful and democratic Palestine, and state clearly that they will live in peace with Israel: Now, therefore, be it

Resolved by the House of Representatives (the Senate concurring), That Congress-- (1) strongly endorses the principles articulated by President Bush in his letter dated April 14, 2004, to Israeli Prime Minister Ariel Sharon which will strengthen the security and well-being of the State of Israel ; and (2) supports continuing efforts with others in the international community to build the capacity and will of Palestinian institutions to fight terrorism, dismantle terrorist organizations, and prevent the areas from which Israel has withdrawn from posing a threat to the security of Israel .

Passed the House of Representatives June 23, 2004.

LEGAL CONSEQUENCES OF THE CONSTRUCTION OF A WALL IN THE OCCUPIED PALESTINIAN TERRITORY: ADVISORY OPINION OF THE INTERNATIONAL COURT OF JUSTICE

(July 9, 2004)

The Court finds that the construction by Israel of a wall in the Occupied Palestinian Territory and its associated régime are contrary to international law; it states the legal consequences arising from that illegality

THE HAGUE, 9 July 2004. The International Court of Justice (ICJ), principal judicial organ of the United Nations, has today rendered its Advisory Opinion in the case concerning the *Legal Consequences of the Construction of a Wall in the Occupied Palestinian Territory* (request for advisory opinion).

In its Opinion, the Court finds unanimously that it has jurisdiction to give the advisory opinion requested by the United Nations General Assembly and decides by fourteen votes to one to comply with that request.

The Court responds to the question as follows:

(1) By fourteen votes to one: The construction of the wall being built by Israel, the occupying Power, in the Occupied Palestinian Territory, including in and around East Jerusalem, and its associated regime, are contrary to international law;

(2) By fourteen votes to one: Israel is under an obligation to terminate its breaches of international law; it is under an obligation to cease forthwith the works of construction of the wall being built in the Occupied Palestinian Territory, including in and around East Jerusalem, to dismantle forthwith the structure therein situated, and to repeal or render ineffective forthwith all legislative and regulatory acts relating thereto, in accordance with paragraph 151 of this Opinion;"

(3) By fourteen votes to one: Israel is under an obligation to make reparation for all damage caused by the construction of the wall in the Occupied Palestinian Territory, including in and around East Jerusalem;

(4) By thirteen votes to two: All States are under an obligation not to recognize the illegal situation resulting from the construction of the wall and not to render aid or assistance in maintaining the situation created by such construction; all States parties to the Fourth Geneva Convention relative to the Protection of Civilian Persons in Time of War of 12 August 1949 have in addition the obligation, while respecting the United Nations Charter and international law, to ensure compliance by Israel with international humanitarian law as embodied in that Convention;

(5) By fourteen votes to one: The United Nations, and especially the General Assembly and the Security Council, should consider what further action is required to bring to an end the illegal situation resulting from the construction of the wall and the associated régime, taking due account of the present Advisory Opinion.

Reasoning of the Court

The Advisory Opinion is divided into three parts: jurisdiction and judicial propriety; legality of the construction by Israel of a wall in the Occupied Palestinian Territory; legal consequences of the breaches found.

Jurisdiction of the Court and judicial propriety

The Court states that when it is seized of a request for an advisory opinion, it must first consider whether it has jurisdiction to give that opinion. It finds that the General Assembly, which requested the opinion by resolution ES-10/14 of 8 December 2003, is authorized to do so by Article 96, paragraph 1, of the Charter...The Court then rejects the argument that an opinion could not be given in the present case on the ground that the question posed in the request is not a legal one...

Legality of the construction by Israel of a wall in the Occupied Palestinian Territory

Before addressing the legal consequences of the construction of the wall (the term which the General Assembly has chosen to use and which is also used in the Opinion, since the other expressions sometimes employed are no more accurate if understood in the physical sense), the Court considers whether or not the construction of the wall is contrary to international law.

The Court determines the rules and principles of international law which are relevant to the question posed by the General Assembly. The Court begins by citing, with reference to Article 2, paragraph 4, of the United Nations Charter and to General Assembly resolution 2625 (XXV), the principles of the prohibition of the threat or use of force and the illegality of any territorial acquisition by such means, as reflected in customary international law. It further cites the principle of self-determination of peoples, as enshrined in the Charter and reaffirmed by resolution 2625 (XXV). As regards international humanitarian law, the Court refers to the provisions of the Hague Regulation of 1907, which have become part of customary law, as well as the Fourth Geneva Convention relative to the Protection of Civilian Persons in Time of War of 1949, applicable in those Palestinian territories which before the armed conflict of 1967 lay to the east of the 1949 Armistice demarcation line (or "Green Line") and were occupied by Israel during that conflict. The Court further notes that certain human rights instruments (International Covenant on Civil and Political Rights, International Covenant on Economic, Social and Cultural Rights and the United Nations Convention on the Rights of the Child) are applicable in the Occupied Palestinian Territory.

The Court ascertains whether the construction of the wall has violated the above-mentioned rules and principles. It first observes that the route of the wall as fixed by the Israeli Government includes within the "Closed Area" (between the wall and the "Green Line") some 80 percent of the settlers living in the Occupied Palestinian Territory. Recalling that the Security Council described Israel's policy of establishing settlements in that territory as a "flagrant violation" of the Fourth Geneva Convention, the Court finds that those settlements have been established in breach of international law. It further considers certain fears expressed to it that the route of the wall will prejudge the future frontier between Israel and Palestine; it considers that the construction of the wall and its associated régime "create a 'fait accompli' on the ground that could well become permanent, in which case, . . . [the construction of the wall] would be tantamount to *de facto* annexation". The Court notes that the route chosen for the wall gives expression *in loco* to the illegal measures taken by Israel, and deplored by the Security Council, with regard to Jerusalem and the settlements, and that it entails further alterations to the demographic composition of the Occupied Palestinian Territory. It finds that the "construction [of the wall], along with measures taken previously, . . . severely impedes the exercise by the Palestinian people of its right to self-determination, and is therefore a breach of Israel's obligation to respect that right".

The Court then considers the information furnished to it regarding the impact of the construction of the wall on the daily life of the inhabitants of the Occupied Palestinian Territory (destruction or requisition of private property, restrictions on freedom of movement, confiscation of agricultural land, cutting-off of access to primary water sources, etc.). It finds that the construction of the wall and its associated regime are contrary to the relevant provisions of the Hague Regulations of 1907 and of the Fourth Geneva Convention; that they impede the liberty of movement of the inhabitants of the territory as guaranteed by the International Covenant on Civil and Political Rights; and that they also impede the exercise by the persons concerned of the right to work, to health, to education and to an adequate standard of living as proclaimed in the International Covenant on Economic, Social and Cultural Rights and in the Convention on the Rights of the Child. Lastly, the Court finds that this construction and its associated régime, coupled with the establishment of settlements, are tending to alter the demographic composition of the Occupied Palestinian Territory and thereby contravene the Fourth Geneva Convention and the relevant Security Council resolutions.

The Court observes that certain humanitarian law and human rights instruments include qualifying clauses or provisions for derogation which may be invoked by States parties, *inter alia* where military exigencies or the needs of national security or public order so require. It states that it is not convinced that the specific course Israel has chosen for the wall was necessary to attain its security objectives and, holding that none of such clauses are applicable, finds that the construction of the wall constitutes "breaches by Israel of various of its obligations under the applicable international humanitarian law and human rights instruments".

In conclusion, the Court considers that Israel cannot rely on a right of self-defence or on a state of necessity in order to preclude the wrongfulness of the construction of the wall. The Court accordingly finds that the construction of the wall and its associated régime are contrary to international law.

Legal consequences of the violations found

The Court draws a distinction between the legal consequences of these violations for Israel and those for other States.

In regard to the former, the Court finds that Israel must respect the right of the Palestinian people to self-determination and its obligations under humanitarian law and human rights law. Israel must also put an end to the violation of its international obligations flowing from the construction of the wall in the Occupied Palestinian Territory and must accordingly cease forthwith the works of construction of the wall, dismantle forthwith those parts of that structure situated within the Occupied Palestinian Territory and forthwith repeal or render ineffective all legislative and regulatory acts adopted with a view to construction of the wall and establishment of its associated régime, except in so far as such acts may continue to be relevant for compliance by Israel with its obligations in regard to reparation. Israel must further make reparation for all damage suffered by all natural or legal persons affected by the wall's construction.

As regards the legal consequences for other States, the Court finds that all States are under an obligation not to recognize the illegal situation resulting from the construction of the wall and not to render aid or assistance in maintaining the situation created by such construction. The Court further finds that it is for all States, while respecting the United Nations Charter and international law, to see to it that any impediment, resulting from the construction of the wall, in the exercise by the Palestinian people of its right to self-determination is brought to an end. In addition, all States parties to the Fourth Geneva Convention are under an obligation, while respecting the Charter and international law, to ensure compliance by Israel with international humanitarian law as embodied in that Convention.

Finally, the Court is of the view that the United Nations, and especially the General Assembly and the Security Council, should consider what further action is required to bring to an end the illegal situation resulting from the construction of the wall and its associated régime, taking due account of the present Advisory Opinion.

The Court concludes by stating that the construction of the wall must be placed in a more general context. In this regard, the Court notes that Israel and Palestine are "under an obligation scrupulously to observe the rules of international humanitarian law". In the Court's view, the tragic situation in the region can be brought to an end only through implementation in good faith of all relevant Security Council resolutions. The Court further draws the attention of the General Assembly to the "need for . . . efforts to be encouraged with a view to achieving as soon as possible, on the basis of international law, a negotiated solution to the outstanding problems and the establishment of a Palestinian State, existing side by side with Israel and its other neighbours, with peace and security for all in the region".

The Court was composed as follows: Judge Shi, President; Judge Ranjeva, Vice-President; Judges Guillaume, Koroma, Vereshchetin, Higgins, Parra-Aranguren, Kooijmans, Rezek, Al-Khasawneh, Buergenthal, Elaraby, Owada, Simma and Tomka.

[The ruling of the ICJ was adopted by the General Assembly by a vote of *every country in the world* (including a unanimous 25-nation Europe) against the US, Israel, Australia and three island countries of the South Pacific.]

BIBLIOGRAPHY

Abu-Zayyad, Ziad 1997 Land: The Core of the Conflict. *Palestine-Israel Journal* 4(2): 13-16.

Bazbaz, Marwan 1997 Settlement in the West Bank and the Gaza Strip. *Palestine-Israel Journal* 4(2): 31-36.

Benvenisti, Eyal 1989 Legal Dualism: The Absorption of the Occupied Territories into Israel. Jerusalem. Jerusalem Post Press (West Bank Data Project).

Brubaker, Matthew 2001 "The Jerusalem Ring Road." *News From Within* 17(4):11-13.

Campbell, Elizabeth 1998 "'Maximum Territory, Minimum Population' - Jerusalem: THE Laboratory for the Policies of Zionist Colonization." *News From Within* 13(11):8-13.

Cheshin, Amir S., Bill Hutman, Avi Melamed 1999 *Separate and Unequal: The Inside Story of Israeli Rule in East Jerusalem.* Cambridge: Harvard University Press.

de Jong, Jan 2000 "Israel's Greater Jerusalem' Engulfs the West Bank's Core." *Jerusalem Quarterly File* 10.

Dershowitz, Alan 2003 *The Case For Israel.* Hoboken: Wiley.

Falah, Ghazi 1996 The 1948 Israeli-Palestinian War and its Aftermath: the Transformation and De-Signification of Palestine's Cultural Landscape. *Annals of the Association of American Geographers*, 86(2):256-285.

Finkelstein, Norman 2003 *Image and Reality of the Israel-Palestine Conflict.* London: Verso.

Flapan, Simcha 1979 *Zionism and the Palestinians.* London: Croom Helm.

----- 1987 *The Birth of Israel: Myths and Realities.* New York: Pantheon.

Halper, Jeff 2005 Israel in a Middle East Union: A "Two-stage" Approach to the Conflict. *Tikkun* 20(1):17-21.

----- 2004 Paralysis Over Palestine: Questions of Strategy. *Journal of Palestine Studies* 34(2):55-69.

----- 2002 The Three Jerusalems: Planning and Colonial Control. *Jerusalem Quarterly File* 15:6-17.

----- 2000 The Road to Apartheid: The Trans-Israel Highway. *News From Within* 16(5):1-7.

----- 2000 The 94 Percent Solution: A Matrix of Control. *Middle East Report*, Fall.

----- 1999 Dismantling the Matrix of Control. *News From Within* 15(10).
----- 1998 Israel's War on Palestinians: The Campaign of House Demolitions. *Tikkun* 13(5):56-59.

Ir Shalem n.d. *East Jerusalem: The Current Planning Situation.* Jerusalem.

Kaminker, Sarah 1995 "East Jerusalem: A Case Study in Political Planning." *Palestine/Israel Journal* 2(2):59-66.

Khalidi, Rashid 1997 *Palestinian Identity: The Construction of Modern National Consciousness.* New York: Columbia University Press.

Khalidi, Walid 1992 *All That Remains.* Washington: Institute for Palestine Studies.

Khamaisi, Rassem and Rami Nasrallah (eds.) 2003 *The Jerusalem Urban Fabric*. Jerusalem: International Peace and Cooperation Center (IPCC).

Kimmerling, Baruch 1976 *Land, Conflict and Nation Building: A Sociological Study of the Territorial Factors in the Jewish-Arab Conflict*. Hebrew University (mimeo).

----- 1983 *Zionism And Territory*. Berkeley: Institute of International Studies.

Kolatt, Israel 1983 The Zionist Movement and The Arabs. In Shmuel Almog (ed). *Zionism and the Arabs*. Jerusalem: Zalman Shazar Center, pp. 1-34.

Makovskey, David 2003 Taba Mythchief. *The National Interest* (Spring), pp. 119-129.

Matar, Ibrahim 1997 The Quiet War: Land Expropriation in the Occupied Territories. *Palestine-Israel Journal* 4(2): 40-45.

Mansour, Atallah 1997 Arab Lands in Israel: A Festering Wound. *Palestine-Israel Journal* 4(2): 25-30.

Morris, Benny 1979 *The Birth of the Palestinian Refugee Problem, 1947-1949*. Cambridge: Cambridge University Press.

----- 1994 *1948 And After: Israel and the Palestinians*. Oxford: Oxford University Press.

Rummel, R.J. 1994 *Death By Government*. New Brunswick: Transaction Books.

Shavit, Ari 2004 The Big Freeze. *Ha'aretz Magazine*, Oct. 8.

---- 2002 Eyes Wide Shut. *Ha'aretz Magazine*, Sept. 6.

Shehadeh, Raja 1997 Land and Occupation: A Legal Review. *Palestine-Israel Journal* 4(2): 25-30.

Shlaim, Avi 2000 *The Iron Wall: Israel and the Arab World*. New York: Norton.
Sluka, Jeffrey 2000 *Death Squad: The Anthropology of State Terror*. Philadelphia: University of Pennsylvania Press.

Sternhell, Zeev 1998 *The Founding Myths Of Israel*. Princeton: Princeton University Press.
Yiftakhel, Oren 1999 Judaize and Divide: Shaping Spaces in the Israeli Ethnocracy. *News From Within* (December), pp. 13-20.

Zunes, Stephen 2004 *Congress to Sharon: Take All You Want*. www.anti-war.com (June 26)

FURTHER RESOURCES

Reports

Amnesty International 2004 *Under the Rubble: House Demolition and Destruction of Land and Property* (May).

----- 2002 *Shielded from Scrutiny: IDF Violations in Jenin and Nadlus* (November).

----- 2002 Without Distinction: Attacks on Civilians by Palestinian Armed Groups (July).

----- 1999 *Demolition and Dispossession: The Destruction of Palestinian Homes* (December).

Bimkom 2005 *A Planning Snare: Planning Policy and House Demolitions in East Jerusalem* (February, Hebrew).

B'tselem 2004 *Through No Fault of Their Own: Israel's Punitive House Demolitions in the al-Aqsa Intifada* (November).

----- 2002 *Land Grab: Israel's Settlement Policy in the West Bank* (May)..

----- 2001 *Not Even A Drop: Water Crisis in Palestinian Villages* (July).

----- 1998 *The Quiet Deportation Continues.*

Christian Aid 2004 *Facts on the Ground: The End of the Two-State Solution?* (October).

----- 2003 *Losing Ground: Israel, Poverty and the Palestinians* (January).

Human Rights Watch 2004 *Razing Rafah: Mass Home Demolitions in the Gaza Strip* (October).

Israeli Committee Against House Demolitions 2004 *A Destructive Policy: House Demolitions in East Jerusalem: Facts, Intents and Implications* (December, Hebrew).

Palestinian Center for Human Rights 2003 *Demolition of Palestinian Houses by Israeli Occupying Forces as a Means of Punishment abd Determent* (June).

Palestine Monitor (for statistical up-dates, see <www.palestinemonitor.org>).

Pengon 2003 *Stop The Wall in Palestine.*

Books

Beit-Hallahmi, Benjamin 1987 *Israeli Connection: Who Israel Arms and Why.* New York: Pantheon Books.
----- 1996 *Original Sins: Reflections On the History of Zionism and Israel.* Interlink.

Benveniste, Meron 2000 *Sacred Landscape: The Buried History of the Holy Land.* University of California Press.

----- 1996 *City of Stone: The Hidden History of Jerusalem.* University of California Press.

----- 1996 *Intimate Enemies: Jews and Arabs in a Shared Land.* University of California Press.

Bollens, Scott 2000 *On Narrow Ground: Urban Policy And Ethnic Conflict In Jerusalem And Belfast.* Albany: SUNY Press.

126

Carey, Roane (ed) 2001 *The New Intifada: Resisting Israel's Apartheid*. New York: The Verso Press.

Carey, Roane and Jonathan Shanon (eds.) 2002 *The Other Israel: Voice of Refusal and Dissent*. New York: The New Press.

Chomsky, Noam 1983 *Fateful Triangle: The United States, Israel and the Palestinians*. Boston: South End Press.

Cohen, Shaul Ephraim 1993 *The Politics of Planting: Israeli-Palestinian Competition for Control of Land in the Jerusalem Periphery*. Chicago: University of Chicago Press.

Falk, Richard 2000 *Human Rights Horizons: The Pursuit of Justice in a Globalizing World*. New York: Routledge.

Flapan, Simha 1987 *The Birth of Israel: Myths and Realities*. New York: Pantheon.

Grossman, David 1988 *The Yellow Wind*. New York: Farrar, Straus and Giroux.

Hirst, David 1977 *The Gun And The Olive Branch: The Roots of Violence In The Middle East*. New York: Nation Books.

Kaminer, Reuven 1995 *Politics of Protest: The Israeli Peace Movement and the Palestinian Intifada*. Brighton: Sussex Academic Press.

Khalidi, Walid 1988 *All That Remains: The Palestinian Villages Occupied and Depopulated By Israel in 1948*. Washington: Institute of Palestine Studies.

Khamaisi, Rassem, Rami Nasrallah and Michael Younan 2003 *Jerusalem on the Map*. Jerusalem: International Peace and Cooperation Center (IPCC).

Kimmerling, Baruch 2001 *The Invention And Decline of Israeliness*. University of California Press.

----- 2003 *Politicide: Ariel Sharon's War Against the Palestinians*. London: Verso.

Nasrallah, Rami, Michael Younan et. al. 2003 *Envisioning the Future of Jerusalem*. Jerusalem: International Peace and Cooperation Center (IPCC).

Pappe, Ilan 1988 *The Making of the Arab-Israeli Conflict, 1948-1951*. London: Macmillan.

Said, Edward 2001 *The End of the Peace Process: Oslo And After*. New York: Vintage Books.

----- 1979 *The Question of Palestine*. New York: Vintage Books.

Savir, Uri 1998 *The Process*. New York: Vintage.

Sayigh, Yezid 1997 *Armed Struggle and the Search for a State: The Palestinian National Movement, 1949-1993*. Oxford: Oxford University Press.

Segev, Tom 1986 *1949: The First Israelis*. New York: The Free Press.

Sharoni, Simona 1994 *Gender and the Israeli-Palestinian Conflict: The Politics of Women's Resistance*. Syracuse: Syracuse University Press.

Shehadeh, Raja 2001 *Strangers in the House: Coming of Age in Occupied Palestine*. Steerforth Press.

Shlaim, Avi 1988 *Collusion Across the Jordan: King Abdullah, the Zionist Movement, and the Partition of Palestine*. Oxford: Clarendon.

Silberstein, Laurence 1999 *The Postzionism Debates: Knowledge And Power In Israeli Culture.* New York: Routledge.

Tamari, Salim (ed.) 1999 *Jerusalem 1948: The Arab Neighbourhoods and Their Fate in the War.* Jerusalem: Institute of Jerusalem Studies, 1999.

Some Useful Websites

Al-Haq: <alhaq.org>

Alternative Information Center: <www.alternativenews.org>

Arab Association for Human Rights: <www.hra.com>

Ariga: <www.ariga.com>

Badil: <www.badil.org>

Bat Shalom: <www.batshalom.org>

B'tselem: <www.btselem.org>

Christian Peacemaker Team: <www.prairienet.org>

Coalition of Women for Peace: <www.coalitionof women4peace.org>

The Electronic Intifada: <electronicintifada.net>

Foundation for Middle East Peace: <www.fmep.orgt>

Gush Shalom: <www.gush-shalom.org>

Ha'aretz newspaper: <www.haaretzdaily.com>

Hebrew website: <mahsom.org>

Indymedia: <www.indymedia.org.il>

The Israeli Committee Against House Demolitions (ICAHD): <www.icahd.org>

Jerusalem Center for Economic and Social Rights: <www.jcser.org/english>

Jerusalem Center for Women: <www.j-c-w.org>

Jerusalem Media and Communication Center: <www.jmcc.org>

Jerusalem Report: <www.jrep.com>

Jewish Voice For Peace: <www.jewishvoiceforpeace.org>

New Profile: <www.newprofile.org>

Palestine Monitor: <www.palestinemonitor.org>

Palestinian Center for Human Rights (PCHR): <www.pchrgaza.org>

Palestinian Hydrology Group (PHG): <www.phg.org>

The Palestinian Initiative for the Promotion of Global Dialogue and Democracy: <ww.miftah.org>

PalMap: Palestine Mapping Center <www.palmap.org>

PENGON: <www.pengon.org>, <www.stopthewall.org>

PASSIA: <www.passia.org>

Rabbis for Human Rights: <www.rhr.israel.net>

Ta'ayush: <taayush.tripod.com>

Yesh Gvul <yeshgvul.org>